COLLISION COURSE

COLLISION COURSE

The Classic Story of the Collision of
the *Andrea Doria* and the *Stockholm*

Alvin Moscow

THE LYONS PRESS
Guilford, Connecticut
An imprint of The Globe Pequot Press

The Lyons Press is an imprint of The Globe Pequot Press.

10 9 8 7 6 5 4 3 2 1

Printed in the United States of America

ISBN 1-59228-287-3

Library of Congress Cataloging-in-Publication Data

Moscow, Alvin.
Collision course : the classic story of the collision of the Andrea Doria and the Stockholm / Alvin Moscow. –1st Lyons Press ed.
        p. cm.
Previously published: New York : Grosset & Dunlap, 1959.
Includes index.
ISBN 1-59228-287-3 (pbk.)
    1. Andrea Doria (Steamship) 2. Stockholm (Motorship) 3. Shipwrecks—North Atlantic Ocean. I. Title.

G530.A244M67 2004
363.12'3'0916346—dc22
                                                    2004048739

2004

MERRY CHRISTMAS Joe,
WITH OUR VOYAGE STILL FRESH IN YOUR
MEMORY THOUGHT YOU WOULD FIND THIS
ACCOUNT INTERESTING. LOVE
Mom & DAD.

To DEIRDRE, *again*

Contents

An Explanation   7

1. A Calculated Risk   13
2. "Lights to Port"   31
3. "I Can See a Ship"   61
4. "Why Did She Turn So?"   81
5. "Shall I Ring the Alarm?"   95
6. "We're Going on a Picnic"   109
7. "We Need Boats"   133
8. "I Want to See the Captain"   157
9. "Send Down a Ladder"   183
10. "Tell Them I Did Everything I Could"   199
11. "My Schedule is Imperative"   215
12. "Seaworthiness is Nil"   227
13. "I'm Also Wondering About That"   247
14. "Do I Have to Answer?"   273
15. "I Loved the Sea—Now I Hate It"   297
16. Salvaging the *Doria*   311
17. Revisiting the *Doria*   337

Index   359

An Explanation

THIS is a completely factual and true account, within the capabilities of the author, of the worst sea tragedy of our times. The temptation to extend this story to what might have or must have happened has been scrupulously avoided. No words or thoughts have been put into the minds of the survivors beyond those remembered afterwards by each of the men or women who spoke or heard them.

Many facets of the story are steeped in controversy, and, aware of this, I have tried to check and recheck every fact contained in this book. Where accounts conflicted, I have applied the weight of evidence to reach an unbiased conclusion, and where the weight of evidence failed to tilt the scales

7

appreciably to one side, both sides of the story have been presented.

Much of the controversy over the rescue operation stems from the fact that each participant witnessed only a particular segment, be it large or small, of the disaster. The primary purpose of this book is to put into proper perspective for the first time the pertinent aspects of the collision of the *Andrea Doria* and the *Stockholm*.

Having approached this subject as a news reporter with little, if any, aforehand knowledge, I am happy to make known the help I received from many sources.

Firstly, I am indebted to The Associated Press, in general, and to my city editor, Joseph H. Nicholson, in particular, for introducing me to this subject by assigning me to the four months of court hearings on the disaster, and again for granting me an extended leave of absence for further research and the writing of this book.

I wish to thank the Swedish-American Line and its attorneys, Charles S. Haight and Gordon Paulsen, and the Italian Line and its attorneys, Eugene Underwood and Kenneth Volk, for the extent of their cooperation under the circumstances.

I am grateful to the officers and men of the *Andrea Doria* and of the *Stockholm* who individually allowed me to probe their thoughts as well as review their activities on the night of the collision: Captain Piero Calamai, Staff Captain Oswaldo Magagnini, Third Officer Guideo Badano, and Dr. Bruno Tortori-Donati of the *Andrea Doria*; and Captain H. Gunnar Nordenson, Chief Officer Herbert Kallback, Second Officer Lars Enestrom, Third Officer Ernst Carstens-Johannsen, and Chief Purser Curt Dawe of the *Stockholm*.

I needed and received "expert" advice for the understanding of certain technical aspects and background material concerning the disaster, and for this help I wish to thank, among others, H. L. Seward, Professor Emeritus of Mechanical and Marine Engineering at Yale University, who served as consultant to the Committee on Merchant Marine and Fisheries of the House of Representatives in its investigation of the collision; W. R. Griswold, sales manager of the Marine Division of the Sperry Gyroscope Company; Frank O. Braynard, of the American Merchant Marine Institute; and John Sherman, of the U.S. Merchant Marine Academy, Kings Point, New York.

My thanks are due also to the commanders of the major rescue vessels at the scene who submitted to my interrogation, to those passengers who corresponded, telephoned, or spoke with me about July 25 and 26, 1956, and to the many seafaring men who revealed to me shipboard practices that are not to be found in books, periodicals or newspapers.

With the passage of so many years since the original publication of this book in 1959, I have now the rare opportunity of thanking the reading public for their high and continuing interest in *Collision Course*. This was my first book. Its success in the marketplace changed my career and my life. I have a very special affection for it, as my firstborn, and so I would like to express here my appreciation to Robert Markel and Norma Anderson, editors at Grosset & Dunlap, for bringing *Collision Course* back to life in a new edition in 1981. And now I would especially like to thank Jonathan McCullough and Emily Ginsberg, editors at Lyons Press, for their help with this new updating of *Collision Course*.

In writing a new chapter on the *Andrea Doria* as the "Mount Everest" for scuba divers, I was coached by three intrepid and experienced deep sea scuba divers who know the *Doria* so well: David A. Bright, Christina Young, and Bart P. Malone. They are now part of the story, and I thank them.

9

Finally, for moral support and critical editing throughout the writing of the three editions of this book, I am—as I was before for other reasons—forever indebted to Deirdre Meadow Moscow, my wife.

It must be said, however, that with all the help received from persons mentioned above and others not listed, the views and conclusions expressed in this book are solely those of the author.

—ALVIN MOSCOW
ST. GEORGE, UTAH 2004

COLLISION COURSE

Chapter One

A CALCULATED RISK

THE NORTH ATLANTIC, like all oceans, is track-less and free, a no-man's body of water beset by storms and ice in the winter and storms and fog in the summer. This mighty ocean has been made safe for travel by the genius of man. Yet in his frailty man must take care, for despite all the electronic wonders devised through the years of scientific progress, periodically the sea takes its toll.

On a Wednesday, the 25th day of July, 1956, at 2:40 in the afternoon, Superior Captain Piero Calamai, who had devoted thirty-nine of the fifty-eight years of his life to the sea, sensed fog in the air. He made straightaway for the bridge of his ship, the Italian luxury liner *Andrea Doria*.

13

The captain, a tall, well-built man whose swarthy sun-tanned face was dominated by an aquiline nose, was credited by his crew with a sixth sense by which he could smell fog on the horizon before it became evident to the men on watch. It was an unusual occurrence when Captain Calamai had to be summoned to the bridge because of fog. The captain, like masters of all ships, had standing orders that he be called in the event of any kind of reduced visibility at sea. He seemed always to arrive there, though, just before he was needed. The simple explanation for Captain Calamai's "sixth sense" probably was that he was a worrier. He never was away from the bridge of his ship for long. Of the multiple duties incumbent upon the master of a ship, Captain Calamai favored those of chief navigator.

The aloneness forced upon a man by the sea suited the Italian captain. A shy, introverted person, he least enjoyed the social obligations of a captain of a luxury liner. Because he disliked cocktails, liquor and small talk, he discharged his social obligations to celebrities and important passengers aboard by showing them the bridge of his beautiful ship during the morning hours. He preferred conducting a tour of the ship's bridge and instruments to acting as host at the usual cocktail party in the captain's cabin. Neither did he dine with passengers at a "captain's table." He ate with his senior officers in a small room off the First-Class Dining Room.

Nor was he a strong disciplinarian. He was too sensitive and benevolent a man to impose his will upon a subordinate. Although a major part of the time of a ship's master is spent as an administrator overseeing the smooth running of his little community bounded by the rails of his ship, he may impose his discipline through his second-in-command who holds the rank of staff captain or chief mate. Captain Calamai availed

14

himself of his staff captain in disciplinary cases. He never was known to chastise and openly embarrass a subordinate. Instead, he would take an erring man aside when absolutely necessary for private fatherly advice. And his men loved him and respected him for it. Those who served under him knew he devoted himself selflessly to his ship and that in his innate honesty he expected the same of the men serving him. The only criticism admitted by some of his officers was that perhaps Captain Calamai was "a little mild."

That he was an excellent seaman and navigator with a sure hand, none of his men doubted. He had served on and commanded large, fast ships of the Italian Line passenger fleet for almost all of his life. He had been commander of the *Andrea Doria,* Italy's finest, since her maiden voyage in January, 1953.

Captain Calamai saw the unmistakable signs of fog on the horizon as he stood on one of the bridge wings of his ship. The bridge wings, like the wings of an airplane, extended from either side of the wheelhouse to a point slightly beyond the hull of the ship, and being near the top of the ship's superstructure afforded the captain an unrestricted view of the sea before him. Fog was not unusual in the waters off the east coast of the United States for the month of July. The question was how dense and how deep the fog was for this voyage. Captain Calamai often had stood eighteen to twenty-four hours of continuous watch on the final day's voyage into New York. He was not the kind of man who could leave his bridge at such times to his second-in-command, as did most ship captains who would limit their own watch duty in fog to eight or twelve hours.

Depending upon the density of fog, Captain Calamai knew that the law required that he reduce the speed of his fast

15

ship. He knew equally well that any reduction in speed meant a further delay in arriving in New York, where he was scheduled to bring the *Andrea Doria* into the harbor at six A.M. the following day. Although the Italian Line, like all shipping companies, never instructs a captain to break the law to arrive on schedule, Captain Calamai knew, as do all captains, that late arrivals are costly. Fuel costs, the pay of some two hundred longshoremen hired the day before to be at the dock to unload the ship, and the public relations of bringing passengers to their destination on time—all add up in the costly operation of a passenger ship.

Approaching the fog ahead, the *Doria* was then about one hour behind schedule because of a storm two nights before. Her twin turbine engines were on FULL SPEED AHEAD, pounding out 35,000 horsepower. The turbines fed by high-compression steam turned the ship's two giant propellers, each 16 feet in diameter, 134 revolutions per minute. It was a tremendous amount of power and every bit of it was needed to push this colossal ship, 697 feet long and 11 decks high, through the ocean at her full cruising speed of 23 knots. It was necessary to maintain that speed constantly from Gibraltar at the mouth of the Mediterranean Sea to the Ambrose Lightship at the entrance to New York Harbor in order to bring the ship to port on schedule.

But this day, July 25, was the last day of the voyage. Most of the 4,000-mile voyage from her home port of Genoa was behind the *Doria*. Captain Calamai had taken the shortest route across the North Atlantic, the Great Circle route, passing through the Azore Islands and heading almost due west for the Nantucket Lightship, which served as a substitute landfall for the United States. During the winter months, the *Andrea Doria* like other Italian Line ships traveled a longer,

16

more southerly route in an effort to follow the sun across the Atlantic. But in the summer, the Great Circle route offered sunshine as well as economy of fuel consumption. Fuel consumption always has been a major concern of shipowners. The *Andrea Doria*, for instance, burned ten to eleven tons of fuel oil every hour underway, the equivalent of what the average homeowner uses to heat his home for two years. Now, toward the end of her voyage, the *Andrea Doria* was riding light, with many of her fuel tanks empty, rolling more perceptibly with the waves. The previous day Captain Calamai had radioed ahead to New York his request for 2,200 tons of oil to refuel the ship for the return voyage.

Directly ahead, beyond the fog, some 165 miles and less than eight hours' sailing time, lay the Nantucket Lightship for which the *Doria* was being steered. The red-hulled little vessel was anchored in the ocean some 50 miles off Nantucket, beyond the treacherous shoal waters which extended from the shore of the Island. It was the gateway of the North Atlantic for shipping to and from the United States. For the *Andrea Doria*, the small lightship represented the first sighting of the United States and the last lap of the voyage off the shores of Massachusetts, Connecticut and Long Island to New York Harbor.

For another ship, a glistening all-white vessel which resembled a long, sleek pleasure yacht more than a liner carrying 534 passengers on a year-round transatlantic schedule to Scandinavia, the Nantucket Lightship represented the point of departure from the United States. This ship, the Swedish-American liner *Stockholm*, was heading due east toward the Nantucket Lightship as the *Andrea Doria* was approaching it from the opposite direction. For the *Stockholm*, whose white was broken only by a single yellow funnel,

17

mast and kingposts, it was the first day out of New York. The Swedish ship, just three inches short of 525 feet from her sharply raked bow to her round stern, had left her pier at Fifty-seventh Street in New York at 11:31 that morning. The day had ben hot, muggy and overcast in New York and not much better out at sea. A haze blurred the rays of the summer sun, yet there was no fog as the *Stockholm* sailed away from New York. The Swedish ship had followed the French liner *Ile de France,* which had left her pier at Forty-eighth Street at the same time, down the Hudson River and out to sea. But the leviathan black and white French ship pulled steadily away from the *Stockholm* at sea, her engines building up to 22 knots. The *Stockholm* could at best do 18 or 19 knots. It was about 2:40 in the afternoon that the *Ile de France* faded from sight in the haze ahead as the *Stockholm* plowed through the sea toward the Nantucket Lightship. Her course was 90° true on the compass, or due east, designed to take her a mile off the Nantucket Lightship, from where she would swing north toward Scandinavia. It was her usual route, the shortest and most economical for a ship going to northern Europe.

Neither the *Stockholm* nor *Andrea Doria* was under any compulsion, legal or otherwise, to follow the so-called "recognized tracks" across the ocean, for neither the Swedish nor Italian lines were members of the North Atlantic Track Agreement. The Agreement was purely a voluntary arrangement among nine British, one United States, one Belgian, one French and one Dutch passenger steamship company. No government was a party to it. Nor did it apply to freighters, oilers, or any type of ship other than passenger vessels of the member companies. Even to the passenger ships of these companies, all plying between New York and English Channel ports, the tracks were not compulsory. The Track Agreement merely urges those passenger ships to use the routes "so far as circumstances permit."

Thus, on July 25, the *Stockholm* headed eastward on the usual westbound track which the *Andrea Doria* was following from the opposite direction toward the Nantucket Lightship. Yet in this there was nothing unusual, for each ship was plying the same route it had always followed.

The *Andrea Doria*, only three and a half years old, was a maiden in the elite society of luxury passenger ships. To many she was the most beautiful ship afloat. The Italian Line, in designing this ship which was to mark the rebirth of the Italian merchant marine after the second World War, decided wisely not to compete with the United States and Britain for size and speed of their ships. Instead, the *Andrea Doria* was imbued with Italy's matchless heritage of beauty, art and design. The 29,100 gross ton ship, 697 feet long and 90 feet wide, of course was no slowpoke midget. She was among the largest and fastest ships of the world. But there was something special about her. The Italian Line itself tried to put into words that special something which marked the *Andrea Doria* apart among ships of the world. The Italian Line said:

First of all, a ship that is worthy of the name must be a SHIP. She must be able to function as a huge machine ... to provide light and heat and numerous essential hotel services to her passengers. She must be able to cleave the ocean waves efficiently and safely, no matter what the weather conditions. She must get her passengers where they want to go with reasonable dispatch, adhering to a schedule announced in advance.

But today a ship must be more than that. For the period of her voyage she must be a whole way of life for her passengers. She must provide them with an experience that will somehow be

19

different and better than a comparable experience they could have anywhere else. This experience must be one they will enjoy while they have it . . . and one they will never forget as long as they live.

The *Andrea Doria* is, we think, unique. She was designed to be a huge, completely efficient machine, a real ship. She was also designed as a living testament to the importance of beauty in the everyday world.

Works of art were everywhere on the ship, particularly in the public rooms, and there were thirty-one different public rooms, providing an average of 40 square feet of recreational space for each of the 1,250 passengers the *Andrea Doria* could accommodate. Italian artists had created within the ship a small art world in murals and panels of rare woods, in ceramics, mirrors, mosaics and crystals. Four artist-designers were commissioned each to design his idea of a superlative luxury suite consisting of a bedroom, sitting room, powder room, baggage room and bath. The four de luxe first-class suites on the ship's Foyer Deck were completely different. One was wild in a design of blue mythological figures floating on a white background which covered the furniture as well as the walls. Another was sedate in the finest of expensive tastes. But all were modern, unusual and luxurious with thick plush rugs, heavy draperies and push-button conveniences. These cabins were the ultimate in luxury.

The rest of the ship was less luxurious only in degree, according to first, second or third class of accommodations. The entire ship was air-conditioned. Each of the three classes had its own motion picture theater for daily movies. Each had its own swimming pool and surrounding recreational area. In fact, when built, the *Andrea Doria* was the only ship with three outdoor swimming pools emphasizing out-

20

door living on the sunshine route of the Italian Line from the Mediterranean to New York. The swimming pools, each one decorated in distinctive ceramic tiles, were terraced on three decks of the ship's stern in country club settings of tables, sun umbrellas, pool bars and white-waistcoated waiters.

The ship itself was a work of art with exterior lines so graceful that the full length of the huge vessel from its sharply angled bow to its spoon-shaped overhanging stern seemed to thrust forward like a poised missile. Horizontal lines of the ship were rounded and soft while all vertical lines leaned back toward the stern, giving the impression of windswept movement. Her black hull and white superstructure, made of special alloys to minimize top weight, were topped by one slender mast and a single elliptical funnel which bore the red, white and green colors of Italy. Inside, the décor was modern but a gentle contemporary modern predominated by sensible, simple furniture, wood paneling, indirect lighting and the various original art creations. The most prominent art display, priceless in itself, was a mural covering more than 1,600 feet of wall space in the First-Class Lounge. Painted by Salvatore Fiume on eight wall surfaces, it surrounded the lounge with a three-dimensional art gallery showing the painting and sculpture of Italy's masters: Michelangelo, Raphael, Titian, Cellini and others. At the focal point of the lounge, in magnificent perspective to the mural, stood a giant bronze statue of the sixteenth-century admiral, Andrea Doria, staring sternly ahead, in full armor and cape, his right hand resting upon a sword half his own height. It was for him this ship was named.

Genoa, the home port of this ship, produced two of the world's greatest sea captains: Christopher Columbus and

21

Andrea Doria. While Columbus went off in search of new sea routes and new worlds, Doria stayed home and fought off in turn the Spanish, the French and Barbary pirates. One of the most wily fighting men and politicians of his day, Andrea Doria, who is credited as the first man to discover how to sail a ship against the wind, became Admiral of the Genoese Fleet and "father of his country." Like George Washington in the United States, Andrea Doria won independence from Spain for the republic of Genoa. After a long and harrowing career at sea and in politics, he retired to a monastery at the age of eighty-seven, only to be summoned to sea again to fight off the French who were attempting to annex Corsica. He led his fleet against the French and won again, returning to more acclaim from his countrymen in Genoa. He lived to the age of ninety-four, dying, it is said, only after he heard the news that his son had been killed in a campaign in Africa. But his name and reputation as well as his descendants and wealth lived on. Many ships were christened with his name following his death, including a small brig in the service of the American colonies revolting from British rule. The brig *Andrea Doria* was the first ship to be saluted by a foreign nation recognizing the sovereignty of the United States.

Like that of the Borghese, the name of Doria lived on through the centuries as one of the great family names of Italy and it was to Andrea Doria that the Italian Line returned when choosing a name fitting for the great ship it had designed after the second World War. The ship, whose new design was first tested in experimental tanks, was constructed in the famous Ansaldo Shipyards of Sestri, a suburb of Genoa, from 1949 to June 16, 1951, when, amid much fanfare, she was launched. Decorating the interior of this ship consumed another eighteen months and in December, 1952, she was taken out on her trial runs and tested at speeds in excess of 26 knots which well satisfied her owners.

The new ship's first master, who would take her on her maiden voyage to New York, was aboard for the trial runs. Captain Calamai also came from a family whose name in Genoa was connected with the sea, although the Calamai family had neither the station nor wealth of the Doria family. His father, Oreste, had made the Calamai name known in Italy by founding and editing the magazine *The Italian Navy*, the foremost magazine in its field. His older brother, Paolo, who had joined the navy before him, had risen to the rank of rear admiral and commanded the Annapolis of the Italian Navy at Leghorn. Captain Calamai began his sea career at eighteen years of age when he enlisted in the navy as an officer cadet on July 17, 1916. He served aboard two ships as an ensign during the first World War, winning the War Cross for Military Valor, and then completed his enlistment on three other ships after the war before he was released to pursue a career in the merchant marine. He had served as an officer on twenty-seven different ships of the Italian merchant marine before he was chosen as master of the *Andrea Doria*. His career was interrupted by the second World War during which he served at a reserve lieutenant commander, again winning a War Cross for Military Valor. The career of Piero (Little Peter) Calamai of Genoa was an unblemished success.

On the *Andrea Doria*'s first voyage from Genoa to New York in January, 1953, Captain Calamai had been the youngest of the Italian Line's ship masters to command a first-rate ship. Now, in July, 1956, on the fifty-first voyage of the *Doria*, Captain Calamai had reason to suspect, ironically enough, that this would be his last round trip on the *Andrea Doria*. He was due, upon bringing his ship back to Genoa from New York, for his annual vacation, after which he was in line to take command of the *Andrea Doria*'s sister ship, the *Cristoforo Colombo*, which, built a year later, succeeded the *Doria* as flagship of the Italian merchant fleet, whose captain was retiring at the mandatory age of sixty.

Approaching the Nantucket Lightship, the westbound New York leg of the fifty-first voyage was nearly over. The *Andrea Doria* had departed her home port of Genoa July 17 and had made her regular commuter rounds of the Mediterranean, stopping for passengers, cargo, and mail at Cannes on the French Riviera, Naples in southern Italy and British Gibraltar at the entrance of the Mediterranean. After weighing anchor at Gibraltar at 12:30 P.M. on Friday, July 20 and setting out for the North Atlantic, Captain Calamai had noted in his own logbook: *We have a total of 1,134 passengers (190 first class, 267 cabin class and 677 tourist class), 401 tons of freight, 9 autos, 522 pieces of baggage and 1,754 bags of mail.*

The nine-day voyage had been routine, nothing marking it in any way different from any of the previous fifty trips to New York. For the 1,134 passengers, the sea voyage had been a time to unwind, to settle into the luxury of being served and entertained. It was a time to cast off one's everyday cares and worries, to marvel at the vastness and power of the sea and to sense one's own individual place in the world. The routine of shipboard living, adjusting one's walk and digestion to the rhythm and roll of the ship, had become a way of life after a day or two at sea. Each day was marked by certain regular events. There were religious services each morning in the ship's exquisite chapel, the daily movie, the sports events on open deck, cocktails, after-dinner games, drinking, dancing and, above all, the enormous and elaborate meals. The amount of food and drink consumed each day on a ship like the *Andrea Doria* is astonishing: 5,000 eggs, 1,500 pounds of meat and fish, 2,000 pounds of fruits, 150 pounds of coffee, 200 gallons (or 800 bottles) of wine and about 100 gallons of milk (more for cooking than drinking purposes).

For the 572-man crew, each day had its routine of work and rest. Each man and woman in the crew had his or her job to do and knew his or her specific role in the chain of command on the ship. At the top of the command pyramid, of course, was the captain of the ship and upon his head rested the entire responsibility for the safe and efficient operation of the vessel. Thus, at about 3 P.M. on July 25, when Captain Calamai no longer had any doubt that the *Andrea Doria* was in fog, he ordered the usual precautions he prescribed for all occasions when in weather which reduced visibility.

Fog, rain, mist, snow, storms, gales and hurricanes all are facets of the character of the North Atlantic and in the summer months, fog or mist are to be expected in the vicinity of the Nantucket Shoals. Captain Calamai was not in the least surprised, for fog had become virtually part of the routine of the voyage from Nantucket to New York in July. At first, with the Nantucket Lightship some 160 miles ahead, the fog was light and patchy, but Captain Calamai had reason and past experience to suspect the fog would grow thicker as the *Doria* approached the Nantucket Lightship. When he gave the order that fog precautions be taken, his officers knew exactly what was expected of them.

Of the two radar sets on the bridge, the one to the right of the helm was switched on to the 20-mile range and one of the two watch officers posted himself at the radar screen as a lookout for any ship or object within twenty miles of the *Andrea Doria*. The ship's fog whistle, operated by compressed air, was flicked on and began to boom warnings at 100-second intervals through the fog. The twelve watertight doors, interconnecting the ship's eleven watertight compartments below A-Deck, were closed by the control panel on the bridge. And since fog settles down upon a ship at sea like a heavy cloud of minute water particles, which it is, the lookout in the crow's-nest was ordered forward to stand his watch on the peak of the ship's bow. There, closer to the level of the water, he was expected to sight anything ahead of the ship before it was seen by the lookouts and officers on the bridge. Such are the precautions, prescribed by law, taken on all ships proceeding in reduced visibility. They are as ordinary and routine as turning on the windshield wipers of an automobile in the rain.

Nor did Captain Calamai neglect to telephone down to the Engine Room. "We're in fog," was all he had to say. The engineers knew what to do. There are two ways to reduce the speed of a ship. One could throttle down by reducing the number of nozzles feeding high-compression steam from the boilers into the turbines. Or, one could reduce the steam pressure in the boilers. The latter was the practice on the *Andrea Doria*. It was cheaper to reduce steam pressure and burn less fuel although cutting steam pressure reduced the power and maneuverability of the ship in event of emergency, for it takes far longer to build up boiler pressure than to open closed turbine nozzles.

In any event, the reduction of speed on the *Doria* was only a token gesture to the requirement of reducing speed in fog. Steam pressure in the four boilers which drove the turbines was eased from 40 to 37 kilograms per square centimeter, reducing the speed of the ship just a little more than one knot. The engine telegraphs on the bridge and in the Engine Room remained at full speed ahead. The *Doria* was making 21.8 knots through the sea and fog instead of 23 knots.

The law governing speed in fog is contained in Rule 16 of the so-called Rules of the Road, officially entitled "Regulations for Preventing Collisions at Sea." *Every vessel shall, in fog, mist, falling snow, heavy rainstorms or any other condition similarly restricting visibility, go at a moderate speed, having careful regard to the existing circumstances and conditions,* Rule 16 says. The key words "a moderate speed" have been interpreted in the courts of the United States and throughout the world to mean a speed at which a vessel can come to a dead stop in the water in half the distance of the existing visibility. The theory behind this interpretation is that if two ships approaching each other can stop in half the distance of their visibility, a collision is *per se* impossible. If visibility is nil, the rule requires a ship to stop or go at the minimum speed sufficient to maintain steerage—at least until the weather clears. Actually, this has never or seldom been done in the open sea either before or after Rule 16 was promulgated and adopted in 1890.

Shipmasters facing the choice between delivering their passengers and/or cargo to port on schedule or slowing down for safety's sake in fog have consistently chosen to risk traveling at top or near top speed through fog. On-time arrivals have always been the measure of a captain's ability. Anyone could stop in a fog and wait for a day, two days or a full week, losing money for the company all the time and incurring the wrath of passengers and shippers. But it is the skillful captain who can bring his ship into port safely and

27

on schedule voyage after voyage. For the *Andrea Doria* to continue at full speed through fog was no careless undertaking. It was the kind of calculated risk considered necessary by sea masters, much as automobile drivers exceed legal speed limits on the highways.

In the Engine Room of the *Andrea Doria* a standby watch was posted, with a man at each of the large wheels which controlled the two turbines of the ship. At the instant of notice from the bridge, the men stood ready to stop and reverse the ship's engines.

Of the precautions taken and not taken, the passengers generally were oblivious. The turn of weather sent those who had been lounging near the three swimming pools back into their cabins for the final day's packing. Cabin luggage, with the last of the party dresses and evening suits, was collected by the room stewards during the afternoon and stacked along the starboard side of the Promenade Deck in anticipation of expeditious unloading at the pier the following morning. The Captain's Farewell Dinner and Ball had been held the previous evening. No parties or formal dress were scheduled for the final night at sea. It was meant to be a quiet, restful and relaxed evening for the passengers.

On the bridge of the ship, however, all was quiet but not quite relaxed. The afternoon fog patches grew closer and thicker as the day wore on. Only twice was Captain Calamai able to leave the bridge during two clearings in the fog. Once, at about 4 P.M., he went down to his cabin for some necessary paper work, and toward evening he left the bridge to change from his white summer uniform to his evening blues. As he left his cabin for the last time he took with him his navy-blue beret which he liked to wear as a protection for his head from the night sea air. Captain Calamai fully expected to spend the whole night on watch, guiding his beloved ship through the fog to New York. He ordered his dinner on the bridge, a light repast of soup, a small piece of meat and an apple. No omen of disaster disturbed the captain. Everything about him on the bridge of the *Andrea Doria* was being done in accordance with his instructions. All was routine.

Chapter Two

"LIGHTS TO PORT"

THE GLEAMING, white motorship *Stockholm* of the Swedish-American Line, bound for Copenhagen and Gothenburg, was seven hours and some 130 miles out of New York when its young third officer came up to the bridge for his 8:30 to midnight watch on July 25, 1956. It was the 103rd eastbound crossing of the North Atlantic for the small passenger liner launched in 1948. For the third officer, who had joined the ship two months earlier, it was his fourth eastbound trip aboard.

Johan-Ernst Bogislaus August Carstens-Johannsen at twenty-six years of age was a heavy-set, big-boned and handsome young man who stood six feet high and weighed 185 pounds.

31

His broad shoulders and barrel-shaped chest were offset in the mind's eye by a boyish face with a rosy-pink hue, smooth texture and expression of youthful candor. His dark chestnut hair, wavy and long, came down in a sharp widow's peak to his broad unwrinkled brow. He had the appearance of a man without a worry in the world. Ashore in one of his rough tweedy sports jackets, he could be easily taken for ten years younger—perhaps a high school football player.

Carstens—as he was called by all who knew him—stopped in the chartroom behind the wheelhouse for the routine check of the ship's navigational papers before relieving the watch. A quick perusal of the three-by-four-foot navigational chart spread out on the table showed him the course and approximate position of the *Stockholm*. The course, as always, was 90° true, or due east, from the Ambrose Light vessel stationed at the mouth of New York Harbor, to the Nantucket Lightship anchored beyond the shoals of Nantucket Island. The course, indicated by a straight penciled line, had not been changed since Carstens' last watch earlier that day. The ship's rough log contained the usual notations. Carstens flipped through several weather forecasts, one of which indicated fog beyond the Nantucket Lightship, but that was not unusual for the Nantucket area.

In the wheelhouse, Lars Enestrom, the senior second officer, greeted Carstens warmly and filled him in on the routine of the watch. The captain was in his cabin, the radar set was on for the night, no ships were within sight or within the 15-mile scope of the radar, the night lights had been switched on at 8 P.M. There was nothing unusual to report. The course was still 90 degrees. Enestrom told his younger friend that he thought the ship was perhaps somewhat north of course. He had taken a distance bearing on Block Island by radar at 11 minutes after 7, but he could not vouch for its accuracy. Block Island had been forty miles away. But anyway, Enestrom said, it seemed that the ship was about one and a half miles north of course. Carstens had better keep an eye on that, the second officer suggested.

Enestrom, a tall, slender Swede thirty years old with closely cropped blond hair, had become a friend of the young third officer. He often remained on the bridge for an hour or so beyond 8:30 to keep company with Carstens on the night watch. But this evening, the first night out, Enestrom was fatigued from the long work hours in port in preparation for sailing that morning. He excused himself politely, saying he was going straight to bed.

The day of departure is always a long, hard day for the officers and most of the crew of every passenger ship. Carstens, up since 6 A.M., had supervised the securing of passengers' automobiles aboard before sailing. But now, seven hours out of New York, he felt cleansed of the city's humid mugginess. He had had a hearty dinner, followed by a steam bath and shower in the ship's *aquasanium* and an hour's rest in his cabin before coming up for duty.

With Enestrom gone and the captain in his cabin, Carstens was in sole command of the *Stockholm* as it surged on toward the Nantucket Lightship. Three seamen constituted his watch. They divided the four-hour watch into equal 80-minute periods, taking turns as helmsman, lookout in the crow's-nest and standby-lookout. A feeling of confidence and well-being pervaded the young officer as he went through the routine of his watch.

"Every ship has its own long splice" is a saying familiar in many forms to men of the sea. It means in effect that each ship is a reflection of the "old man" or each ship is operated differently, according to the working philosophy and habits of the captain.

Captain Nordenson at sixty-three years of age, with almost forty-six years of sea life behind him, was a hard taskmaster. And the *Stockholm*, the oldest and smallest ship of the White Viking Fleet of the Swedish Line, was a compact, tightly run vessel. Like virtually all other passenger ships, the *Stockholm* had developed a personality and a character that reflected her eight years of life, her captain and crew, her owners, and above all, Sweden.

She was actually the fourth of the Swedish Line to bear her name. The first *Stockholm*, 565 feet long and almost 13,000 tons, was launched in 1904 and served a full and useful life until the 1930's. The second and third *Stockholms* had been ill-fated. The second ship, a luxury vessel of 28,000 tons, was launched at the Cantiere Riuniti Shipyards in Trieste in May, 1938. Scheduled for delivery to Sweden by the Italian shipyard the following April, the ship was mysteriously destroyed by fire at her shipyard pier. Nine months later the Swedish Line contracted with the same yard to build a third *Stockholm*, using the same design, keel and motors of the destroyed ship. This ship was launched in March, 1940, but then World War II prevented delivery. The third *Stockholm* was sold the following year to the Italian Line for $8,000,000. But she was never to leave the shipyard. When Italy surrendered to the Allies in 1943, the Germans, in control of Trieste, seized and stripped her and towed her out to the shallow waters of San Sabba where she was sunk by Allied bombing.

The Swedish Line by this time had had enough. Their technical staff began drawing plans for a smaller ship, one which could be built safely in one of Sweden's own shipyards. The plans for the second and third *Stockholms* went back into

34

the file. Gone were the ideas for a luxury ship with three swimming pools (one for the crew), ten decks, wide corridors, large windows, an outdoor dancing area and de luxe cabins with private verandas.

Instead of a 28,000-ton luxury ship, the fourth and present *Stockholm* was planned during the war years as a 12,165-ton ship, with seven decks, one indoor swimming pool, and the necessary public rooms and accommodations for 395 passengers instead of 1,300.

The *Stockholm*, launched early in 1948, was the first new passenger ship to cross the North Atlantic after the second World War. She was the largest ship ever built in Sweden but at the same time she also was the smallest passenger liner in the North Atlantic trade. Those were the days when all steamship companies were building small vessels. The thinking was that air travel would replace sea voyages in the postwar tourist traffic to Europe. No one foresaw the tremendous postwar surge in tourism that was to boost transatlantic shipboard travel to more than a million passengers a year despite and in addition to air transportation.

Seeing the error of its ways, the Swedish-American Line in 1953 had the *Stockholm*'s superstructure enlarged to increase its passenger capacity from 395 to 548. The ship still retained the sleek appearance of a racing yacht. She was 525 feet long, 69 feet at the beam, with a long forecastle, severely raked destroyer bow and gracefully rounded cruiser stern.

As her owners pointed out, the *Stockholm* was a ship built for comfort rather than luxury. The personal comfort resulted from the unexcelled service of her crew, the practical but not luxurious accommodations, and the engineering ingenuity of providing an outboard cabin for everyone, passengers and crew alike. From the senior officer down to the lowest and

35

newest pantry boy, each crewman reflected the Scandinavian concept of rigid devotion to duty and work. The company cared for the welfare of the crew as well as the passengers. No more than two crewmen were assigned to any one cabin, and each crew cabin was the equal if not better than the passenger accommodations.

The Swedish Line expected and received a full day of work from every crewman. The ships of the line were among the very few which assigned only one officer to each watch. While most ships assigned two officers to the bridge, so that one could remain lookout while the other tended to radar or navigational aids in the chartroom, Scandinavian liners believed one hard-working officer could discharge the necessary duties with no undue strain. The *Stockholm* had only three officers to stand regular watches around the clock. The captain and chief officer, who stood no regular watches, shared command of the bridge in times of need, such as reduced visibility, major changes of course, or approaches to landmarks, navigational aids and harbors.

In the wheelhouse, the nerve center and brain of the ship, Carstens felt in familiar, friendly surroundings as he went about the routine duties of the watch. The three seamen had their prescribed, limited duties and, in effect, Carstens was alone on the bridge. There was no smoking or coffee drinking permitted on the bridge of the *Stockholm*. Officers were not to fraternize with the seamen lest familiarity break down the chain of command rigidly adhered to on the ship. Conversation was limited strictly to matters in the line of duty.

There was nothing at all unusual about this night. All was routine. The ship was cutting through a calm sea on the first leg of the eastbound journey. After Ambrose, the next point of departure would be the Nantucket Lightship, located some

36

200 miles east of New York. The engine telegraphs, one on each wing of the bridge, were on FULL SPEED AHEAD. They had been set on leaving New York Harbor and would remain at full speed until the breakwaters of Copenhagen Harbor.

Pacing the breadth of the wheelhouse, Carstens glanced into the scope of the radar set near the right door. The illuminated sweep hand, rotating like a second hand on a watch, showed all clear, no ships within the 15-mile range of the radar beacon. The helmsman, Ingemar G. Bjorkman, a twenty-year-old lad with three years of sea duty behind him, kept both hands clasped on the spokes of the ribbed steering wheel, his eyes concentrated on the gyrocompass to his left. He stood on a raised wooden platform leaning his back against the rear wall. Ahead of him was the curved forward wall of the room, with its large square windows stretching across the 20-foot breadth of the room. Directly below the center window was the course box which held three oversized wooden dice, with the numbers 090 so that the helmsman would never be in any doubt as to the course to steer. The helmsman's only duty was to turn the wheel from side to side, compensating for the movement of the ship, keeping the vessel on the desired course. Carstens from time to time in his pacing of the wheelhouse stopped to glance at the compass. The purpose was to check the steering of the helmsman and also to remind him that the officer was keeping tabs on him.

The sky was cloudy and overcast when Carstens had come on watch. With the ship's clocks still set at New York's Eastern Daylight Time, at 8:30, it was not yet night. But the light of day was fading fast and the sea seemed a deep gray, turning to a dull black. Although it is extremely difficult to judge distances with any degree of accuracy in the open sea with no

landmarks to guide the eye, Carstens vaguely estimated that
the horizon was some five or six miles distant.

At about 9 p.m., Captain Nordenson came up to the
bridge for his postprandial look around. The captain, as
was his custom on the first night out, had dined in his cabin
one deck directly below the wheelhouse. Captain Nordenson, who had commanded at one time or another every one
of the Swedish-American Line ships, was a strict disciplinarian who spared few words in casual conversation with
either his officers or crew lest that relax the discipline of his
ship. Carstens, engrossed in his duties, was unaware of the
captain's arrival until he noticed the skipper pacing the
starboard wing of the bridge.

Captain Nordenson, a man grown portly but not soft with
age, walked with his head down, back and forth along the
narrow passageway on the aft part of the bridge wing. He
responded to Carstens' greeting and then continued his
pacing.

Carstens would have liked to talk. He was a gregarious,
outward-going young man who enjoyed chitchat, bull ses-
sions into the night, parties and general good times. His
nature was open and ingenuous and his life at sea agreed
with him, for it imposed a discipline upon his working hours
and left him fully free to do as he wished during his off-duty
hours. Carstens, at this time of his life, felt about as close as
a man can be to the ideal of being without worry or heavy
care. He had had a turbulent childhood as the youngest child
in a respected upper-class family of Lund, a cultural center
of southern Sweden, where his father, a physician, was the
medical director of the province. He had followed his older
brother and sister in the best private schools of Lund, but
where his brother went on to become a lawyer and legal

counsel to the Bishop of Linkoping and his sister had become a dentist and was seeking a medical degree, Carstens had had trouble adjusting himself to one school after another. He had "found himself" only when he had gone to work on the herring fishing boats of the Baltic Sea during summer school vacations when he had been fifteen and sixteen years of age. When he had completed his compulsory schooling, the equivalent of a high school education in the United States, he had shipped out to sea with a boyhood friend.

Two years later, in 1949, both he and his friend were hired by the Brostrom Concern, the largest shipowning company in Sweden, and they soon learned the value of education even at sea. After three years as an apprentice seaman, Carstens qualified for Sweden's Nautical College and there he worked hard and sweated to pass his examinations for an officer's license in 1953. Later that year he passed his Master's examination, completing all the studies necessary for a Master's license. He needed only time and sea experience to earn the right to command any size ship in the Swedish merchant marine. After nautical school, Carstens served fifteen months in the Royal Swedish Navy's minesweeping operations in the North and Baltic seas and in 1955 he returned to the Brostrom company which gave him varied experience on three cargo ships, a full-sail training ship and the passenger liner *Kungsholm* before he was assigned to the *Stockholm* on May 19, 1956.

On the night of July 25, this young man had every reason to be satisfied with himself. He had made the grade in his chosen field, for he knew that only the better men were assigned to the passenger liners of the Brostrom company. He had, he felt, the confidence of his captain, his fellow officers and his company. His private life also had found some direction. On Little Christmas Eve of the previous year he had married a slim, dark-haired, pretty Alsatian girl, Liliane Martel, and she was waiting for him in a new apartment she had found in Gothenburg, the home port of his ship. They were expecting their first child in five more months.

Carstens went about his duties on the bridge without undue concern. He was not the worrying type. He gazed out at the sea and he glanced at the radar screen at frequent intervals for any sign of another ship, aware of the likelihood of meeting westbound ships head-on en route to the Nantucket Lightship. There would also be ships crossing the *Stockholm* bow from time to time in these heavily trafficked waters. But this was part of the routine and there were rules of the road for ships on the open sea. Carstens had no worries. He checked the navigation lights of the *Stockholm* each time he went out on a bridge wing. The *Stockholm,* like all ships, carried two white masthead lights—one on the tall mast behind the wheelhouse and a forward, lower light— which were required to be visible for five miles. The *Stockholm* also had a green side light below the bridge on starboard side and a red light on her port side, each visible for two miles.

He checked the engine telegraphs, one on each of the bridge wings, whose handles were in the forward position for FULL SPEED AHEAD. Below, in the Engine Room, two huge diesel engines were pounding out 14,600 horsepower to drive the ship's twin propellers 110 times a minute.

Carstens checked his helmsman and his lookouts as well to see that none of them were slipping on their duties. As watch officer he was responsible for everything on the bridge. His watch was young in years. At twenty-six, Carstens was the oldest man on the bridge. Peder Larsen, a Danish

40

seaman, was the next oldest, a few months younger than Carstens, but he was new to the *Stockholm*. The other two seamen, twenty-year-old Bjorkman and Sten Johansson, who was eighteen, were young men with the training and discipline of apprentices who hoped to go to nautical college and become officers in the future.

At 9:20 P.M., one-third of the watch was over and the three seamen changed positions. Johansson, who had been on standby, relieved Bjorkman at the helm. Bjorkman climbed a ladder to the roof of the wheelhouse and motioned for Larsen to climb down from the crow's-nest. Larsen scampered down the mast ladder to become standby and Bjorkman went up for the next eighty minutes to the small enclosure near the top of the mast. It was the best vantage point in clear weather to maintain a lookout, for the higher the distance from sea level the greater the visibility.

Ten minutes later, having checked the navigation chart, Captain Nordenson told Carstens to change course from 90 to 87 degrees. The officer immediately relayed the order to helmsman Johansson, flipped the wooden numerals in the course box to 087 and then went into the chartroom to lay out the new course. Carstens surmised that the captain wished to draw closer to the Nantucket Lightship, although the laconic captain saw no need to explain his actions to the young officer.

As the helmsman eased the wheel to the new course, Carstens in the chartroom calculated the ship's position as of 9:40 P.M. by dead reckoning. He did this by reading off the last two numbers on the ship's SAL log, an instrument which records the mileage of the ship by means of a brass tube projecting from the bottom of the ship, and marking on the course line the number of miles traveled since the last posi-

41

tion, which had been taken at 8 P.M. The two dead reckoning positions indicated the ship had traveled thirty miles in the past hour and forty minutes.

Carstens thus found the approximate position of the ship at 9:40 P.M. and from that position drew a new course line of 87 degrees true. He erased the 90-degree line, which had passed eight miles south of the Nantucket Lightship. The 87-degree line passed the lightship at about three miles, but this too was an approximation. The officer knew that northerly currents would set the ship within the desired one or two miles distance from the lightship when passing abeam. Not less than one nor more than two miles was the usual passing distance from the lightship the captain desired before setting a new course for Sable Island and a clear untrafficked route to the north of Scotland.

With Nantucket Lightship still too far away for accurate bearing measurements by radio or radar, dead reckoning was the only means of navigation at that point. Any error in calculation could be corrected, Carstens knew, when the lightship was sighted within the 15-mile range of radar. Dead reckoning, so misunderstood by so many laymen, should properly be written *d'ed* reckoning, an abbreviation for deduced reckoning. Despite all modern innovations it is still the prevalent method of navigating across a trackless ocean in a small or large ship.

When Carstens returned to the wheelhouse, having noted the change of course on the navigation map and in the logbook, the end of the day was complete. Night had fallen and the sea and sky assumed a different, more luxuriant mood. The gray of day had turned to black with the bright yellow light of an almost full moon glimmering on a calm ocean. The waves appeared long and irregular. The ship rode easily, rolling slowly from side to side, through the undulating water. It seemed, indeed, a beautiful night to Carstens. Little did he realize then that he would never be able to forget afterwards this impression of the moon, full but for a sliver on top, as it cast a spotlight beam of yellow on the right side of his ship. Occasionally the moon ducked behind a cloud but soon reappeared some 20 degrees off to the right of the ship.

The night remained almost as warm as the day, about 70 degrees, and both doors of the wheelhouse leading to the wings of the bridge were left open. Ordinarily the windward door was kept closed to prevent the cross breeze from whipping through the pilothouse. But this night there was only the slightest breeze from the southwest.

Carstens, of course, was not alone in admiring the beauty of the night at sea. Several passengers before retiring enjoyed the unique pleasure of the salty sea air of summer. Miss Colleen E. Bruner, of Des Moines, Iowa, not only remarked on the moon but also pointed out the Big Dipper to her sister.

For Carstens, this watch seemed not only routine but somewhat dull. On each four-hour watch from New York to the Nantucket Light, the *Stockholm* usually encountered one, two or three ships which required the watch officer to take some action. But on this night, Carstens had not sighted a single ship. To pass the time, he switched the radar set range from 15 to 50 miles. The wider range brought on the radar screen the east coast of the United States and Carstens enjoyed trying to identify points along the coast. Martha's Vineyard, an island off the coast of Massachusetts, was easy for Carstens to identify on the radar screen. It showed up as a large blob of yellow. Further ahead, although it was not yet on the radar screen, Carstens knew he would

43

see Nantucket Island and the lightship. On the 50-mile range, ships were too small to show up on the radar screen and the young officer soon turned the radar set back to the 15-mile range so that it served as a lookout for ships beyond man's normal vision.

Shortly before ten o'clock, Carstens noticed that Chief Officer Herbert Kallback had come up to the open deck of the bow where three seamen had been on their hands and knees all evening scrubbing down the wooden deck of the bow. It was to be polished with oil the following morning as a protection against the salt air and sea spray. The chief officer, as usual, was carrying a black flashlight in his left hand like a general with a swagger stick. Carstens watched as the chief officer inspected the work on the foc's'le deck, then apparently approving the progress of the work, called a halt for the night and led the men off the bow.

Shortly afterwards, Captain Nordenson came into the wheelhouse and announced he was going down to his cabin and would be there if needed. "Call me when you see Nantucket," he told the third officer. Neither man could remember the short, casual conversation afterwards. Whether the captain had said anything about the possibility of fog or not, neither man could recall. If he had, it would have been superfluous, they said later. Carstens knew of Captain Nordenson's standing orders that he was to be summoned at any time of day or night in the event of fog or any other potentially dangerous event. Captain Nordenson went down one deck to his cabin to catch up on some paper work for the two hours before he would be needed on the bridge to make the change of course upon reaching the Nantucket Lightship. It was his practice not to retire on the first night out until after the lightship had been passed.

44

When the captain had left the bridge, Carstens noticed the
time and decided to determine the position of the ship.
Nantucket Lightship, about 40 miles ahead, was now within
range of the ship's radio direction finder, Carstens thought.
Before leaving the wheelhouse, however, he checked the
radar to be certain there was no ship within 15 miles of the
Stockholm. He called his standby, Peder Larsen, from a small
room behind the wheelhouse to stand lookout on the bridge
and he glanced at the gyrocompass to make sure the helmsman was steering the desired course of 87°.

In the chartroom Carstens switched on the radio direction
finder, which working on batteries was ready for instant use,
tuned it to 314 kilocycles, and turned the compass wheel
eastward to pick up the radio beacon signal of the Nantucket
Lightship. The signal was loud and clear in his earphones.
Carstens zeroed it carefully to minimum and, reading the
bearing on the compass, he laid off a corresponding line on the
chart. Then he swung the wheel of the direction finder to the
northwest to pick up the radio beacon signal of Block Island,
which the *Stockholm* had passed three hours before, and
drew that bearing line on his chart. Where the two lines
intersected was the position of the ship at 10:04 P.M. by the
electric clock on the chartroom wall. As an additional check
he noted by the ship's echo sounder that the depth of water
beneath the ship was 35 fathoms and that corresponded with
the depth noted for that position on the chart.

Thus, in about three minutes time, Carstens fixed the position of the ship with a fair degree of accuracy. The *Stockholm,* he saw, was two and one-half miles north of the course
set by the captain.

Carstens returned to the wheelhouse and checked the
radar. The flasher showed no ships or obstructions on the

radar scope. Two and one-half miles off course was not very much at this point of the voyage, Carstens thought, but he decided to recheck his position again in a half hour before taking any corrective action. He checked the tide tables too, which convinced him that the currents were setting the *Stockholm* northward.

At 10:30 P.M., he took another RDF position. This time, he not only took bearings on Nantucket Lightship and Block Island but he also took a third bearing on the Pollock Rip Lightship some 60 miles to the north. The three bearings left no doubt. The *Stockholm* was now two and three-quarter miles north of the projected course line. He would have to correct for the northerly currents.

Carstens walked back into the wheelhouse. "Steer 89," he told Johansson.

"Eighty-nine, yes, sir," responded the helmsman, turning the wheel slowly to the right as he watched two degrees click off on the gyrocompass.

Carstens had made his first independent decision of the routine watch, then two-thirds over. He turned the numbers in the course box to read 089. The two-degree change to the south, or to the right, would compensate for the northerly set of the current, he expected. At any rate, he decided he would check his position again in another half hour.

A few minutes later, at 10:40, Peder Larsen took over the helm from young Johansson for the final third of the watch. Johansson relieved Bjorkman in the crow's-nest and Bjorkman went to rest his feet in the standby room.

Carstens continued to pace the bridge on watch. There was a slight haze on the horizon but visibility continued to be good. Each time Carstens walked out to the bridge wing, he glanced up at the crow's-nest to see that the lookout was alert, and further up the mast to confirm that the navigation lights were burning clearly. Every three minutes or so he inspected the radar scope for a sign of any ship.

Carstens, as he paced the bridge, paid particular attention to Peder Larsen at the wheel. This was Larsen's first voyage on the *Stockholm* although he had had eight years of previous sea duty.

Carstens thought Larsen could steer the ship well enough when he kept his mind on what he was supposed to be doing. But the Danish seaman seemed to have an insatiable curiosity about what was going on about him and he carelessly allowed his attention to wander from the compass he was supposed to watch. That was all right for the steering of a freighter or a ferryboat, Carstens thought, but Larsen would have to learn that a helmsman was expected to keep a passenger liner on a tight, straight course within one degree of the desired course line. Larsen allowed the *Stockholm* at times to yaw two, three and even four degrees to either side.

Aware of this trait of his helmsman, Carstens sought to keep a tight rein upon him. Each time he walked through the wheelhouse, which was every three to five minutes, Carstens pointedly stopped to look at the compass by which Larsen was steering. The helmsman could have no doubt that the officer was checking his steering and the wordless reminder was enough to turn Larsen's eyes upon the compass.

As for the helmsman's point of view, Larsen had complete confidence in his own ability to steer the *Stockholm,* or any other ship. He just did not see the necessity for keeping his eyes glued to the compass like a robot. A glance at the compass and the feel of the wheel in his hand sufficed, he thought, and despite the yawing of the ship he did make good the course he was to steer by.

47

Carstens, more concerned about the possible drifting of the *Stockholm* off course, wanted to take another RDF fix to determine what effect his two-degree change of course at 10:30 P.M. had made in the *Stockholm*'s position. He checked the horizon visually and by radar for any other ships and, finding none, called Bjorkman from the standby room to stand lookout watch on the bridge while he was in the chartroom.

Carstens took this fix on the radio beacons of the Nantucket and Pollock lightships. As he did with the other RDF position fixes, Carstens noted on the navigation chart the mileage on the log and the time. It was actually 10:48 P.M., if one computes the time by the ship's speed and distance from the previous fix, but Carstens noted the time as 11 P.M. Why he did this, he could never explain. This inaccuracy was to plague him in the months ahead, but he could not know that at the time. Nor could he foresee even 21 minutes into the future.

What concerned Carstens at the moment was that the *Stockholm*, despite the two-degree change in course, was now three miles north of the projected course. The tide was causing the ship to drift progressively farther to the north. At 10:04, the ship had been two and one-half miles off the course line; at 10:30, she was two and three-quarters miles off, and now three miles off.

Carstens strode back into the wheelhouse and ordered another two-degree turn to the right. Larsen eased the wheel to 91 degrees as Carstens checked the radar scope. This time he saw the "pip" of a ship.

The pip was small and faint, a yellow dot appearing at a distance of 12 miles and just slightly off to the left of the *Stockholm*'s heading flasher. Bending over the radar, with his eyes focused on the spot where he had seen the pip, Carstens tried to adjust the set for added brightness to bring the pip into better focus. But it remained dim and small. He decided to wait until the pip showed the vessel to be 10 miles away. Then, he told himself, he would plot the course of the ship on the Bial Maneuvering Board set up beside the radar scope. The maneuvering board, 14 by 18 inches, corresponded to the radar scope. By plotting the other ship from 10 miles away, he could allow one mile for each concentric ring of the maneuvering board and obtain a larger diagram than by plotting from 12 miles and halving the value of the ten concentric distance rings.

Radar is one of the most simple devices of the electronic age, so simple as to be deceiving. It is in the misuse of the instrument or the misinterpretation of what it tells you, that navigators go wrong so often.

The radar set on the bridge of the *Stockholm*, which is not materially different from those on any other ship, has a round television-like screen which is dark except for illuminated hands originating in the center of the scope like the hands of a watch. The scope is a cathode tube which always shows the home ship to be in the center and stationary. One hand, the ship's heading flasher, always points upward to 12 o'clock. Another hand, the flasher, circles the scope about 12 times every minute continuously, in synchronization with the ship's revolving radar antenna atop the mast. Any object struck by the very high-frequency radio signals emitted by the set through the antenna appears on the radar scope at the appropriate distance and bearing. The outer rim of the circular scope is marked off with the 360 degrees of a compass. With the heading flasher on the course of your own ship, you can determine the relative position of the other

49

ship at that given instant by noting its bearing in relation to your ship. This is done by putting the third hand, called the cursor, which is similar to the alarm setting hand of a clock, on the pip and noting the number of degrees it is away from the heading flasher.

Because one observation is true for only the instant it is made, at least two observations must be plotted on a paper or device similar to the radar scope in order to determine the course of the other ship in relation to your own ship— provided neither ship changes course. Only by plotting at least three observations can one see if a ship is changing course. And only by timing the various positions can one determine the speed of the other vessel. And then, with a bit of trigonometry, one can simply determine the true course of the other vessel.

In the dark of the wheelhouse, Carstens switched on and adjusted the light beneath the plastic surface of the Bial Maneuvering Board, lighting it like the dashboard panel of an automobile so that the numbers and lines on the board could be seen and yet no light reflected into the dark wheelhouse. He adjusted the compass ring around the radar scope to the 91-degree course of the ship and watched the pip of the other vessel until it reached 10 miles distance. At that exact moment he asked the helmsman for the actual heading of the *Stockholm*. Larsen sang out, "Ninety degrees." The pip at that moment was one degree to port. Adding the one degree difference from 90 to 91, he marked an X on the plotting board two degrees to port and 10 miles away. With a glance back at the chartroom wall clock, which he could see through the open door, Carstens noted the time of his observation. Later he could not recall it.

The young officer watched the pip on the radar for several

seconds to determine that it represented a ship coming toward the *Stockholm*. This was not unusual on the *Stockholm's* route from New York to Nantucket. It was expected.

Carstens, informing Bjorkman of the ship, ordered him to stand lookout on the port wing of the bridge. After the ship had been safely passed would be time enough for Bjorkman to rest in the standby room.

Carstens walked from the radar to one wing of the bridge, looked out to sea, walked back to the radar to check the pip of the other ship, and then went to the other bridge wing to scan the horizon. The night, it seemed to Carstens, had not changed. The moon shone overhead and the sea remained calm.

He plotted the pip of the other ship again with the help of the helmsman. It was six miles away and four degrees to port. Giving his entire attention to the exact marking of the other ship's position, he was unaware of the bridge clock ringing six bells for 11 P.M. Larsen at the wheel, however, responded by pulling the lanyard over his head for six chimes on the ship's bell above the wheelhouse. It was his duty as helmsman to sound the hour to the whole ship.

Captain Nordenson in his cabin below the wheelhouse noted the six bells and, pausing in his writing, thought he would soon have to go up to the bridge for the approach to the Nantucket Lightship. But he did have a half hour or so before the lightship would be picked up on radar. He continued to write in his personal diary: *Beautiful weather and warm, a slight haze on the horizon. 1131 departed from New York. Sent a letter to my Sonia, darling* [his wife]. *It's very nice to get away from the heat in New York.*

Carstens on the bridge neglected to note the time for his six-mile observation. He looked out at the black night beyond

51

the port bow of the *Stockholm,* expecting to see the mast-head lights of the other ship.

He had, of course, full confidence in his radar. The set had been checked and calibrated for accuracy the day before the ship sailed from New York. Yet good seamanship, as Carstens had learned it in school, called for him to wait if possible until he visually sighted the lights of the other ship before taking action. And he expected to see the lights then or at any moment at about 20 degrees off his port bow.

He had marked an X on the plotting board corresponding with the range of six miles and four degrees to port. Then he ruled a straight line between the X's, noting that it showed the bearing of the other ship was increasing and that the ship would pass—if neither one changed course—to the left of the *Stockholm* at a distance of between one-half and one mile. He decided he would have to turn to the right to increase the passing distance because Captain Nordenson's standing orders were never to allow another vessel to come within one mile of the *Stockholm.*

He expected to have plenty of time before the ships met to turn the *Stockholm* to the right and execute the usual port-to-port, or left-to-left, passing. This was in accordance to Rule 18 of the International Rules of the Road: *When two power-driven vessels are meeting end on, or nearly end on, so as to involve risk of collision each shall alter her course to starboard, so each may pass on the port side of the other.*

Having plotted the course of the other ship, Carstens walked to the starboard wing of the bridge where he told lookout Bjorkman, "Keep a sharp lookout for a ship on the port!"

This was all routine. Carstens was not in the least concerned. He had executed this maneuver many, many times before. Port-to-port passings were the pactice at sea. It is only when meeting a ship at sea starboard-to-starboard that a navigator must make a basic decision. The accepted practice in a right-to-right passing situation in open waters is for both ships to turn to their right early enough to execute the usual port-to-port passing. It is only when the two ships are so far to the right of one another that it would be dangerous to attempt to cross over for a port-to-port passing, that the starboard-to-starboard passing is acceptable. And then, the law courts have held, the ships must pass on each other's right side without having to alter course. But Carstens did not have this to concern him: the ship he saw on his radar was on his port or left side.

As he peered into the dark night, however, he began to wonder why he did not see the lights of the other ship. The radar told him the other ship was a fast one. But what size ship or what type ship, he could not tell. He saw the radar pip of the ship advance to within five miles of the *Stockholm* and still he could not sight the vessel.

The underlying principle for all the Steering and Sailing Rules of the Rules of the Road is stated in the preliminary: *In obeying and construing these Rules, any action taken should be positive, in ample time, and with due regard to the observance of good seamanship.* This is the basic safety rule of all the regulations promulgated to prevent collisions at sea. It means that in taking advantage of the relatively slow speed of ships, and overcoming the disadvantages of poor braking or stopping power of ships, every change of course taken to avoid a collision must be taken early and must be a bold or sharp action or change of course. Only a bold alteration of course, one of at least 20 degrees, can be easily seen from another ship. And it must be taken far

53

enough away from the other ship that NO MATTER what the other ship does, there can be no collision. This is prudent seamanship!

When the oncoming ship was four miles away, Carstens turned the knob of the radar set to the close-up range of five miles. The pip became enlarged, taking the shape of a yellow bean on a black background. The illuminated flasher circled the screen indicating no other ships in the vicinity. Although Carstens did not bother to notice the time, the bridge clock showed 11:03 P.M.

Again he peered into the night and now he began to wonder why he did not see the lights. No definite reason occurred to him. Not for a single moment did he think that there might be fog. To him the night seemed clear enough. He assumed visibility was as good for the other ship. It occurred to him that the lights of the other ship might be defective. That did happen sometimes. Ships did steam through the night without running lights, contrary to law. It was possible also that the other ship was a naval vessel on maneuvers, running with her lights blacked out.

If he had thought of fog, he could have called the captain up to the bridge instantly. A speaking tube directly to the captain's cabin was not more than 18 inches away from the radar set, on the starboard wall of the wheelhouse.

For a fleeting moment Carstens thought of summoning the captain, but he dismissed that idea. He was sure he would see the other ship in a moment. Still the thought of fog or of a fog patch blacking out the lights of the oncoming ship did not occur to Carstens. Nor was he worried. He was not the worrying type of man or officer. He was aware of the easy maneuverability of the *Stockholm*. She handled well, responded instantly to the wheel and had tremendous stopping power. The great advantage of diesel motors which ran the *Stockholm* was that, like the motor of an automobile or truck, they had 100 per cent backing power. Steam turbines, more efficient than diesels in running larger ships, were rated with only 30 to 60 per cent backing power.

The bridge clock showed 11:06 P.M. The *Stockholm* was plowing full speed ahead at more than 18 knots when Carstens went once again to look at the radar scope. The radar pip was still there, off to port, closing in on the *Stockholm* when Bjorkman sang out, "Lights to port."

Carstens, standing at the corner of the radar set, looked through the square window to the left of the radar set and there, where he had expected them to be, he saw the two white dots of the ship's lights. He could make out also a weak red light, the portside light of the other ship.

He looked down into the radar scope. The pip showed the ship to be about 1.8 or 1.9 miles away. It was just inside the two-mile ring of the radar scope.

Picking up binoculars from a ledge on the aft wall some ten feet away, Carstens strode to the port wing of the bridge for a better look at the lights. The forward light was a bit to the left of the aft light as he saw them, indicating the ship was heading still farther away from the *Stockholm*.

Now, certain in his mind of the position and course of the other ship, he decided he would increase the safety margin for the passing. "Starboard," he called out. Larsen turned the wheel steadily two complete turns to the right.

Carstens watched the *Stockholm* bow swing away from the approaching vessel and called out, "Amidships." Larsen turned the wheel back to its center position. Meanwhile, the bridge telephone rang.

Carstens watched the *Stockholm* straighten out on her new

55

course. She had swung some 20 degrees to the right. Then he ordered "Steady so," and Larsen steadied the ship on her new course.

The orders had been given calmly in a voice hardly raised from a normal speaking tone. To Carstens, again, this was a routine maneuver. He no more suspected disaster within three minutes than does a sleeping man fear being struck by lightning.

He took one more look at the masthead lights of the unknown ship to the left, satisfied himself the ships would pass safely port-to-port, and then went to answer the telephone. He walked at a normal gait across the darkened wheelhouse to the telephone mounted on the rear wall on the starboard side of the wheelhouse. So sure was he of a safe passing, the young officer did not bother to look again at the other ship.

Turning his back on the approaching ship, he picked up the telephone. "The bridge," he said.

"Lights 20 degrees to port," reported Johansson from the crow's-nest.

"All right," said Carstens, and hung up. He stood with his left shoulder toward the wall as he spoke, facing the helmsman.

Johansson, replacing the phone in the crow's-nest, looked out at the lights of the other ship. In that instant the eighteen-year-old youth saw the position of the lights begin to change. He stared in disbelief as the forward light crossed under the aft light. The lights now, as he saw them, were in a switched position, the forward light to the right of the rear light. The other ship was going to cross the bow of the *Stockholm*. The seaman reached for the telephone and then stopped the motion. He didn't call the bridge again. His duty as lookout

56

was to report the sighting of other vessels to the bridge. Now it was up to the bridge.

Lookout Bjorkman on the starboard wing of the bridge also saw the lights change. He started across the wheelhouse to tell the mate. But then he saw the officer also had seen the lights.

Carstens, having walked back to the port wing, stood with his binoculars focused on the lights. He had stopped for a glance at the radar before returning to the port wing. While on the telephone, he had not seen the other ship start her swing across the *Stockholm* bow. The changed position of the radar pip had not registered in his mind. His glance at the ship through the windows of the *Stockholm* as he walked to the bridge wing also failed to alert him.

But when he reached the bridge wing, the situation roared up at him. No longer was this the safe passing situation he had assumed. He saw the enormous broadside of a giant black ship, sparkling with lights like Copenhagen's Tivoli. The ship was heading across his bow. Amidst this phantasmagoria, he saw the glow of the ship's green running light. It was the starboard side of the other vessel!

Carstens lunged at the engine telegraph in front of him. Heaving his body over the telegraph stanchion, he gripped a handle in each of his huge hands and pulled the twin levers together to the upright STOP position and an instant later plunged them down to FULL SPEED ASTERN.

"Hard a-starboard," he cried out to Larsen, as he cursed the unknown ship ahead of him. The engine telegraph clappers clanged out their harsh brassy cry as Carstens moved the handles. At the same time, he thought he heard a whistle signal from the other ship, but because of the bells of his own engine telegraph, he could not be sure.

Larsen reacted immediately. As fast as he could reverse one hand over the other he swung the power-driven wheel to the right. It spun around once, twice, three, four and five full turns and then it would go no farther.

Captain Nordenson below reacted immediately. Upon hearing the telegraph cables to the Engine Room moving inside his wall, he pushed his chair back from his desk, grabbed for his cap and started off for the bridge. Fog, he thought. The ship had come upon sudden fog and Carstens topside had reversed the engines, the captain thought as he left his cabin.

Next door, Acting Chief Engineer Gustav Assargren also reacted immediately. He had just finished reading a book and had turned off his light when he heard the bells of the engine telegraph on the bridge. He hopped out of bed and began shedding his pajamas. Any engine maneuver at sea was unusual and, he decided, his place was in the Engine Room.

In the Engine Room the telegraph repeaters clanged out the startling order for full speed astern, and two officers and three motormen reacted immediately. While the men in the Auxiliary Engine Room came running into the Main Engine Room, Second Engineer Justra Svensson, posted on the maneuvering platform between the controls for the two giant diesel motors, turned the wheel of the starboard motor to STOP. Motorman Alexander Hallik at the same time turned a smaller wheel to open an air valve necessary to reverse the engine. Then Svensson lunged across the 10-foot platform separating the two motors, and stopped the port engine. The forty-seven-year-old officer raced back to the starboard engine and turned the wheel to FULL SPEED ASTERN. It was like bringing an automobile to a full stop before going into reverse.

On the bridge, Carstens and the two seamen felt the ship shudder as the braking action began to take hold. But a ship does not screech to a stop like a car. They felt the braking, but they saw the *Stockholm* plunging ahead on her starboard turn still heading for the unknown ship ahead.

Terror welled up inside Peter Larsen, making his first voyage on the *Stockholm,* as he saw the enormous black hull of the unknown ship fill the square windows before his eyes. One sharp thought cut through his mind. A shiny brass alarm button was not more than five feet away. He could, he thought wildly, dash from the wheel in an instant, push that button and alarm the entire ship of the catastrophe which was seconds away. He might save hundreds of lives. The passengers should have the chance of at least this warning. The thoughts raced through Larsen's head, but he remained at the wheel, obeying his orders, holding the rudder at hard right, watching disaster happen, and muttering to himself, "I'm a goner ... this is the end for me."

One passenger at least, Dr. Horace Pettit, a devoted amateur yachtsman who never failed to carry a compass in his pocket, had been alerted by the distant sound of a whistle signal from another ship. Without a moment's hesitation, he dropped the book he was reading, thrust his head through the open porthole of his cabin and saw a ship, her lights aglow, speeding across the *Stockholm*'s bow. "Brace yourself," he yelled to his wife, "we're going to crash!"

Up until the very last instant, Carstens just did not believe the ships would collide. Somehow they would miss one another, his mind insisted. He gripped the engine telegraph on the port wing of the bridge and watched with horror the sight which afterwards he would discover he could never drive from his mind for very long.

"The watertight doors!" The thought screamed through Carsten's mind at the last moment. The watertight doors, which would protect the *Stockholm* from possible sinking, were still open. And the two ships drew closer and closer together.

Chapter Three

"I CAN SEE A SHIP"

ON THE BRIDGE of the *Andrea Doria*, the watch changed at 8 P.M. The ship was surrounded by a thick, opaque fog which cut visibility to about one-half mile. At times the wet mist even cut off the bow of the ship from the view of the men on the bridge. The wheelhouse was turning dark as the two officers of the eight-to-midnight watch came up to the bridge together. They were unalike in appearance and personality. Senior Second Officer Franchini was a tall, thin, dark-complexioned man of serious mien, thirty-seven years old, while his colleague, Junior Third Officer Eugenio Giannini, was blond, light-skinned, short and stocky, a cheerful, eager officer of twenty-eight.

First Officer Luigi Oneto, the senior watch officer, passed the watch to Franchini while Giannini, the youngest officer on the ship, relieved Second Officer Junior Guido Badano at the radar. "Come, I'll show you the position on the chart," Oneto said to Franchini. The two men went into the chartroom where the first officer pointed out the approximate position of the ship. Franchini glanced at the rough log as Oneto, who was leaving the watch, spelled out the various fog precautions which had been taken. The course of the ship was 267° true. The numerals were written on a small blackboard over the chart table and on a blackboard in front of the helmsman.

Giannini performed the usual functions which began each watch by checking the three compasses on the bridge to see that they were properly adjusted to one another. He then checked the panel controlling the watertight doors. He saw the twelve small red lights gleaming in the wheelhouse.

At the radar to the right of the helm, Badano pointed out in the scope the pips of three ships which showed in the 20-mile range of the Raytheon radar set. "They are all going with us," Badano said. Giannini saw that two ships were about nine miles ahead of the *Doria*, one bearing some 40 degrees to the left and the other about 40 degrees to the right. The third ship was about six or seven miles behind the *Doria* and to her left.

Franchini stopped to glance into the radar scope long enough to fix in his mind the positions of the two ships ahead and then went out on the wing of the bridge. There he chatted casually with Captain Calamai as the two men peered into the thick, impenetrable fog.

Giannini, who could hear the subdued voices of the two older men through the open wheelhouse door, silently watched the radar scope. He could see that the fast *Andrea Doria* was steadily gaining on the two ships ahead. He was not concerned with the ship behind, which the *Doria* was rapidly outpacing. From time to time the captain asked for the bearings and distances of the two ships ahead and Giannini called out the figures. He read the distance from the ships by the concentric rings on the scope which represented miles. He determined the angle bearings by adjusting the cursor on each of the pips and reading off the degree of bearing on the outer rim of the scope. The radar set was of a later model than that of the *Stockholm.* It had a built-in compass synchronized with gyrocompass by which the helmsman was steering. Thus at any one given moment he could read off the relative bearing of other ships.

But unlike the *Stockholm,* the *Andrea Doria* radar set had no plotting device nearby which the radar man could use. In order to plot the precise position, course and speed of an observed ship it would be necessary for the second officer of the watch to plot on a maneuvering board in the chartroom where there was light. The plotting device was in the top drawer of the chart table, unused. Unlike the *Stockholm* regimen, it was not the practice on the *Andrea Doria* to plot radar observations of other ships. The officers merely approximated the course and speed of other ships by what they could see and remember of the changing positions of pips on the radar scope.

The rule of thumb followed by many ship officers is that if the angle of the pip changes appreciably, you will pass the other ship safely. If the angle does not change substantially, the two ships are on a collision course and one or both must change course depending upon the circumstances.

As the *Andrea Doria* plowed on through the misty wet fog

and calm black sea, overtaking and passing the two slower ships that had been ahead, there was no sense of foreboding on the bridge of the modern luxury liner. Captain Calamai had navigated his ship through fog many times during his forty-one round-trip crossings of the North Atlantic on the *Andrea Doria*. He had missed only ten voyages of the *Doria* during her three-and-a-half-year life because of vacations. He himself, while master of the Italian liner *Saturnia* and other ships, had crossed the North Atlantic more than one hundred times and the South Atlantic even more often while voyaging from the Mediterranean to South America.

Second Officer Franchini, in his eighteen years at sea, half his lifetime, also was familiar with fog and the vicissitudes of ocean travel. He had served as an ensign on two Italian submarines during World War II until he was captured escaping from a torpedoed submarine in 1943. He spent the next three and a half years as a prisoner of war in England. After the war he had served on five other Italian Line ships before being assigned as second officer on the *Andrea Doria* in October, 1955.

For Giannini however, making his fifth voyage, this was the first time he had been on watch in fog since he had come aboard the *Doria* three months ago. The *Doria* was his first ship since being hired by the Italian Line, although he had served on six other vessels since going to sea as a junior deck boy in 1949 at nineteen years of age. But he had the same schooling as his senior officer and captain. All three officers on the bridge held captain's papers. Gianinni had earned his that January when he graduated from the Italian Naval Academy in Leghorn.

Several minutes after nine o'clock the staff captain, Osvaldo Magagnini appeared on the bridge. It was his second visit to the bridge since the onset of the fog. "Would you like to go below for some rest?" Captain Magagnini asked his superior officer. The second-in-command knew the answer before Captain Calamai replied, "No, thank you." His query was more a gesture of courtesy than anything else for in the years Captain Magagnini had known Captain Calamai, he never knew the commander to trust the bridge of his ship to anyone but himself in fog.

Captain Magagnini, who stood no regular deck watches since his promotion to staff captain the previous February, remained on the bridge, chatting with Captain Calamai for a while and then walking about the wheelhouse, checking the radar, the helmsman, the charts and getting the feel of the bridge.

Captain Calamai, as was his practice, paced the bridge incessantly. He walked from the outer end of the bridge wing, extending beyond the side of the ship, to the inner end of the bridge wing, a distance of some 20 feet. He walked through the wheelhouse, glancing at the radar from time to time, and he stopped at the chartroom to estimate the position of his ship at fairly frequent intervals. Then back into the wheelhouse and out again to the wing of the bridge, where he could feel the wet sea air in his face and sense the movement of his ship. The wing of the bridge is the best vantage point to see or hear the approach of another ship, and old seafarers like Captain Calamai trusted to his senses more than he did to radar.

Somewhat after 9:20 a pip appeared in the radar scope seventeen miles almost dead ahead of the ship's course. Giannini called out his observation as he watched the yellow pip appear closer and closer to the center of the radar scope. The center of the scope, stationary, represented the moving

Andrea Doria, and the moving pip turned out to be the stationary Nantucket Lightship. The lightship was expected at about that time. The officers on the bridge gathered at the radar set and, observing the positions as the flasher swept around the scope, concluded that it must be the lightship at last.

Franchini went to the chartroom and took a position fix of the ship by loran, a long-distance radar-type instrument, and then checked it by turning his radio directional finder on the lightship. There was no doubt left that directly ahead lay the Nantucket Lightship, the first checkpoint for the *Doria* since the Azore Islands. In fact, it appeared that if the *Andrea Doria* continued on course she would split in half the small anchored ship.

At fourteen miles distance from the lightship, Captain Calamai ordered a change of course six degrees to the left. Carlo Domenchini, the fifty-nine-year-old seaman at the wheel, swung the helm to port as the compass needle clicked off the degrees to 261. Second Officer Franchini took over at the radar for the important approach to the lightship. Staff Captain Magagnini, who had instructed most of the officers aboard in the use of the *Doria*'s radar equipment, looked over the second officer's shoulder, watching the pip that was the Nantucket Lightship draw closer and closer. Third Officer Giannini went about the more menial chores of changing the course numbers on the two blackboards, laying off the new course on the chart, and recording the changes in the rough log.

On the wing of the bridge, Captain Calamai peered out into the fog which enveloped the bulbous bow of his ship. If he were to obey the Rule of the Road which called for ships to be able to stop in half the distance of visibility, the Italian superliner should have been stopped dead in the water. But the *Andrea Doria* also had an obligation to dock her 1,134 passengers in New York early the following morning. About 250 longshoremen had been hired to be on the dock ready for work at 8 A.M., and they would be paid some $2.50 an hour from 8 A.M. on whether or not the ship arrived on time. And so the *Andrea Doria* sped on, as undoubtedly did virtually every other vessel traveling in the fog-shrouded waters.

The fog itself grew thicker as the *Andrea Doria* approached the Nantucket Lightship, lying outside the shoal waters—for the origin of the fog that night was at these shoal, or shallow, waters where the warm Gulf Stream traveling up the east coast of the United States from Florida collided with the cold-water streams which originated in the Bay of Fundy, off Nova Scotia, and flowed past Maine down the east coast of the United States. The extent of the fog was unknown to the men aboard the ships in that area. It was only afterwards that it could be computed that the fog shelf extended some 160 miles west of the Nantucket Shoals to some 18 or 19 miles east of the shoals and the Nantucket Lightship.

In this fog, of course, Captain Calamai could not see the Nantucket Lightship, nor did he expect to. Franchini at the radar inside the wheelhouse called out the distances and bearings as the *Doria* approached the small anchored vessel. At 10:20 P.M., the second officer called out, "We are abeam of Nantucket. Distance—one mile." He turned at that instant and looked at the wall clock in the chartroom, which he could see through the open door. Giannini in the chartroom noted the time and distance when abeam of the lightship. It was an important fact to mark down for it accurately reflected the exact position of the ship in the ocean at that given minute.

67

As the *Andrea Doria* sped by the unseen lightship, Captain Calamai called out the new course which would take the ship on a direct line to Ambrose Lightship at the mouth of New York Harbor. "Steer 268," he ordered. The helmsman swung the wheel sharply again, this time to the right, bringing the ship to her new course just two degrees less than due west. The captain heard only six blasts of the lightship's foghorn as the liner sped by and then the lightship was gone. Its position could be noted only on the radar scope where its pip faded into the distance behind the speeding liner. The very high frequency of the radio signals emitted by the radar set pierced the fog sharply in a straight line. But the sound waves of a foghorn are muffled and distorted by fog. Foghorns designed to carry four, six or eight miles are generally considered not reliable beyond a distance of two miles. Even then, a thick fog can radically change the direction of the sound of a horn or whistle.

In the chartroom, Third Officer Giannini marked off on the navigation chart the ship's position one mile south of Nantucket and noted the time. Computing the distance and time from the last loran fix taken by Franchini, the third officer computed that the ship was traveling at 21.8 knots.

The ship was traveling in the open sea and the course ahead to New York was clear and direct. The *Doria* was on her last lap to New York. The fog outside persisted. Giannini, after finishing his work in the chartroom, reported the speed of the ship to Captain Calamai on the wing of the bridge. Staff Captain Magagnini and Franchini were conversing softly in front of the radar set.

The quiet of the bridge was broken by the ringing of the telephone. Giannini, the most junior officer, answered. It was a radio operator reporting a telephone call from New

68

York for a passenger. The young officer relayed the report to the captain and Calamai said, "You go."

The young officer left the bridge to deliver the message to the purser who, in the turn of the chain of command, would send a steward to find the passenger wanted. Before long Giannini returned to the dark and quiet wheelhouse, where he had to adjust his sight once again from the well-lighted passenger section of the ship to the blacked-out wheelhouse.

He walked over to Franchini who was standing near the radar. "Would you like me to take over the radar watch?" he asked the older officer.

"No, I'll stay," Franchini said with a sort of casual shrug. Peering into a black radar screen on the lookout for tiny yellow pips is perhaps the most onerous part of a bridge watch, but the third officer had been at the radar for the first two hours of the watch. Franchini decided to take the radar watch for the last two hours.

Approximately 20 or 25 minutes after passing the Nantucket Lightship, Franchini observed a small, barely definable pip at the outer edge of the radar scope. He thought it represented a slow ship which the *Andrea Doria* was overtaking. He kept his eye on the spot of the pip as the illuminated flasher swept the scope, lighting the pip every eight seconds. In a few moments he saw he had been wrong. It was a ship but it was not going in the same direction; it was coming in the opposite direction.

"It's a ship!" he yelled out. "I can see a ship coming against us!"

"What's the bearing?" Captain Calamai queried.

Captain Magagnini and Giannini walked to the radar set to peer over Franchini's shoulder as the second officer put the adjustable cursor on the pip, and announced, "She's seventeen miles away, four degrees to starboard."

The three officers at the radar watched the progress of the pip with interest. By the rate at which the gap between the pip of the other ship and the center spot of the radar, which represented the *Doria*, closed, it became more and more apparent the two ships were coming on opposite tracks. No one bothered to plot the course or speed of the ship. No one foresaw any difficulty or danger in passing a single ship in the open space of the ocean. In fact, there was such an absence of foreboding that Captain Magagnini chose this time to leave the bridge.

The genial staff captain renewed his offer to take over from Captain Calamai who had been up on the bridge since three o'clock that afternoon. But the captain declined again. Captain Magagnini said "Good night" and retired to his cabin one deck below the bridge to catch up on some paper work before going to bed.

Despite the calm sea that night, the *Andrea Doria* rolled considerably. It was the last night out. In the eight-day crossing the huge ship had expended some 4,000 tons of fuel oil and fresh water which had served as ballast in the bottom of the hull. The *Andrea Doria*, like most modern passenger liners, was a tender ship. She was top-heavy, especially at the end of her voyages, because of her large superstructure, needed to provide public rooms and recreation space, in comparison to the shape and weight of the hull underwater, streamlined for speed. Like a huge pendulum, the ship rolled slowly and steadily on one side of her rounded hull; then she rolled back to an even keel and swung over lazily on her other side. The rolling increased the usual yawing of the ship as the bow headed first to the right and then to the left as the liner made her way forward in the water. No ship travels in a straight line. But this was the last night out and passengers, or most of them, had become quite accustomed to the incessant motion of the ship as she throbbed, rolled, pitched and yawed through the water. Certainly the crewmen on the bridge took no notice.

Both Captain Calamai and Third Officer Giannini from time to time walked into the wheelhouse to observe the pip of the other ship on the radar. Franchini hardly left the set as he continued to observe the pip advance down toward the center of the radar screen on a course generally parallel to the heading flasher of the *Doria*. It indicated that the other ship was coming on an opposite and parallel course slightly to the starboard of the *Doria*. The identity of the ship, he did not know. But it mattered little. As long as it was a ship, the *Andrea Doria* had to avoid any danger of collision.

As the two ships drew closer and closer together Franchini reported from time to time that the other ship was still to the starboard, or right, and on an opposite, parallel course to that of the *Doria*. He was estimating the other ship's course in his mind's eye without plotting. This was akin to doing long division mentally to find an approximate answer. At sea this approximate answer usually suffices, although radar experts shudder at the inherent danger of the practice. The approximation is safe as long as the navigator remembers to take bold and positive action early enough to avoid any collision which might result from incorrect radar observations. The ideal is to keep one's ship far enough away from any other ship so as to make a collision physically impossible no matter what unexpected turns are executed on the other ship.

Franchini was following the rule of thumb known to all

71

seamen, that if the angle of the radar bearing on the other ship increases, there will be a safe passing; if it remains constant, there is danger of collision. To Franchini this night the angle appeared to be increasing.

To Captain Calamai it seemed that a ship to the right of the *Doria* on this westbound track to New York must be heading toward shore, probably Nantucket. He assumed vaguely that the other ship probably was a fishing trawler or some sort of small vessel heading for Nantucket Island. Fishing boats were not uncommon in these waters. With the east coast of the United States to the right of the *Andrea Doria* and the open sea to her left, Captain Calamai decided to keep to the left.

Despite the Rule of the Road which required ships meeting head-on or nearly head-on to turn right for a port-to-port passing, Captain Calamai believed there was sufficient passing distance for a starboard-to-starboard passing. By keeping to his left, Captain Calamai was keeping his ship toward the open sea rather than encountering the dangers of coming too close to land. There was always the possibility that if he turned right toward land and shallow water, he might encounter another ship which would require him by law to turn farther to the right and even closer to the shore.

Whether or not he consciously considered each one of these possibilities, the captain was not unduly concerned. He had an officer posted at the radar, keeping the other ship under observation at all times. On the wing of the bridge he could see nothing except fog and hear nothing but the bleating of the *Doria's* own fog whistle. He noted, however, the fog was beginning to thin out somewhat. Visibility increased to perhaps three-quarters of a mile, more or less. It was next to impossible to judge distances on the open sea without the benefit of a landmark by which to gauge the eye.

Captain Calamai, pacing the quiet, dark bridge of his luxury ship, had full confidence in the speed of his ship and his own ability to navigate safely. This was a confidence, not of any daredevil venture such as obstinately refusing to give ground, but rather of his two-score years of sailing without an accident. At his command was one of the finest, fastest, and most maneuverable ships of the world. He had spent most of his years at sea navigating the large, fast liners of the Italian Line and felt he could rely on the speed of the *Andrea Doria* and his ability to maneuver her.

Without any plotting of the exact course and speed of the other ship, Captain Calamai did not realize that the ship bearing down upon him was also a fast vessel and therefore more likely to be a large, modern vessel than a fishing boat. Plotting would have told him the combined speed of the two ships was 40 knots: closing in two miles every three minutes.

When the two ships were about seven miles apart, Franchini switched the radar to a close-up range. The round screen on the close-up range reflected a radius of eight miles instead of twenty miles. The pip of the other ship appeared larger and set back near the outer rim of the radar scope. Franchini watched the pip progress faster now down toward the center of the radar screen. He estimated that the other ship, if it continued on its present course, would pass the *Doria* on the starboard side at a distance of perhaps a mile, perhaps a bit less. The second officer reported this to Captain Calamai, who came in to see the radar scene himself.

There was an aura of concentration on the bridge as Captain Calamai prepared to take action, if necessary. Yet there

73

was no tension. There was only one ship seen on the radar and miles of ocean on all sides of the *Andrea Doria.*

Helmsman Domenchini asked if he could be relieved at the wheel to go below for a cigarette. Captain Calamai gave his permission, and Seaman Giulio Visciano took the helm.

Visciano, a forty-three-year-old seaman, was at the wheel when Captain Calamai gave his first order since the other ship had been sighted at a distance of seventeen miles. The captain gave the order when Franchini reported the oncoming ship to be some fifteen degrees to starboard at a distance of . . . Here the captain and the radar officer differed on a vital point later when they tried to reconstruct the events. Franchini said the distance was three and one-half miles. The captain said it was five miles. The importance of this difference was to become evident at the Federal Court pre-trial hearing which followed.

But whatever the distance, it was at this point that Captain Calamai told the helmsman, "Four degrees to the left . . . and nothing to the right." The captain had decided to increase the passing distance between the two ships for safety's sake. Believing the ships would pass safely starboard-to-starboard even without his change of course, he saw no reason for any "positive" change of course taken "in ample time." He was confident in the knowledge of the speed of the *Andrea Doria.*

Helmsman Visciano turned the wheel to the left until the compass reading came to 264 degrees and then he straightened the wheel on the new course. As the ship yawed, however, he kept the helm from coming back to the right, thus making a slow and even left turn. His action was what the captain had wanted by his order, "Nothing to the right." It was an order peculiar and common only to the Italian

74

merchant marine, used as a means of veering gradually in one direction so as to increase a passing distance without getting too far off course. It had the advantage of saving fuel and computations expended in taking a zig and zag "positive" action to steam around another ship. It had the disadvantage of being so slight an action as to be unobservable by the navigator of the other ship.

Franchini at the radar next reported the other ship two miles distant and still on a parallel course (despite the four-degree turn and subsequent veering of the *Doria*).

Captain Calamai, followed by Giannini, walked to the railing halfway out on the bridge wing, listening for the foghorn of the other ship. They heard only the long blast of the *Doria*'s fog signal every 100 seconds. Both the captain and the young junior officer assumed that because the *Andrea Doria* was in fog, sounding fog whistles, the other ship also should be blowing her fog warning.

Giannini, standing next to the captain, wondered aloud, "Why don't we hear her whistle?" Captain Calamai remained silent, looking into the fog. "She should whistle," said the third officer plaintively. The other ship was within two miles of the *Doria* and the two officers could see and hear nothing of it.

Giannini strode into the wheelhouse for a glance at the radar. He saw the pip of the ship less than two miles off and about 30 degrees to the right. Snatching up a pair of binoculars, he returned to the wing of the bridge and scanned the sea ahead with the aid of the powerful lens.

In a moment he saw a faint, diffused glow of light in the nighttime fog. "There she is!" he exclaimed, pointing. "Do you see?"

"Yes, I see," the captain replied, straining to distinguish

from the vague glow of light two separate masthead lights so that he could determine the direction of the other ship.

Franchini, overhearing the conversation, assumed the other ship had been sighted visually from the wing of the bridge and that it was no longer incumbent upon him to follow the radar pip of the other vessel. He abandoned the radar to join the captain on the bridge wing and to see the ship for himself.

As he walked toward the door of the wheelhouse, the bridge telephone rang. He changed his direction to answer the phone. It was the lookout on the bow, Salvatore Colace, reporting. "I see lights on my right."

"That's all right," replied Franchini. "We are seeing lights too." Actually, at that time Captain Calamai and Giannini could see only the diffused glow of lights.

Giannini was the first to see the masthead lights of the *Stockholm*. The impression of the two lights flashed through his mind in an instant as he peered with his binoculars through the wet mist which hung upon the wing of the bridge. For the first instant, the lights seemed to indicate the other ship was heading off to the right. The forward lower light was to the right of the aft higher light. But in the next instant, the lights seemed to reverse themselves. He now saw not only the two masthead lights but also the red glow of the light on the left side of the other ship.

"She is turning, she is turning!" the young officer screamed. "She is showing the red light!" He gasped for air. "She is coming toward us!"

Captain Calamai saw the two white lights then and hesitated, perhaps for a split second. It must have seemed though like an eternity. It was impossible to believe this was happening. The masthead lights were opening. The other ship

76

was turning to her right and heading toward the *Doria*. The red side light, shouting catastrophe to the captain, glared brighter and brighter as the ship closed in. She seemed less than a mile away.

This was the moment of decision, immeasurable in time, for the master of the *Andrea Doria*. There were so many miles of ocean around and now so little room. His lifetime knowledge of the sea and ships had to be used for the correct instinctive maneuver, if he were to have any hope of avoiding a collision. Should he go right? Left? Straight ahead? Stop?

The decision made, Captain Calamai called out, *"Tutto sinistra* . . . all left."

Helmsman Visciano spun the power-driven wheel as fast as he could to the left. When the wheel would turn no more, he bent over, pressing all his weight on the wheel, holding one of the spokes with both his hands in a desperate attempt to make the ship turn faster.

Giannini dashed to the center window of the wheelhouse to get a better perspective view of the other ship. One can easily mistake visual bearings sighted from a side wing of the bridge.

Franchini rushed to the automatic fog signal while at the same time he shouted to his commander, "Captain, the signal . . . the two whistles."

"Yes, yes, give the signal," shouted Captain Calamai from the bridge wing.

The second officer switched off the automatic fog signal and sounded two sharp blasts, the required signal for a left turn. Then he was struck with the thought that the ship was still plunging on at full speed.

In three strides, he was at the engine telegraph, ready to

77

jerk the handles back to stop the ship. "Captain, the engines!" he cried.

"No, don't touch the engines," the captain yelled at him. "She turns faster."

Captain Calamai had decided that it was too late to try to stop the *Andrea Doria*. Her turbine engines, with only 40 to 60 per cent backing power, could not halt the 29,100-ton ship in fewer than three miles. His only hope was in the *Doria*'s speed. He had decided that he must outrace the other ship, turning left faster than she could swing to her right. If that failed, he thought, perhaps the two ships might brush one another side by side as they turned in tangent arcs and escape serious damage.

But the huge *Andrea Doria* could not be turned like an automobile. Captain Calamai gripped the bridge railing, unconsciously trying to push his ship around in her turn. But the speeding ship, under the impetus of her forward motion, skidded forward in the water perhaps a full half-mile before she even began to turn.

"Is she turning? Is she turning?" Giannini screamed at the helmsman.

"Now, she is beginning to turn," Visciano said as the gyro-compass could be heard to click off the degrees—two clicks for each degree—as the giant liner began to swing crabwise in the water, the bow turning left first as the ship plunged on forward and then the bulk of the ship finally skidding after the front end as the rudder took effect.

But it was then too late. Captain Calamai saw the dim outline and then the bow of the other ship as it came out of the night at the *Doria*.

The slender bow seemed aimed directly at him as he stood
78

transfixed on the bridge of his ship, realizing that no matter what he did, his ship could not get away. At the last moment, instinct for self-preservation prevailed. Captain Calamai retreated from the horror before him, backing away toward the door of the wheelhouse. Then the *Stockholm* struck!

Chapter Four

"WHY DID SHE TURN SO?"

A SHIP BECAUSE of the mass of weight above water leans away from her turn, and the *Andrea Doria* under a hard left rudder heeled over on her right side, toward the *Stockholm,* when she was struck just aft and beneath her starboard bridge wing. Teen-ager Martin Sedja, Jr., standing on deck near the *Doria's* cabin class swimming pool, saw the lights of the *Stockholm* and thought the ship was swerving to avoid the *Doria.* "It was coming in at an angle, like it was trying to keep from hitting us, but it couldn't get away in time." He didn't wait there to see it happen.

On the *Stockholm* Dr. Pettit literally risked his neck to see it. After warning his wife, he jutted his head out of Cabin

81

M-6, on the forward port side of the *Stockholm,* and watched.

The *Stockholm,* driven by 14,600 horsepower, sliced through the *Doria's* steel hull like a dagger stabbed into an eggshell. The *Stockholm* bow was constructed of two rows of extra-heavy steel plating an inch thick, separated by an air space two feet wide. It was designed not as an icebreaking bow but rather to follow an icebreaker through ice fields off the Scandinavian coast.

With the force of a battering ram of more than one million tons, the *Stockholm* prow plunged into the speeding Italian ship, crumbling like a thin sheet of tin, until her energy was spent. With the *Stockholm* pinioned in her, the *Andrea Doria,* twice her size, pivoted sharply under the impact, dragging the *Stockholm* along as the giant propellers of the Italian liner churned the black sea violently to white. Only then did Dr. Pettit draw back into his cabin to see his wife rigidly stretched out in her lower bunk, both hands clutching the sides of the bed.

Death and destruction had been wrought in a matter of seconds. Then the two ships separated. The *Doria,* her turbine engines still producing 34,000 horsepower, broke free of the dagger in her side. The *Stockholm,* her entire forward force expended in the penetration of the *Doria,* slid and bounced against the side of the Italian liner, from the hole beneath the bridge to the extreme stern of the ship. Steel scraped steel and a fiery blast of sparks shot up skyward and cascaded back to the sea in a shower of orange and yellow flashes on the black background of the night.

Even before the sparks lighted the night, Carstens had been impelled to act. Numb in the shock of catastrophe, he had clung to the engine telegraph on the bridge wing until the two ships struck. The *Stockholm* sliced through the hull of the *Andrea Doria* so cleanly that Carstens hardly felt a jolt. His mind was on the watertight doors at the moment of collision, for he thought the *Stockholm* could very well sink in a matter of minutes if he did not shut the watertight doors. Leaving the engine telegraph at FULL SPEED ASTERN, he flew into the wheelhouse, pressed the alarm button to signal the closing of the doors and then he cranked a small wheel which controlled two doors on B-Deck aft. The other doors were closed manually at the sounding of the alarm by men stationed at the door locations.

So fast did he move that he still saw the sparks from the collision as he headed blindly and instinctively toward the chartroom and the stairway beyond it to summon the captain.

Captain Nordenson was halfway up the stairway to the bridge when the ships collided. Jogged only slightly, the sixty-three-year-old seafarer did not miss a step. He never "dreamed" the true meaning of the jolt as he pounded up to the bridge.

The captain and third officer collided at the door between the wheelhouse and the chartroom. "What happened?" demanded the captain. At worst he thought the ship had brushed a submerged wreck.

Carstens sputtered out disjointed words. "Collision . . . we collided with another ship . . . she came from the port . . . from the port . . ."

"Shut the watertight doors."

"They're closed," said Carstens.

A glance at the five-by-ten-inch control panel with the two red button lights shining in the dark wheelhouse confirmed for Captain Nordenson that the doors indeed were closed. Without breaking his long stride, the captain reached the port wing of the bridge, with Carstens tagging at his heels, in time to see the stern of the other ship about one ship length away. She appeared to be speeding away, ahead of the *Stockholm* to the north.

"Who is she?" the captain demanded, peering into the dark night.

"I don't know," said Carstens almost with a wail.

From the shape of the round spoonlike stern, Captain Nordenson thought it might be the old *Kungsholm*, which he had once commanded. The ship, sold and resold, was now sailing as the *Italia* of the Home Lines.

The fog which had engulfed the *Andrea Doria* earlier now moved slowly in on the two ships as the captain and third officer stood on the bridge of the *Stockholm* watching the lights of the other ship grow dim as distance between the two vessels increased.

"Why didn't you call me?" the captain demanded, turning on Carstens.

"There was no reason in the world to call you," exclaimed Carstens. "I had good visibility . . ." the young officer started to explain in a sputter of words, but the captain had no time then for disjuncted explanations. As Carstens kept repeating that the other ship had turned to port for no reason, the captain noticed the engine telegraph was still on FULL SPEED ASTERN, although he did not notice that the *Stockholm* was making no headway in the water. The captain moved the handles up to STOP and then he strode across the wheelhouse to the radar set.

Meanwhile, the lights of the other ship had faded away. Captain Nordenson could see only one white spot of a light in the distance. "Now, I must find out the distance," he told himself and strode into the wheelhouse to the radar set near

84

the starboard door. A glance showed him the other ship was 1.9 miles away to the port of the *Stockholm.*

Officers and men, meanwhile, were rapidly streaming into the dark wheelhouse. Perhaps all of two minutes had passed since the collision.

Engineer Svensson, having reversed the starboard engine, had just reached the port engine control wheel when the collision hurled him ten feet away, sprawling on the steel deck grating. But then he scrambled to his feet and stumbled to the port engine wheel to complete the maneuver for full astern. By that time Third Engineer Edwin Bjorkegran, who had seen the signal on the telegraph repeater in the Auxiliary Engine Room, had reached the control platform in the Main Engine Room. He had been only a yard away from the starboard engine controls when the collision threw him forward on his face. When Captain Nordenson's order came down to stop both engines, Bjorkegran handled the starboard engine while Svensson stopped the port engine.

Chief Engineer Assargren was in the embarrassing posture of having his trousers half on and half off when the collision sent him sprawling in his cabin on the Sun Deck. Hurriedly he struggled into his trousers, threw on a shirt, grabbed a flashlight and headed for the Engine Room. The hallways and stairways were crowded with passengers, lost and confused by an unexpected shock on the first night out on a strange ship. One woman passenger on A-Deck, not far from the main entrance to the Engine Room, was most distraught, thinking she was the cause of all the chaos. She had flicked the light switch in her cabin at the precise moment of the collision and now she was running through the hallway trying to explain that she must have set the emergency brake of the ship.

Chief Officer Gustav Herbert Kallback, who had started out of his cabin next to that of the captain when he had heard the telegraph bells, was the first officer after the captain to reach the bridge. Second Officer Enestrom and Second Officer Junior Sven Abenius, both asleep at the time of collision, reached the bridge some minutes later.

The officers headed toward the captain for orders. "What shall I do?" asked Kallback as soon as he could get the attention of the captain. The officers all came away with the same impression of Captain Nordenson under stress. He was calm and commanding. He moved about the bridge with a nervous agility that was surprising for a man of his years. The captain himself set about checking the various indicators on the bridge, the inclinometer, the engine speed indicator, the lights of the ship.

As each of the officers reached the bridge, he was sent forward to check the damaged area of the ship and ordered to report conditions on the bow to the bridge. One after another, first Kallback, then Enestrom and then Abenius, went forward to the bow.

Carstens meanwhile wandered about the bridge in a daze. He felt alone and left out. The captain seemed to have no time for him. Lost in the hubbub on the bridge, his teeth began to chatter, shivers ran up and down his back and he found himself unable to control his vibrating body. The attack came upon him suddenly. Wandering about the bridge, he tried to force his attention upon his colleagues. No sooner had Enestrom reached the bridge, not fully awake from a deep sleep, than Carstens grabbed his arm and demanded, "Why did she turn so? Why did she turn to port, why?" But all this was incoherent to the sleepy second officer.

Carstens, in those terrible moments, felt the weight of the

86

world fall upon him. What had he done? Everything had been routine and then the terrible thirty seconds and the collision. Had he done something wrong? He didn't know. He could not think of anything that he had done contrary to what he had been taught at school. Yet there had been a collision. It seemed it was all because the other ship—whatever ship that was—had turned left when no ship under such conditions is supposed to turn left. Why did she turn left? Why? In his bewilderment, he kept asking that question on the darkened bridge of the *Stockholm*. But no one had the time or inclination to answer him.

The trim indicator on the bridge showed the ship was down three and one-half feet by the bow and listing four degrees to starboard. Captain Nordenson telephoned the Engine Room. "Start the ballast pumps on the bilges. Check the forwards compartments for water. Correct the list for four degrees to starboard."

To the ship's carpenter he ordered, "Take soundings around the ship, starting forward and working aft and report back to the bridge." Soundings of water in the bilges would indicate the amount of sea taken into the *Stockholm* and hence the amount of her loss of buoyancy.

Meanwhile, Chief Officer Kallback led the first work party forward to the bow. He took the open deck route, free from passenger traffic, down the ladder from the bridge to the Verandah Deck and then forward to a stairway leading to the forecastle, which was the open deck extension of Upper Deck. At the head of the stairway he saw a view of the bow, where an hour earlier he had had three men scrubbing down the deck. Despite his thirty years at sea, Kallback's stomach turned and for an instant he thought he would be sick. Before him what had once been a slender, graceful bow had been crumbled into a mass of ugly, jagged steel, heaped with debris and wreckage. He went swiftly down the stairway to the deck, into a doorway, and down to the crew's quarters on Main Deck inside the ship.

Chief Purser Curt Dawe, reporting to the bridge, was told to organize his stewards and pursers. All passengers were to be instructed to wear lifebelts and report to the ship's public rooms until further word. Every cabin was to be checked. Every porthole on the starboard side of the ship was to be closed, bolted shut and secured. The names of all passengers were to be checked from the passenger list and all crewmen were to be checked off the roster to determine if anyone was missing or injured. The hospital was to be organized for care of the injured. The ship was to go on an emergency basis. All crew was to stand by emergency stations until further orders.

There was no sense in sounding the general alarm for the passengers, Captain Nordenson decided. There had been no emergency drill on the first day out. It was scheduled for the following day, which would have been the first full day at sea, the usual time for lifeboat and emergency drills on the *Stockholm* as on other vessels. The crew had been alerted by alarms which went off automatically at the moment of collision.

The collision in smashing back the entire bow had ruptured all of the water-pipe lines in the forward end of the ship. Water splashed everywhere, adding to the general confusion in the crew's quarters in the bow of the ship. The rupturing of the sprinkler-system pipes set off the wailing typhoon siren of alarm in the crew's quarters, sending the men fortunate enough to survive the collision dashing to their emergency stations even before they had realized what had happened.

88

Chief Purser Dawe relayed the captain's orders via the ship's assistant chief pursers and head stewards to the 150 men in his department. The stewards found that most of the passengers, even without a drill, had indeed found their own lifejackets and were only too eager to be told what to do and where to go. A surprising number of passengers, according to the stewards, had slept through the collision and had to be awakened.

Of panic, there was none. The damaged area of the ship had been confined to the crew's quarters in the bow. Passengers in other parts of the ship could sense little or nothing wrong. The lights were burning brightly throughout the ship, she seemed to be on an even keel, there was no sign of any damage or danger that any passenger could see, with one exception. The water freed from the ruptured pipes in the bow flowed rapidly through the corridors of A-Deck and the Main Deck. Salt water mixed with fresh water soon rose to a level of between 18 and 24 inches in the main fore-and-aft corridor of the two decks. The water flowed toward the rear of the ship against an uphill incline, reaching about the midway point of the ship before leveling off.

On the bridge, Captain Nordenson could see from the inclinometer that the *Stockholm* was down by the bow three feet seven inches and listing four degrees to starboard. The question was: Would the *Stockholm* survive?

The *Stockholm* was a nine-compartment ship built to the highest construction standards of the Lloyd's Register of Shipping. She was designed to withstand the flooding of any one of her nine watertight compartments. That is to say, if her largest compartment was open to the sea, the *Stockholm* would remain afloat, but if two compartments became flooded, she might, although not necessarily, sink. It was the

1948 International Conference which raised the standards for all passenger ships. Ships whose keels were laid after the 1948 convention had to withstand the flooding of any two compartments, even the two largest adjacent compartments.

The forward compartments on the *Stockholm*, as of any ship, were the smallest, and the danger of sinking was less with the forward compartments flooded than if the larger sections of midships had been flooded. Yet there was the danger.

In the damaged area, Chief Kallback, a sensitive, quiet man who had devoted his life to the sea for the past thirty years, fought to control his emotions. He fortified himself with the reminder of a Swedish rule of life which he had always lived by. "In a bad situation, you make the best of it." Sloshing through the flowing water in the dark of the narrow corridors, Kallback and an advance party of seamen surveyed the damage. As they worked their way forward, Kallback assigned men to organize other work parties to force their way into each cabin in the area. The cabins had been smashed back, one on top of the other, like a closed accordion, their sizes reduced to half and less. Inside several jammed cabins the rescue party could hear the cries and moans of trapped kitchen and pantry workers.

The chief officer could force his way forward only to the ship's collision bulkhead, the first transverse wall 53 feet behind the bow. The bulkhead, designed to protect the ship from flooding in the event of collisions, had been shattered. Behind the collision bulkhead, on Main Deck, the first six cabins on the port side of the ship and the first five on the starboard side also had been smashed. The first of these cabins had been torn open, the others compressed one into the other.

90

On A-Deck below, where the cabins began farther aft, the forward cabins on each side of the ship, 1-A and 2-A, had been smashed open. But access to these cabins still was possible because they were above the C-Deck waterline. Crew's cabins were located on B-Deck behind the second watertight bulkhead some 127 feet behind the bow.

It soon became apparent to Kallback that the safety of the ship depended on this second bulkhead. The No. 1 cargo hold, 80 feet behind the bow, had been opened to the sea, apparently from the concussion of the impact. The cargo hold was filled to the 11-foot mark with sea water, reaching the beams of B-Deck. If the water rose one deck more, to A-Deck, it would overflow the top of the bulkhead and successively flood the whole ship.

The Engine Room had the ballast pumps working on the bilges soon after the collision. Captain Nordenson, informed of the situation forward, ordered the Engine Room to set the main pumps working on emptying the forward hold. The ship's entire water supply was cut off by the engine-room controls to stop the flooding from the torn sprinkler system in the bow.

Chief Assargren went forward from the Engine Room to the area of No. 3 hold, which had been converted to the ship's stabilizer room, where the giant Denny-Brown stabilizing fins were located. The room was dry. The chief then turned the pumps on for No. 2 hold, but only air was pumped. The captain was pleased at the report that No. 2 hold, located behind the second watertight bulkhead, was dry and tight. But all the pumping in No. 1 hold was to no avail.

Captain Nordenson checked the trim indicator on the bridge and found the ship was down another seven inches by the bow. The second report, from Enestrom, was that

91

water in No. 1 hold had risen to thirteen feet. Meanwhile, the second bulkhead had been inspected. It was tight and holding up well, Kallback reported.

But Captain Nordenson was worried about the pressure on the bulkhead, which, in effect, was serving as the new bow of the ship. The farther the front end of the ship dipped into the water—and it was now four feet two inches below the normal waterline—the more pressure the sea exerted on the bulkhead.

Captain Nordenson sent word back to the radio shack behind the chartroom to try to find out the identity of the other ship. No one on the *Stockholm* at that time knew either the identity of the ship or the amount of damage she had sustained in the collision.

The *Stockholm*'s third radio operator, Sven Erik Johansson, had been alone in the radio room, telegraphing his fourth message of the voyage to Gothenburg, when the collision impact hurled both him and his chair through the air. The thirty-four-year-old radioman, formerly with the Swedish air force, landed with a resounding thud on the floor. Lying on his back, he noticed the wall clock said 11:10 before he got to his feet. With the singlemindedness of a Swedish sailor, he tried to contact Gothenburg again to explain the interruption. SORRY, WE HAVE COLLIDED, he started to message, but then his feet slipped from under him and he fell again to the floor strewn with books and papers from the radio room shelves.

When Captain Nordenson sent word to the radio room that he wanted to know the identity of the other ship, all three radiomen of the *Stockholm* were in the radio room. Chief Radio Operator Bengt Mellgren, who had taken command of the radio shack, scribbled a message which he

92

handed to Second Radio Operator Ake Reinholdsson at the Morse key. The message, sent out on the airwaves of 500 kilocycles, was the first notification to the world of the collision off Nantucket.

Reinholdsson first sent a series of three repetitions of X X X, clearing the distress channel for an urgent message, followed by the radio call sign of the *Stockholm*, SEJT, and then the message:

WE HAVE COLLIDED WITH ANOTHER SHIP. PLEASE—SHIP IN COLLISION—INDICATE

The radio operator had not finished spelling out the last word when the message was interrupted by an SOS from the other ship.

A formal photograph taken in the Mediterranean of the *Andrea Doria* when she was new in 1953.

A portrait of the yacht-like *Stockholm*, built in 1948, as she looked with her enlarged superstructure of 1953.

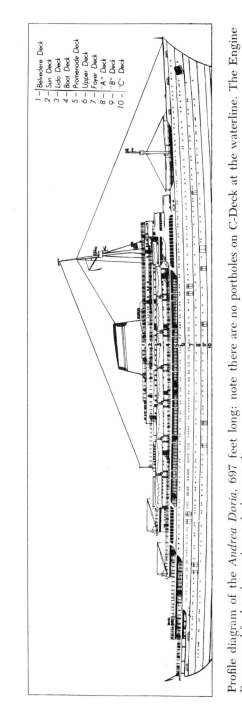

1 – Belvedere Deck
2 – Sun Deck
3 – Lido Deck
4 – Boat Deck
5 – Promenade Deck
6 – Upper Deck
7 – Foyer Deck
8 – "A" Deck
9 – "B" Deck
10 – "C" Deck

Profile diagram of the *Andrea Doria*, 697 feet long: note there are no portholes on C-Deck at the waterline. The Engine Rooms and fuel tanks are beneath the waterline.

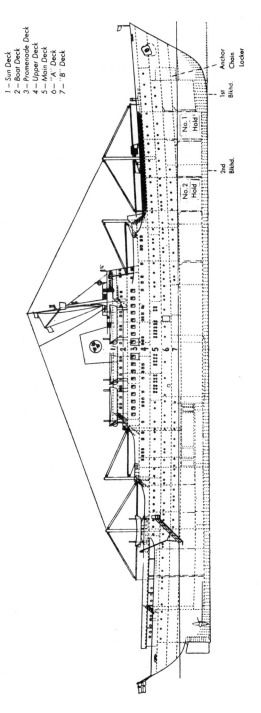

1 – Sun Deck
2 – Boat Deck
3 – Promenade Deck
4 – Upper Deck
5 – Main Deck
6 – "A" Deck
7 – "B" Deck

Profile diagram of the *Stockholm*, 525 feet long: The sea was held back by the watertight bulkhead midway between holds No. 1 and No. 2.

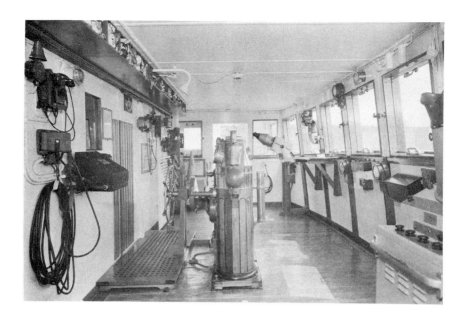

The third mate of the *Stockholm* used the radar set barely seen here on the extreme right and the telephone on the aft wall in the foreground.

A close-up of the radar set, which had been checked for accuracy the day before the collision, and the plotting board to the right.

The spacious wheelhouse of the *Andrea Doria* contained two engine telegraphs, two radar sets and two helms. The metal wheel automatic pilot was switched off when fog was encountered.

The *Doria*'s chartroom behind the wheelhouse. The radar plotting device was in the top drawer.

Captain Nordenson of the *Stockholm* in a contemplative mood.

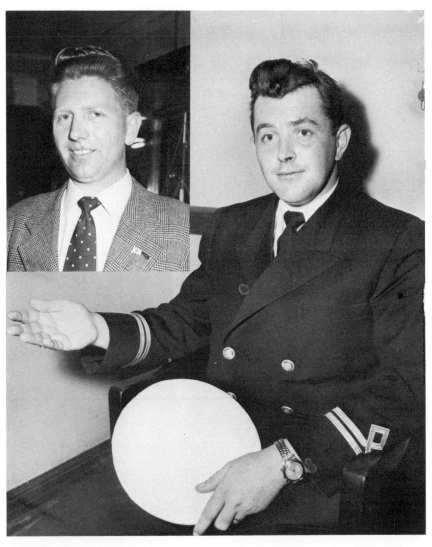

Third Mate Carstens-Johannsen in a typical ingenuous pose, explaining something after the collision.

(INSERT) Peder Larsen, the helmsman whose attention wandered.

A portrait of Captain Calamai at the time of the *Doria*'s maiden voyage.

The three officers who were on the bridge of the *Doria*. Captain Calamai seated, Third Officer Giannini on his right, and Second Officer Franchini on his left.

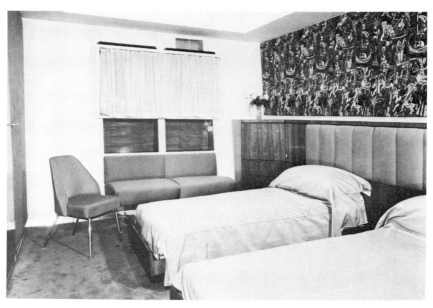

The de luxe bedroom occupied by Ferdinand Thieriot, business manager of the San Francisco *Chronicle*, and his wife, Frances.

A typical first-class cabin, not unlike that occupied by the Cianfarras, the Petersons and the Dilworths.

A view of the *Doria*'s First-Class Lounge.

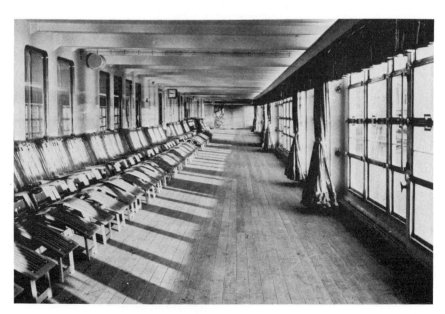

The Promenade Deck with its glass escape doors.

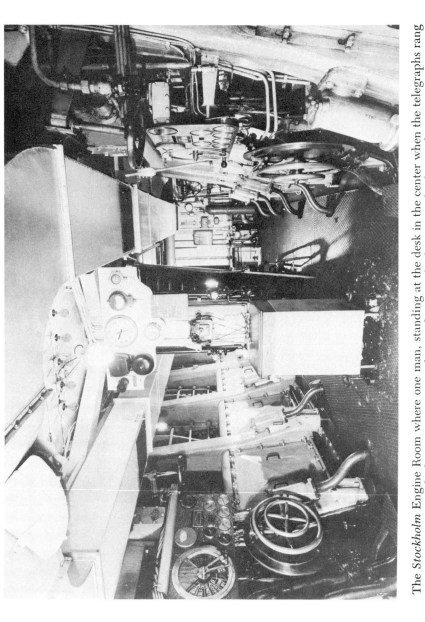

The *Stockholm* Engine Room where one man, standing at the desk in the center when the telegraphs rang FULL SPEED ASTERN, had to open two air valves and reverse both engine wheels seen here.

The names of the rescue ships *Pvt. William H. Thomas*, *Ile de France* and *Cape Ann* will be perpetuated in American merchant marine history as "Gallant Ships." Louis S. Rothschild, Under Secretary of Commerce for Transportation (on left) presented the awards to Captain Shea of the *Thomas*, Captain de Beaudean of the *Ile de France* and Captain Boyd of the *Cape Ann*, and a letter of commendation to Captain Blanc of the *Robert E. Hopkins* (standing left to right).

This and the spectacular picture on the next page of the listing *Andrea Doria* were taken at night from the deck of the *Ile de France* by vacationing Ken Gouldthorpe, then staff photographer for the St. Louis *Post Dispatch*.

St. Louis Post-Dispatch

He used an exposure of about two seconds on his 35 mm. camera and hoped for the best because he had no flashbulb equipment with him.

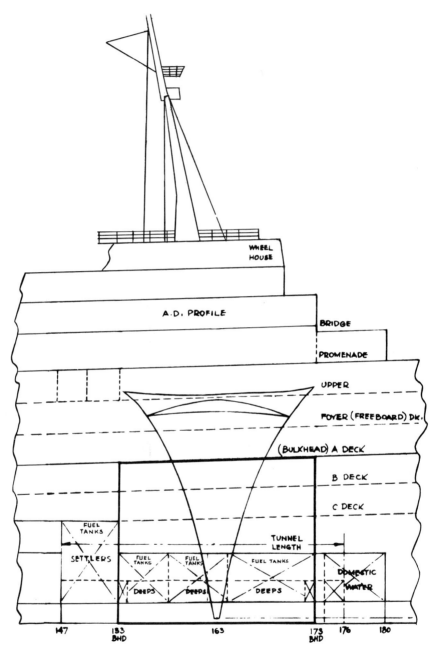

A diagram of the *Stockholm* bow, at its deepest penetration, superimposed on the *Andrea Doria* at the approximate place it struck.

Chapter Five

"SHALL I RING THE ALARM?"

THE SEA POURED into the *Andrea Doria*. Thousands of tons of water flowed through the hole in the right side of the ship. No one ever put a tape measure to the damage but the best evidence indicated that the hole was about 40 feet across at the top and, because of the shape of the *Stockholm* bow, progressively narrower on the lower decks. Seven of the eleven decks of the Italian liner had been ripped open, from the Upper Deck of the ship down to the double-bottom tanks of fuel and oil. The penetration was estimated to be close to 30 feet within the ship on the Upper Deck, less farther down—probably only 18 feet at the water level at C Deck and about seven feet at the bottom deck below the level of the sea. From all appearances, calculated afterwards, only one of the ship's eleven watertight compartments was open to the sea.

Yet the *Andrea Doria* shuddered under the tremendous blow of the collision and suddenly, within a minute, leaned sickeningly over on her right side. Captain Calamai staggered hurriedly to the edge of the bridge wing in time to see the *Stockholm* disappear beyond the stern of his ship. He had felt one or two, perhaps three, distinctive bumps as the white ship had slid along the side of his ship. He leaned over the bridge railing to inspect the damage but all he could make out in the night fog was the huge black hole darker than the black hull of his beautiful ship. It began slightly aft and four decks below the bridge wing and extended down and beneath the sea. Furniture, luggage and all sorts of unidentifiable objects poured out of the gaping hole and floated aft as the ship zigzagged out of control.

Realizing that the *Doria* was still at full speed ahead, Captain Calamai rushed to the engine telegraph inside the wheelhouse. He saw Franchini transfixed at the wheelhouse entrance and shouted, "The watertight doors—see that they're closed!" The captain ran to the engine telegraph and jerked both handle controls to FULL STOP. He stood there trembling. A nightmare had come to pass.

Franchini ran across the dark wheelhouse and as he passed Giannini he shouted to the younger officer to check the time. The fancy wood panel of levers which electrically controlled the twelve watertight doors of the ship was located on the rear wall near the left side of the room. Reaching there, Franchini saw that each of the twelve small levers was in the closed position. The twelve red button lights glowed red, indicating the watertight doors were closed.

96

Giannini grabbed a flashlight from the ledge beneath the center window and played the beam upon the bridge clock. It showed 11:10 P.M.

Within that first minute or two after the collision, the men suddenly realized that the *Doria* had not righted herself from the starboard list. The tilt of the deck was severe and it was difficult to maintain one's balance.

"What's the list?" cried out the captain and Giannini turned his flashlight on the trim indicator on the forward wall of the wheelhouse. The indicator needle fluttered at 18 degrees. This seemed incredible to the young officer for he knew that the modern *Doria*, built to the standards of the International Conference for Safety of Life at Sea of 1948, was not supposed to list more than 7 degrees initially and 15 degrees at the very worst. But he reported the trim indicator reading to the captain. No sooner did he call out the 18-degree list than the needle crept to 19 degrees and 20 degrees.

To Captain Calamai, the report of the severe list came like a second stroke to a man who had just suffered his first, unexpected heart attack. It meant that his ship was sinking immediately after the collision. He rushed to the telephone for a report from the Engine Room below.

The Engine Room consisted of three cavernous chambers in the center section of the 697-foot ship. The first room forward was the Generator Room, 47 feet long and 75 feet wide, containing five huge diesel generators, lined side by side across the breadth of the room, which provided for the main electrical needs of the ship. Behind that was the Boiler Room containing two boilers to supply hot water for passenger services and four huge boilers to supply high-compression steam to drive the ship's turbine motors. The third chamber was the Main Engine Room containing the twin turbine engines and most of the controls for the ship's pumps and machinery. Twenty-two officers and men were on watch in the three rooms at the time of the collision because of the fog precautions taken on the *Doria*.

The impact of the collision ruptured the starboard turbine motors, which began to spurt oil. First Assistant Engineer Giuseppe Mondini, in charge of the engine-room watch, shut down the starboard engine even before Captain Calamai's order came down on the engine telegraph. When the telegraph signaled FULL STOP, he switched off the port engine. He sent men forward to the Boiler Room and the Generator Room, and aft to the rear of the ship where the rudder machinery was located, to check for damage. In the bowels of the ship, it was impossible to know what had happened. The men had felt a violent double thump but they could not be certain whether it came from fore or aft.

The *Andrea Doria* was designed and constructed as a two-compartment ship in conformity to at least the minimum standards of stability established by the 1948 International Conference. Her 697-foot length was divided into eleven watertight chambers in such a way that if any two of the chambers became fully or partially flooded in an emergency, the other chambers would contain enough air and buoyancy to keep the ship afloat. Since it is difficult to conceive of any more than two chambers of those eleven chambers being ripped open to the sea at the same time, the *Andrea Doria* was theoretically "unsinkable."

The watertight chambers were formed by the watertight bulkheads which extended across the width of the ship and from the bottom up to the level of A-Deck. The bulkheads were of solid steel tested to withstand the maximum pressure of water from a flooded compartment. The only openings in these bulkheads were the watertight doors, which when closed were as watertight as the bulkheads themselves. Thus water entering any one or even two compartments would be contained, and since the ship was designed to list no more than 15 degrees at the worst, she should remain afloat under the worst conditions imaginable.

The *Andrea Doria* was built with a safety margin of 5 degrees because she would have to list some 20 degrees before water filling any one compartment would overflow the top of the watertight bulkhead at the A-Deck level.

Yet, in fewer than five minutes after the collision, the *Andrea Doria* was listing more than 20 degrees and to the men on the ship who understood stability matters it meant that water would overflow one compartment into the next compartment progressively until the ship sank—if she did not capsize first.

In the time it took the ship's chief engineer, Alcisio Chiappori, to run ten decks down from his cabin to the Engine Room, the list had increased to 22 degrees. The fifty-three-year-old engineer with one look at the trim indicator realized that unless he could correct the list, the ship was lost.

The engineers who had gone forward from the Main Engine Room discovered the source of water pouring into the ship. The *Stockholm* bow had ripped open the compartment immediately forward of the Generator Room. It was the deep-tank compartment, 55 feet long, which contained ten huge tanks with a capacity for 1,000 tons of fuel oil. The tanks were arranged with three outboard and two inboard tanks on each side of the compartment, with an access tunnel, about seven feet high and four feet wide, running from the Generator Room to a small pump and control room, a sort of cul-de-sac, at the forward end. The tunnel had four laterals branching

off toward the hull at the forward and rear ends of the compartment. The tunnel and its laterals permitted access through
manholes to the fuel tanks below the compartment, which
were called "double bottoms." The *Doria*, like all modern
ships, had a complete double bottom made up of a series of
fuel- and water-storage tanks the entire length of the ship.
The double bottom, besides being an excellent storage space,
served the double purpose of adding ballast weight to the
lowest part of the ship and protecting the vessel from being
punctured by underwater objects. For added protection, the
Andrea Doria also had a series of wing tanks for carrying
fuel and water along the sides of the three engine rooms. Extending up to the top of the engine rooms, the tanks served
as a double hull protecting the three largest compartments
from being punctured by possible minor collisions or scrapes.

If the *Stockholm* had hit at any one of the three engine-
room compartments, or even at a bulkhead connecting two
compartments, the *Andrea Doria* could have withstood the
damage. The sea would have flowed across the open compartments the width of the ship and there would have been
hardly any list. The *Doria* would have settled lower in the
sea but on an even keel and could have been towed safely to
shore.

But in smashing open the deep-tank compartment, the
Stockholm had struck a vulnerable spot. Her bow pierced
the five fuel tanks on the starboard side of the compartment
and left intact the portside tanks. The ten fuel tanks near
the end of the voyage had been empty. Thus some 500 tons or
240,000 gallons of sea water gushed into the starboard tanks,
providing that much dead weight on one side of the ship,
while the air-filled port tanks rose out of the sea like a bal-
loon. The more the ship listed to starboard, the more hun-

dreds and thousands of tons of water poured into the 40-foot hole in the side of the *Doria*, and the more water that flowed into the starboard side, the more the ship listed. It seemed only a matter of time before the ship would roll over on her starboard side and go down.

The engineers discovered there was no way they could stop the flooding of the Generator Room because, incredible as it may seem, there was no watertight door protecting the Generator Room from the access tunnel in the deep-tank compartment forward. The sea entering the tank compartment surged through the tunnel and into the unguarded Generator Room. Without a watertight door between the two compartments, it was as if there was no watertight bulkhead between them at all.

Sea water, mixed with the black oil of the ruptured double-bottom tanks and the residue of the deep tanks, flowed into the Generator Room. The water found its natural way to the starboard side of the room, adding to the list of the ship. Slowly it rose up the inclined deck toward the center of the room, threatening to short-circuit successively the five dynamos that produced 3,750 kilowatts of electricity for the ship.

There was nothing Chief Engineer Chiappori could do to save the Generator Room. He had put to work all the suction pumps of the ship, but they were unable to stem the rising water. As the water level approached the electrical parts of the No. 5 generator, which was closest to the starboard wall, he had that generator switched off. It was merely a matter of time before all the generators would be useless, but he posted an electrician at the generator control board with orders to shut off each generator only at the last possible minute when the rising water threatened to touch an electrical part. The point was to prolong the operation of the electrical plant because as the electricity supply decreased, fewer pumps could be used to cope with the flooding water.

To his distress, Chiappori, who was a vacation replacement for the regular chief engineer, learned that there was no practical way he could flood the port tanks of the fuel-tank compartment. That had been his best and most obvious hope of righting the list of the ship. But the pumps and controls for flooding these tanks were located in the cul-de-sac room at the forward end of the flooded tunnel. It did not seem possible to him or the other engineers who felt they were risking their lives even by remaining in the Engine Room to attempt to forge one's way through the 55-foot flooded tunnel to the pump room.

The engineering officers and men worked furiously against time and the inrushing sea. The air-conditioning had been shut down to conserve electricity and the three engine rooms had become unbearably hot and steamy. The list of the ship made it almost impossible to maintain one's footing on the wet and slippery grating of the deck. The men stripped down to their trousers and curled their toes for a griplike tread on the cross-sectioned grating that served as a floor.

The Boiler Room and the Main Engine Room had been dry for some time after the collision, but slowly the water and oil which had drained from the upper decks into the bilges began to overflow through the floor gratings into the Boiler Room and Engine Room. Even with every available pump on the ship in operation, it was, the engineers knew, a losing battle.

The situation had been reported to the bridge by telephone. The bridge telephoned back with a question: Could the ship's engines be used? Chief Engineer Chiappori interrupted his work on the pump controls to check. He reported back that while the starboard engine was out, the port engine was available.

On the bridge, the men expected the ship to capsize before long. The list hovered at about 22 degrees and many ships had gone into the death throes at a lesser degree of list. The wheelhouse was in a furor as Captain Calamai reeled off orders for the men and officers streaming up to the bridge. Fearing his ship would soon go down, the captain ordered virtually everyone on the bridge to turn to and launch the lifeboats. He directed them first to the portside lifeboats on the high side of the ship. He ordered Second Officer Badano to summon the lifeboat crews to their stations. The stocky second officer flipped on the loudspeaker channels to the crew's quarters and twice announced: *"Il personale destino alle imbarcazioni si portino ai propri posti!"*

All the ship's outboard lights were switched on, including the two powerful searchlights atop the ship's mast. The whistle signal was reset to sound continuous double blasts, the signal for a ship out of control.

Staff Captain Magagnini, who had rushed to the bridge from his cabin in his pajamas and slippers, led the way to the port side lifeboats. The ship's two first officers, Luigi Oneto and Carlo Kirn, followed. Before long the high side of the ship was swarming with boat crews. Eight lifeboats hung there in a row at the level of the Lido Deck, one below the bridge, stretching out almost the full length of the superstructure. The boat crews with the officers working alongside them feverishly ripped the tarpaulin covers from the boats, hammered away the chucks that secured the keels, and released the winch brakes. The davits were supposed to slide down

103

to launching position over the side of the ship and the boats were supposed to fall of their own weight. But, much as Captain Calamai had feared, this did not happen.

The men and officers pushed, shoved and heaved against the inert metal lifeboats but neither they nor the davits moved. Since the modern *Andrea Doria*, like other ships, had been designed to list no more than 15 degrees, the modern davits had been designed as launchable up to 15 degrees. But now that the *Doria* was heeling some 22 degrees, the davit arms holding the boats were facing skyward instead of toward the sea. To free the boats they had to be pushed uphill and that was impossible.

The men continued to struggle against the mechanics of launching the eight boats on the high side of the ship, and Captain Calamai watched the situation from the wing of the bridge. After about five or six minutes Captain Magagnini, who had kicked off his slippers, padded back up to the bridge and reported the hopelessness of trying to launch the boats from the high side of the ship. Captain Calamai told him to see to the launching of the eight boats on the starboard side. Both men still feared the likelihood of imminent capsizing. They both realized also that with the eight portside lifeboats useless, the remaining eight boats on the starboard side could accommodate at absolute full capacity 1,004 persons. There were 1,706 passengers and crew aboard.

Resigning himself as best he could, after consultation with his staff captain and others, to the loss of his ship, Captain Calamai turned to saving the passengers. Second Officer Badano was sent again to the loudspeaker system, and with the captain standing beside him, dictating, Badano announced: "*Si pregano, i signori passeggeri di portarsi ai propri posti di reunione."* He repeated it in Italian and then made the same announcement twice in English: "If you please, passengers are requested to go to their muster stations."

Badano, after making the announcement, turned to the captain. "Is there any more?"

"No, no more," said Calamai.

"Shall I ring the alarm?" asked the younger officer.

"No, no, we have only half the lifeboats," said the captain. He told Badano to go into the chartroom and plot the ship's present position for a distress message. He wanted to send an SOS for help in getting the passengers off the ship.

Captain Calamai had resolved not to sound the regular abandon-ship alarm, required by law. The prescribed alarm was the sounding of six or seven staccato blasts followed by one long blast on the ship's sirens or bells, or both. All passengers had supposedly been instructed how to respond to the alarm during the abandon-ship drill which had been held the day after the *Doria* left Naples. But Captain Calamai had been around ships and the sea long enough to know that drills during a pleasure voyage were no measure of what passengers or crew would do in response to a real alarm on a listing ship that might sink. The captain, in short, feared panic if the ship's alarm sirens were set off. He feared a stampeding of the starboard lifeboats if it were learned that there were not enough lifeboats available for everyone on the ship.

Captain Calamai had one slight hope for saving the *Andrea Doria.* It was he who had telephoned the Engine Room concerning the use of the engines. Sixteen years before, when he was executive officer of the torpedoed Italian converted cruiser *Duilio,* he had saved that ship by running her up on a nearby beach before she sank. Now, he decided to try the

105

same thing with the *Andrea Doria*. The shallow off-shore waters of the United States were to the north. Although he did not stop to compute the actual distance, he knew that if he could reach shallow water or a sandbar, the *Doria* could be inexpensively refloated. Actually, the nearest haven was Davis Shoal, some twenty-two miles to the north near Nantucket, where the water depth was twenty feet, shallow enough for the *Doria's* keel to rest on the sandy bottom with her A-Deck and the tops of her watertight bulkheads above water.

The captain, with hope in his heart, pushed the left handle of the engine telegraph gently forward to the position SLOW AHEAD. The bell signal of the telegraph was answered from the Engine Room and the ship began to rumble with the vibrations of the motor. The ship moved slowly in the water for perhaps an instant or more and then she wobbled precariously. The captain jerked the telegraph handle to STOP and he realized that the last hope for saving his ship was gone. To try to run the ship with a 40-foot hole in its side was too dangerous for the welfare of his passengers. It would increase the risk of capsizing. It would prevent the safe launching of the starboard lifeboats and even if the *Doria* did reach the shoals, no rescue ship could be expected to follow her into shallow waters. The captain decided to rest his hope in the speedy arrival of rescue ships. He hoped there were many ships nearby in these heavily traveled waters between New York and Nantucket.

When Second Officer Junior Badano arrived in the chartroom behind the wheelhouse, he discovered Senior Second Officer Franchini and Third Officer Giannini there before him. Giannini had reached the chartroom first and had begun to take a quick dead-reckoning position of the ship. Before he

106

had finished, Franchini arrived to take a more accurate posi·
tion by loran. Badano entered the small room in time to
help. As Franchini called out the readings of the loran signals,
Badano scribbled them down on a scrap of envelope and then
he laid positions off on the navigational chart. The men
worked with extreme care. With the mood of imminent
disaster upon the bridge, they knew that the accuracy of
their work might mean the difference in being rescued before
the ship sank.

Badano handed the captain the scrap of envelope with the
ship's position written on it and Captain Calamai added the
few words needed to complete the distress message. The captain did not notice his chief radio operator, Francesco Guidi,
who had been standing by for orders unseen in the dark
wheelhouse, reluctant to approach the busy and distraught
commander of the ship. Captain Calamai handed the message
to the nearest man, Third Officer Antonio Donato, who rushed
the message to the Radio Room. Radioman Guidi scampered
after him.

The important message was given to Radio Operator Carlo
Bussi, who had been on the eight-to-midnight radio watch.
The transmitter was warmed up and tuned to 500 kilocycles
for the expected distress message. Bussi tapped out three dots
three dashes three dots, known the world over. Next he sent
the ship's call sign, ICEH, and then he flicked the switch of
the automatic radio alarm. The automatic device emitted
over the airwaves twelve long dashes, each exactly four seconds long, designed to trigger automatic alarms set on all
ships which did not maintain a round-the-clock watch for
distress messages on 500 kcs. When the automatic alarm
signal was completed, the radio operator of the *Andrea Doria*

107

tapped out the message that was to set in motion the greatest sea rescue operation in peacetime history:

SOS DE ICEH
SOS HERE AT 0320 GMT
LAT. 40.30 N 69.53 W
NEED IMMEDIATE ASSISTANCE

Chapter Six

"WE'RE GOING ON A PICNIC"

AS THEY WERE designated in law, the 1,134 passengers on the *Andrea Doria* were indeed innocent parties. Happenstance or fate—call it what you will—decided life and death. Marion W. Boyer, a director of the Standard Oil Company (New Jersey) and former general manager of the Atomic Energy Commission, probably owes his life to his wife's whim for a second cup of coffee. As the hour approached eleven, he suggested they retire for the night. He was tired and they had to rise uncommonly early for the morning arrival in New York. But Mrs. Boyer wanted another cup of coffee and then she wanted a cigarette. "Let's stay up a while," she pleaded. "There may be some excitement yet."

109

The last night out on the *Doria,* as it is on so many ships, was rather dull. The now familiar luxury and carefree bliss of shipboard life was ending. Party clothes had been packed away that afternoon. The time had come for reality: the handclasp with gratuities for waiters, stewards, and bartenders, and the goodbyes and the address exchanging with shipboard friends for whom you would never find time ashore. The night altogether had been a quiet one. There was dancing in the small Belvedere Lounge but the First Class Ballroom was dark and empty. The Grand Bar was sparsely occupied. Most people had turned in early. The Boyers, though, were in the Salon, Mrs. Boyer dawdling over her last cigarette waiting for something to happen, at the moment the *Stockholm* bow wrecked their de luxe two-cabin suite below on the Foyer Deck. Enough "excitement" followed.

Walter G. Carlin, an elderly and successful attorney, chairman of the board of a bank and a political leader in Brooklyn, also was tired and sleepy, but he prevailed upon his wife. They declined an invitation of friends for a cup of coffee and retired to their first-class stateroom on Upper Deck, one deck above that of the Boyers. Mrs. Carlin propped herself in bed with a book while her husband finished the last-minute packing and went to brush his teeth in the bathroom at the end of a long corridor of their stateroom. The collision smashed him against a wall and to the floor. When he staggered back into the main section of his cabin, his wife was gone. Her bed was gone and the night table and light she had been reading by were gone. Beyond the wreckage in the room, he saw a gaping hole in the wall and beyond that was the night air, the fog and the sea.

The hole in the *Doria*'s side extended at the Upper Deck from the Carlins' Cabin 46 to Cabin 56. In the latter cabin.

110

Mrs. Martha Peterson also had been reading a book in bed but a few minutes before eleven she and her husband switched off their bed lights and rolled over for a night's sleep. Mrs. Peterson occupied the inside twin bed, separated from her husband's bed by a built-in chest of drawers. Her husband, Thure Peterson, a giant of a man, tall, broad and muscular and well known in his own circle as a chiropractor and president of the Chiropractic Institute of New York, probably was the only man aboard who saw the *Stockholm* bow inside the *Andrea Doria* and survived. Awakened from his short sleep, he was conscious of a tremendous thud, the sound of steel ripping and the vision of a grayish-white hulk which was the *Stockholm* prow passing by him. It occurred to him that he was flying through space and then he lost consciousness.

He heard none of the commotion in the corridors as first-class passengers poured out of cabins on the starboard and port sides of Upper Deck. The ceiling came crashing down upon Kenneth F. Merlin and his wife in Cabin 60 but they managed to crawl through the debris to the corridor. People streamed from their cabins, trying to walk on the slanting decks and slipping and falling to the smooth, polished linoleum floor. A thick acrid white smoke drifted down the passageway.

Ten doors down on the starboard side, in Cabin 80, Richardson Dilworth, Mayor of Philadelphia, awoke on the floor between the twin beds of his cabin. His wife, sitting beside him, was flabbergasted. "I think we hit an iceberg, like the *Titanic*," she suggested. Dilworth, a Marine Corps rifleman in World War I and a captain in World War II, holder of the Purple Heart medal, survivor of the slaughter on Guadalcanal, also had read the bestselling book, *A Night*

111

to Remember, but he reasoned calmly. "No, Ann," he told his wife, "there are no icebergs off the coast of Massachusetts." It was something else, and although he did not know what, the handsome fifty-seven-year-old mayor convinced his wife there was nothing to be unduly concerned about on a modern ship such as the *Doria.* They dressed in the clothes they had laid out for the next morning and left their cabin.

Across the hall, in Cabin 77 on the port side, a young couple half the age of the Dilworths and of an entirely different social background, scampered from their cabin in their underclothes. They were Nora Kovach and her husband Istvan Rabovsky, Hungarian ballet dancers who three years earlier had fled Communist rule to dance in the West. The dancers, having completed a successful European tour, had boarded the *Doria* in Genoa and, because of a misunderstanding concerning the price of the first-class cabin assigned to them, they had switched to the small and less expensive First Class Cabin 77. The cabin for which they had been booked was number 56.

In Cabin 56, the fifty-five-year-old Mrs. Peterson awoke to find herself racked from her shoulders to feet in a tangle of splintered furniture and ceiling fragments. She was unable to move. Her body seemed numbed and aching as if it in some detached way was in pain and she herself could not feel it. The cabin, or what was left of it, was dark, a grayish-black. All she could see was wreckage about her but she became numbly aware that she was not alone in this purgatory. Almost directly above her legs within arm's reach—if she could raise her arm, which she could not—was someone else.

Jane Cianfarra, who had turned off her night light in Cabin 54 where she had occupied the outboard bed near the portholes, regained consciousness in the wreckage of Cabin 56.

She was aware immediately of her husband, Camille Cianfarra, nearby. She could hear him groan, murmuring as if in
excruciating pain, but she could not see him. She strained to
locate him, but then he was silent.

Of her two daughters in what had been the adjoining cabin,
number 52, Mrs. Cianfarra knew nothing. She feared the
worst. She remembered bidding the girls good night before
she and her husband had gone to bed and she recalled the
girls talking and giggling before they dropped off to sleep.
Linda was fourteen years old, the child of her previous marriage to Edward P. Morgan, the radio news commentator.
Joan was eight, the daughter of her marriage to Camille Cianfarra, foreign correspondent for *The New York Times* in
Spain. Linda, being the older, had taken the outboard bed
beneath the two portholes, leaving the bed on the opposite
wall for Joan.

Mrs. Cianfarra, in a state of severe shock, realized she had
heard her husband die. She believed her own life was ebbing.
Her head and face were wet with blood, one hand was
smashed and her legs somehow were trapped. Her body, im-
movable in a crouched half-sitting position, was pinned
against the steel wall of an elevator shaft which backed on
the Peterson cabin.

The two women, after discovering one another, oriented
themselves to their situation. They had concluded they were
alone and lost and would go down with the ship, and then they
heard the voice of Mrs. Peterson's husband. He had been
hurled through a connecting wall into Cabin 58 where he
regained consciousness half buried in debris. But the six-foot
200-pound chiropractor from Upper Montclair, New Jersey,
wriggled free, called to his wife and staggered out into the
corridor and then back into Cabin 56. In the dark of the

113

wrecked hallway leading into the main section of the cabin, Peterson, crawling on his hands and knees, brushed by the lifeless body of Cianfarra, his shipboard neighbor.

Ironically, Cianfarra, returning from Madrid for a vacation, had in a way prognosticated the collision. The fog which had clung to the ship since that afternoon had been the major topic of conversation through the day and dinner that night. Cianfarra, perhaps with a touch of wishful thinking indulged in by every newspaperman, joshingly told his daughters at dinner that there might be a collision, a major catastrophe, and then he would have to go to work and write a story. Mrs. Cianfarra, noting that the two girls might be taking their father seriously, reassured them. The captain had not come down for dinner as usual, she said, so he must be up on the bridge taking good care of the ship's navigation.

Hours later, as the body of Cianfarra lay still in the hallway of Cabin 56, he was the object of the poignant envy of his colleagues in the third-floor newsroom of *The New York Times*. As rewrite men pieced together stories from scant pickings of radio messages and old news clippings in the files, they talked of a newspaperman's dream come true: being on the scene of a major newsbreaking story. They had no doubt they would soon hear from Cianfarra. The office talk, what time there was for it, revolved about how lucky Cian— as he was known by his friends—was to happen to be aboard the *Doria*. City Editor Frank Adams, who rushed from his suburban home to the office at 4 A.M., listed Cianfarra's name for an eyewitness account among the twenty-one stories he scheduled on the collision. As the early morning hours wore on, the men thought and talked of how each of them, if they were on the scene like Cian, would manage to telephone or radio their story to the paper.

114

Later, when the first casualty list came in, the men in the *New York Times* office were struck with a rare sense of shock as they realized the chasm between the view they as journalists held of a disaster in which 50 or 100 unknown persons were killed and their reaction to the death of a single colleague.

Peterson reached his wife and Mrs. Cianfarra only by returning to Cabin 58 and wriggling his massive body under the wall partition which divided the cabins. Actually only half of the wall remained and that was attached only to the ceiling. The half of the wall closer to the hull had been torn away completely with that section of the cabin. Inside Cabin 56, he was surrounded by the wreckage which held the two women trapped. Beyond the wreckage was the hole in the side of the ship. He tried to move debris but it was too heavy to do alone. He needed help if there was to be any chance of saving the women. Both his wife and Mrs. Cianfarra, in the quiet of the wrecked cabin, told him to leave them and save himself. But he assured them he would return shortly with enough manpower to move a mountain of wreckage.

One deck below, on the Foyer Deck, Ferdinand M. Thieriot, business manager of the San Francisco *Chronicle,* and his wife, the former Frances de Figuera, were killed instantly in the bedroom of de luxe Suite 180, one of the four specially designed luxury suites of the ship. Their eldest son, Peter, survived only because the Thieriots, having made a last-minute change in plans not to fly from Gibraltar, were only able to book the bedroom of the two-room suite. The sitting room, with its sofa-bed and wall bed, had been taken in Genoa by the Max Passantes of Denver, Colorado. Peter Thieriot, who was thirteen years old, was given a solitary single cabin about fifty feet aft from that of his parents. His

115

cabin was on the other side of the ship's Main Foyer, which served as entrance from the pier to the ship's first-class quarters. On one side of his cabin was the First-Class Dining Saloon and on the other a telephone booth and the ship's bank. It was to this cabin that his father escorted him shortly after ten o'clock, when they had finished playing at the ship's horse races, bade him good night for the last time and walked across the foyer to his own cabin where Mrs. Thieriot had retired a half hour earlier.

The collision barely awakened the thirteen-year-old boy from his deep slumber. He rubbed his eyes, donned some clothes, looked out into the corridor, saw nothing, and returned to his bed and sleep.

He failed to see that the spacious foyer was heaped with rubble. The ceiling had exploded from the shock of the collision into thousands of pieces, the plate-glass front of the Gift Shop splattered across the floor. Two third-class pursers, Adolfo Bonivento and Emilio Bertini, on the way to their cabins, threw themselves against a wall in poses of hide-and-seek, shielding themselves from the avalanche. Behind that wall, on the starboard forward side of the foyer, three steel vaults in the Purser's Office withstood the pressure of the impact and saved the bewildered pursers from injury.

Diagonally across the foyer, in the aft left-hand corner, the door to the chief purser's cabin flew open and from the cabin rushed Chief Purser Franchesco Ingianni, and the two ship's doctors.

"My God, the boiler's exploded!" exclaimed Dr. Bruno Tortori Donati, chief surgeon and medical director of the ship. The other men hastily agreed with him. The boiler casings rose through the ship to the funnel just aft of the foyer and there was every reason to believe the damage in

116

the foyer was caused by the concussion of an explosion in the Boiler Room.

While the chief purser headed for the bridge, Dr. Tortori Donati and his associate, Dr. Lorenzo Giannini, pushed their way through crowds of passengers to the ten-room hospital on A-Deck below. "It is nothing, nothing, a little explosion in the Engine Room," the handsome thirty-five-year-old ship's doctor told passengers who clutched at his uniform. The two physicians assembled the two men and three women nurses billeted in the hospital, and they set about preparing for the arrival of casualties.

Dr. Tortori Donati stopped in at the women's hospital to comfort his two patients, both elderly and pathetic women whom he had come to like personally. One was an unlucky farmer's wife, Mary Onder, who with her husband had hoarded their meager savings for years for "just one last visit to the old country," and then spent the visit in hospitals. They had sailed the previous April on the *Cristoforo Colombo,* where, on the second day out, the sixty-five-year-old woman had fallen and fractured her left thighbone. Her visit to Italy was confined to the International Hospital in Genoa, where her leg did not set properly. From the *Colombo* hospital she had gone to the Genoa hospital and from there to the *Doria* hospital, and Dr. Tortori Donati sympathized. His other patient had been carried aboard close to death on a stretcher at Naples. Mrs. Rosa Carola, whom the doctor came to know as "Grandma Rosa," was seventy-one years old and frightened. She was suffering, according to her medical report, from acute pulmonary edema, an unstable heart condition and cancer of the larynx. The ship physician, when he had first seen her, felt in his heart that she would not survive the eight-day voyage.

117

Finding the two women terrified by the crash and the subsequent list, Dr. Tortori Donati with a characteristic warmth reassured them that they would not be deserted in their beds. He personally would care for them no matter what happened to the ship, he explained. The *Andrea Doria* was in no danger, the doctor told the women, but he was needed in the main hospital ward to receive injured crewmen. Assuring them that he would soon return, the doctor left to check the men's ward.

He glanced into the ward but saw no one there. An abscessed tooth and a slight fever apparently had not stopped the flight of cabin boy Gaetano Balzano. The doctor hurried back to the hospital main receiving room, unwittingly leaving behind in the men's ward an American sailor named Robert Hudson who was sleeping peacefully, oblivious to the furor throughout the ship. Although not confined to the ship's hospital, Hudson had been assigned a bed in the men's ward rather than in a cabin when he had boarded the ship in Gibraltar. The New Orleans seaman, a slim, dark-haired young man, had injured his back and severely lacerated his right arm in two separate mishaps on the Stockard Steamship Company freighter *Ocean Victory*. His ship had been diverted to leave him in Gibraltar where he had waited in a hospital for repatriation to the United States on the *Andrea Doria*.

The doctor, returning to the receiving room of the hospital, found Dr. Giannini and the five nurses ready for action, but no word of any injured had been received from the Engine Room or the bridge. The doctor was perplexed. Unable to reach anyone on the hospital telephone, he set out for the bridge for direct word from the captain. He instructed Head Nurse Antonia Coretti to stay with the two women patients,

118

told the others not to leave the hospital, and began the long climb to the bridge.

He was surprised at the angle of the decks and the difficulty he had climbing the stairs. Although water had begun to enter A-Deck in the damaged area of the starboard side, the port side was high and dry in the hospital area midships. Dr. Tortori Donati, wearing the blue uniform of an officer, found himself besieged by passengers asking questions and demanding answers he could not supply. Nor could he push ahead of the throng moving with him toward the upper open decks of the ship. The doctor reached the Promenade Deck, three flights above the hospital, when he heard the loudspeaker announcement for passengers to go to their emergency muster stations. Realizing this meant abandon ship, he turned in his tracks and pushed his way against the throng back to the hospital. He was barely conscious of numerous hysterical and incoherent pleas for help. Most of them, it seemed, were demands that he help find lost relatives. But the doctor pushed on. His first duty, as he saw it, was to get his patients ready to abandon ship.

The doctor, considering stretchers impractical for the task, had the two women carried up to the Promenade Deck. Two male nurses transported Mary Onder, with the help of her husband, who had come to the hospital. Dr. Giannini and two women nurses carried blankets and hospital supplies while Dr. Tortori Donati and Head Nurse Coretti carried Mrs. Carola, who had been put under sedation. The old woman gazed wildly in fear at the doctor as he carried her beneath her arms. As the doctor and nurse stumbled along the corridor with their awkward burden, the old woman cried out in her thick, rasping voice that she was dying and that before she died she wanted to see her daughter Margaret

119

once more. The doctor was skeptical about the old woman's chances of surviving but he reassured her constantly, telling her again and again what she wanted to hear. She would live, the doctor told her, and her daughter would soon be at her side.

This did not come to pass, however. The seventy-two-year-old woman did survive that night to live out the few months remaining to her, but her daughter Margaret was killed with two other women in Cabin 230 on the starboard side of A-Deck in the direct line of collision. The fourth bed in the cabin, booked for the sick "Grandma" Rosa Carola, was unoccupied.

Outside Cabin 230, Benvenuto Iazzetta pounded on the closed door with all the strength of his seventy-two years. As acrid fumes of smoke and dust wafted into the corridor, a steward implored the old man to join the passengers fleeing from A-Deck. But Iazzetta insisted that his wife, Amelia, and her sister, Christina Covina, were trapped alive inside the cabin. The steward tried to force the door open, but when water began to flow through the tilted corridor of A-Deck, he promised the old man that he would send for help and Iazzetta finally consented to go topside as the smoke became thicker in the corridor. For a time, passengers fearfully mistook the smoke as evidence of fire somewhere on the ship. Actually the smoke and white dust fumes came from the smoldering of a fireproof lining which separated the steel plating of the ship's hull from the wood paneling of the cabins. It was this lining, in fact, which probably saved the ship from catching fire from the tremendous friction of steel against steel produced by the collision.

Cabin 230 was an outboard cabin with a single porthole.

Its door opened on a narrow passageway off the main corridor. In the adjacent cabin forward, four women traveling singly were killed. And in the next outboard cabin, two Italian nuns, en route to study hospital methods in Worcester, Massachusetts, lost their lives. As did many of the clergy on the *Doria,* they had retired early, at the suggestion of the ship's chaplain, Monsignor Sabastian Natta, in order to attend the 5:30 A.M. mass, the first of nine masses scheduled for the next morning. In all, ten women, traveling Tourist Class, lost their lives in four outboard cabins on A-Deck.

Below these cabins, on B-Deck, the *Doria's* famous fifty-car air-conditioned garage, providing direct access to the pier, was inundated. The sea quickly flooded the nine cars in the spacious garage, including a $100,000 "idea" car of the Chrysler Corporation which had taken fifteen months to build, and a Rolls-Royce of socialite Edward Parker, of Miami Beach, Florida, returning from a honeymoon in Paris.

But the *Stockholm* prow struck its cruelest blow that night on C-Deck, where the smallest and cheapest cabins of the *Andrea Doria* were crowded together. The families in the cabins in the line of collision, most of them Italian immigrants, never had a chance. The death toll on this deck was confined to the area of penetration, between the watertight bulkheads at frames 153 and 173, indicating further that no more than one compartment was breached by the *Stockholm.* But the death toll in the thirteen cabins on the starboard side was greater than in the rest of the entire ship. Death must have been swift for the twenty-six persons killed in eleven of the cabins. Those not immediately killed by the *Stockholm* bow undoubtedly were drowned seconds later as the stricken *Andrea Doria* heeled on her side never to rise

121

again and C-Deck, normally at the ship's waterline level, sank beneath the waves.

One smashed cabin in the starboard section was empty at the time. Its occupants, single men, were still up in the public rooms, enjoying the last night out. In the thirteenth cabin of that section, number 664, a fourteen-year-old Italian boy, Antonio Ponzi, on his way to join his mother in Newark, New Jersey, was trapped against the ceiling in his upper bunk on the left side of the small room as the right wall collapsed and water poured into the cabin. The boy cried out to his cabin mate, whom he knew only as Antonio, who had unlocked the cabin door but could not open it. Knee-deep in swirling black water, the young Rhode Island man, Antonio Lombardi, reached up and dragged the teen-age boy through the narrow opening between his upper bed and the ceiling. He then returned to jerking and rattling the jammed door. But it remained a bar to freedom and safety. Then suddenly an iron beam crashed to the floor. Lombardi seized the beam and, using it as a battering ram, smashed the door down with the desperate force and swiftness of a man fighting for his life. They were the only two known to have escaped from the starboard collision section of C-Deck.

In the wake of death, a wave of incipient terror and confusion swept through the ship as smoke, dust and water, mixed with a slime of fuel and diesel oil from ruptured tanks and pipelines, poured through the corridors.

The 697-foot ship quavered from stem to stern from the shock of the collision. Liquor bottles trembled on their shelves and toppled to the floor in the bars and lounges of the Promenade Deck. Three simultaneous dances going on at the time came to a crashing halt. Couples fell upon one another in a tangled mass on the dance floors. In the First-

Class Belvedere Room, the ship's most luxurious night club, musicians playing the popular "Arrivederci, Roma," for the umteenth time, toppled from their podium with their instruments. The bartender vaulted over the bar and sped from the room. The white-haired headwaiter rushed about wiping up spilled drinks and reassuring the bewildered passengers that everything was all right. Most of the passengers, after the first moment of stunned surprise, seemed intent upon reassuring one another that nothing could be seriously wrong. Morris Novik, founder and president of the Italian-language radio station WOV in New York, was stopped short by the collision, one hand in the air (holding a drink), as he was making a fine point to his table companions on his favorite subject: politics.

"It's really nothing," he said. "Let's sit tight until we find out what's wrong."

Most people in the room did sit tight. Some rushed to the draped windows but saw nothing in the night fog outside. The mothers in the room who had children sleeping below acted like mothers.

Actress Ruth Roman, for one, kicked off her high heels, forgot her dancing partner and rushed from the room. She made straight for her double cabin 82-84 where she found her three-year-old son still sleeping. "Wake up, Dickie," she said softly, shaking him by the shoulder. "We're going on a picnic." She gathered lifejackets and blankets from the cabin and with a firm grasp on her sleepy son's left hand set off for the "picnic."

In the Belvedere Lounge, speculation started moments after the collision. "We've hit an iceberg," exclaimed one woman loudly. "It's an explosion in the ship's machinery," one man stated firmly. Others suggested the ship had hit an unexploded mine ... or a submerged wreck ... or a small fishing boat ... or a large freighter. There was plenty of speculation and very little fright. The first-class passengers in the lounge expected an announcement would soon be forthcoming and while some headed for their cabins, many waited for some word, some instructions.

There was less calm in the Cabin-Class Ballroom where the band had also been playing the popular "Arrivederci, Roma" to a capacity audience. The musicians in the crowded ballroom tried gallantly to pick up the interrupted strains of the song, but after a few bars, the lights flickered off and that put an end to the music. Chairs and tables were uprooted and sent flying across the room along with waiters, dancers, observers, drinks, glassware. In the few seconds before the lights flashed on again, everything seemed topsy-turvy. Chaos ensued as chairs and tables slid across the floor and people scrambled about trying to flee. At the same time, other passengers were fighting their way into the ballroom which was the emergency muster station for cabin-class passengers.

In the Tourist-Class Lounge one deck down, where an amateur band of crewmen were providing music for what gratuities they could collect, the situation was the same: confusion, shock, bewilderment and much noise. Yet, for Dr. Franco Fusco, a young Genoese physician traveling on a Fulbright Scholarship to Ohio State University, everything seemed to stop, like a moment in eternity. Then above the din he heard a "squawking voice" from the loudspeaker. The young doctor listened, but the Italian words were indistinguishable.

As might be expected following an explosion or fire in any darkened movie house, sheer panic tore across the

124

Tourist-Class Dining Room, one deck farther down where passengers were engrossed in the antics of Jane Russell and Jeff Chandler in a movie called *Foxfire*. One passenger though had been momentarily distracted before the collision. Miss Theresa LaFlamme, a thirty-year-old registered nurse returning from a three-month vacation in Europe, was surprised to see her cigarette lighter sliding across the table in front of her. Inside the ship in the dark room, she could not sense the ship was on a hard left turn, and the crash of the collision took her unawares. She was hurled to the floor, as tables toppled over and screams pierced the black room until the lights went on. Then she saw the bedlam of people struggling to get off the floor and falling again, of screams and cries, and she told herself, "There must be no panic." She tried to calm a screaming woman near her, but the woman ran off, and she tried to help another woman and then another. Almost everyone seemed to be running, and those who weren't scurrying off were on their knees praying or weeping, or doing both.

One of the first to escape from the scramble in the movie-dining room was Jack Grubenman, who happened to be near an exit. Heading for a lifejacket in his cabin one deck below, he dashed down a nearby stairway to A-Deck and then fell to his knees as the suffocating fumes of smoke and dust in the corridor caught him full in the face. The descent down the stairway had been simple, but it took him almost an hour, or so it seemed, to push his way from the stern of the ship to his cabin midships on the starboard side. The corridor was jammed with people in nightclothes pushing toward the stairways, and each door along the corridor became a roadblock. To get through the door, Grubenman had to plunge in against the throngs moving in the opposite direction. Cabin 290, which he shared with three other men, was empty. Jack hastily grabbed three lifejackets, thinking of his brother Don and sister-in-law Violet whose next-door cabin had been empty when he passed it. But when he reached the main corridor carrying three bright orange kapok jackets, two huge Italian passengers spied him and without a word pounced upon him. He managed to hold on to one of the lifejackets which he hastily wrapped and tied about himself.

He need not have fought for a jacket for his sister-in-law, Mrs. Violet Grubenman, who had tied a lifejacket securely over her nightgown before rushing from Cabin 288. Jolted in her bed by the crashing which seemed to be directly outside her cabin, she guessed immediately what had happened. She and several friends had discussed that afternoon, when the fog set in, what each would do in the event of a collision. But her plans of that afternoon did not quite work out. The corridor was a nightmare of smoke and panic. People were running in both directions. There was wailing and screaming. Mrs. Grubenman headed for a nearby stairway but before she reached it, lost her footing on the tilted deck, crashed into a wall and fell to the floor. People ran over her and past her. "Get going," shouted one man, who stopped short at her prostrated body. But when she turned up her bleeding face to look at him, he reached down to help her to her feet.

Her husband, Don, at the Tourist-Class Bar, looked out of the window in time to see the white superstructure of the *Stockholm* slip by beneath a shower of sparks. Then he took off at a run for the cabin where he had left his wife. Down one deck he went, but there in the stern of Foyer Deck he became enmeshed with passengers fleeing from the movie theater and was carried back in the wave of hysteria to the

126

Tourist-Class Lounge a deck above, which became an impromptu muster station for some 200 passengers.

What panic there was on the *Andrea Doria* immediately after the collision, even in the darkened movie theater, soon abated into general confusion. From the sundry lounges, bars, card rooms and reading rooms as well as the ballrooms on the upper decks of the ship, passengers headed for their individual destinations. Panic, terror, fright or calmness are all subjective and relative concepts, it must be admitted, and what one person saw as panic another judged as remarkable calm under the circumstances. But if one could measure terror with a geiger counter, the clicking would have become sharper and faster the farther down one went on the eight decks accommodating passengers on the *Andrea Doria.*

Actress Betsy Drake, wife of Cary Grant, occupying one of the twenty-nine airy first-class single cabins on the Boat Deck, needed only to put on the clothes she had just taken off and walk down a short corridor to be on an open deck in sight of the lifeboats on the high side of the ship. Only later did she discover the boats to be useless. Two decks down, in a small portside cabin aft, Mrs. Angela Grillo of Brooklyn fought desperately for twenty minutes with her luggage, which had slid against the door of her cabin, before she could escape with her three-year-old son Anthony. Two more decks down, Mrs. Fanny Wells, of Birmingham, who shared an A-Deck cabin with her three young children, was hysterically desperate. Although her cabin door was open she couldn't leave, for her youngest child, three-and-a-half-year-old Rosemary, was trapped by an arm caught between her bunk and bulkhead.

Farther aft on A-Deck a bewildered young American tourist, who thought the ship had been blown up, leaped from her bed nude and dashed from her cabin. Amid screams and confusion, she was caught up in the press of human traffic in the corridor before she noticed the stares of others. She had to fight her way back to her cabin for her pajamas neatly folded beneath her pillow.

A twenty-six-year-old American secretary returning from an overseas job, who also slept *au naturel,* awakened alone in her cabin, trapped beneath a fallen upper bunk. She struggled futilely in the dark, crying and screaming all the while, until her door was thrown open by a husky, tall steward who lifted her from the wreckage of her bed and carried her to the corridor. As he started down the passageway and she realized she was safe but naked, she pleaded that he release her. "Put me down!" she screamed, but he ran on. She beat her fists upon his chest until he, apparently unaware in his shocked state that it was a woman and not baggage in his arms, dropped her, and she retreated to her cabin for appropriate clothing.

There were some who fled from their cabins without clothes and left the ship in that condition, but they were the exceptions. Most decided to take the time to dress or throw a bathrobe over nightclothes. Many left the ship with suitcases. Ellis D. Hill, an Aramco official returning from Saudi Arabia, toted bottles and sterilized water for his two-month-old twins.

And there were others who dressed "sensibly" for the emergency at hand. Mrs. Josephine Fornaro, returning to Roxbury, Massachusetts, from her first visit to Italy in forty-six years, donned a dress, stockings, shoes, two sweaters, a jacket and a hat. The only thing this seventy-two-year-old lady could not find was her lifejacket. But she was calm and

128

unworried as she left her cabin on the port side of the Boat Deck. It was only later when she saw people from the lower decks coming up to the Boat Deck in their nightclothes and covered with oil, that she began to have her doubts. "I'm going to die," she whispered to herself.

A-Deck was the waistline of the *Andrea Doria*, marked on the outside of her black hull by a thin belt of white. As C-Deck was at the normal water line of the ship, A-Deck was at the emergency line. It was known in marine engineering as the ship's bulkhead deck, serving as a steel cover over the transverse bulkheads which divided the ship into watertight compartments. Ideally, if the deck were an unbroken cover, no water flooding one compartment could overflow into another. But then how could anyone pass through the cover to the decks below? Some compromise in this ideal must be made. Warships, designed to withstand as much punishment as possible, have as few and as small stairway openings in the bulkhead deck as practicable. But passenger liners are built to accommodate passengers. The *Andrea Doria*, designed for luxury and beauty, had seventeen stairways running through A-Deck, and these necessary accommodations for passengers on the long ship now served as openings for the sea, flowing in at the level of A-Deck, to pour down to the decks below.

Passengers on B- and C-Decks who did not escape in the first five or ten minutes following the collision found themselves struggling against a stream of oil-blackened water flowing down the slippery, slanting stairways. It was a terrifying thing. People learned quickly that it was easier to crawl than to walk, better to help your neighbor than to try to push ahead, wiser to recite the Rosary as one progressed

129

step by step from a purgatory than to cry out in helpless anguish.

The weak, the elderly and children were helped in the flight from the lower decks toward safety by crewmen and other passengers. People were not only going up the stairs; many were struggling and tumbling down. Parents carried their little ones on their shoulders and on their backs. Belief that the boilers had exploded spread rapidly through the tourist-class spaces on B-and C-Decks as the black oily water spread. Worst of all was the compartment in which the *Stockholm* had struck. There smoke and paint dust were thick and the decks awash with water. Crewmen quickly closed the door hiding the wrecked starboard side of C-Deck from the passengers on the port side.

People poured into the corridor in their night clothes and gasped for breath in the smoke and dust. "Abandon ship," cried two cabin stewards who remained at their posts. Mrs. Liliana Dooner, an attractive twenty-four-year-old Italian woman en route to rejoin her New Jersey husband, whom she had married when he was stationed with the navy in Naples, hoisted her two-year-old daughter Marie to her shoulders and headed for the stairway.

Paul Sergio, a fifty-six-year-old cobbler on the Notre Dame campus in Indiana, and his wife, Margaret, tried to force their way to the starboard side of the compartment. They had fled their cabin in nightclothes, leaving behind their lifejackets, all their belongings, and a letter Mrs. Sergio had written to their parents in Italy telling of their pleasant and safe trip. A cabin steward, working desperately in the port corridor, untangled legs and arms of those struggling on the sloping deck in the scramble toward a center stairway. Another steward blocked the Sergios' attempt to enter the starboard corridor. "The ship is sinking," he shouted at them above the uproar. "You must go up, up, up," he insisted, pointing to the stairway.

As others rushed by him, Sergio tried to explain. On the starboard side, in Cabin 656, were his brother's wife and her four children whom he was taking to America. For twenty-seven years he had worked and prospered as a shoe-maker in South Bend. Two years before, he had sent for his brother Ross, a carpenter, who had come with his seventeen-year-old son Anthony. Now he and his wife had gone to the old country to visit their relatives and bring his brother's family back to America. There was his brother's wife, Maria; Giuseppe, thirteen years old; Anna Maria, ten; Domenica, seven; and little Rocco, four.

But the steward insisted there was no one left behind the door to the starboard side. "Everyone has gone up and you must go up too. The ship is sinking and everyone must abandon the ship."

Paul and Margaret Sergio, with no alternative, began the long climb to safety. Their search, if it had been possible, undoubtedly would have been in vain, for Cabin 656 was in the direct line of the collision. Maria Sergio and her four children had perished. Their C-Deck cabin had sunk beneath the waves instantly. Three cabins away, Michael and Maria Russo and their two daughters, also seeking a new life in America, died.

It was a long climb topside for Paul and Margaret Sergio and the hundreds of tourist passengers like them on B- and C-Decks. Everyone feared the listing ship was sinking, yet the climb toward safety had to be taken slowly, a single step at a time. Amid the cries, shouting and wailing, each step required concentration lest one slip and be trampled in the

131

crowd. On most of the stairways as men, women and children climbed up, water mixed with oil flowed down. The sea entering the gaping hole in the side of the *Andrea Doria* flowed down A-Deck the length of the ship and as the ship rolled, the sea found its way down the successive stairways to B-Deck and C-Deck and the engine rooms below. Adding to the turmoil there were those who were fighting the crowds, pushing their way down the stairways to their cabins below in search of loved ones, material valuables or lifejackets. In all, there probably were more than 1,000 people on the move throughout the ship during the first few minutes following the collision. The longest journey from C-Deck up five decks to the Promenade Deck required some ninety minutes of hard labor for men and women, young and old alike. It seemed like an eternity of limbo between life and death.

Chapter Seven

"WE NEED BOATS"

THE IMPENETRABLE FOG, from which the *Andrea Doria* had emerged for so few minutes, only to meet catastrophe, once again wrapped its shroud around the luxury liner, which drifted on its side in the black sea. Two red lights, which had been hoisted to the ship's single mast behind the wheelhouse, and the mournful two-blast fog signals indicated to all who could hear that the ship was out of control. As far as the eye could see from the bridge, the *Andrea Doria* was alone, enveloped in fog. Visibility seemed no more than fifty yards, perhaps less. The radar screen showed the yellow blip of only one ship—the one that had smashed into the *Doria's* side, and, for all Captain Calamai knew, that ship too might be sinking.

The *Doria* was now listing 25 degrees. The men on the bridge wondered how much more time remained. Franchini and Giannini, who had been on the bridge since the collision, found time to return to their cabins for lifejackets. Giannini, before leaving his cabin, tucked beneath his shirt a crucifix given him by his mother when he had gone to sea as a junior deck boy seven years before.

In the Radio Room behind the wheelhouse, an awful stillness followed the sending of the SOS as protracted seconds ticked away. Then the answers came in rapid succession. The SOS was acknowledged as received first by the South Chatham radio station in Massachusetts and then from the Mackay shore station in Mackay, New Jersey. The Coast Guard acknowledged the SOS from its radio lookout post in East Moriches, Long Island. The *Stockholm* answered and asked: WAS IT REALLY THE ANDREA DORIA IN COLLISION?

AFFIRMATIVE, the *Doria* replied.

The freighter *Cape Ann* radioed the *Doria,* then the U.S. Navy transport *Private William Thomas* and the Navy transport *Sergeant Jonah E. Kelley,* and a Danish freighter and several ships not listed in the radio call sign book aboard the *Doria.* These responses to the SOS which showed that ships not too far away would soon be coming to the *Doria's* assistance were relayed to Captain Calamai on the bridge. The four radiomen on the *Doria* knew that on all the ships radiomen were delivering the *Doria's* distress message and position to their captains. The *Doria* soon would be receiving position reports from the other ships and then messages that they were on their way.

The *Doria's* distress signal over 500 kilocycles, a medium

low-range frequency, traveled on a ground wave for 300 to 400 miles and on an air wave 2,000 miles. If the ship had been in the middle of the Atlantic, her call for help would have been heard by shore stations in the United States and Europe and presumably all points in between. Her radio signals were in fact picked up by Coast Guard stations in Argentina, Newfoundland, and Bermuda.

But it was Radioman First Class Robroy A. Todd, monitoring messages on 500 kcs at the New York Coast Guard's radio-listening station in East Moriches, on the southern shore of Long Island, who triggered the Coast Guard's Sea and Air Rescue Co-ordination Center into action. Yelling for the other two men on his watch, he handed over the two messages that had come in almost simultaneously from ships with the call signs ICEH and SEJT. The call signs were quickly translated into the names of the two ships and at 11:25 word was sent by a direct teletype circuit to the Rescue Center in New York City: ANDREA DORIA AND STOCKHOLM COLLIDED 11:22 LOCAL TIME LAT. 40-30 N. 69-53 W.

On the tenth floor of an old, dingy loft building at 80 Lafayette Street, one block from the United States District Courthouse in New York City, Lieutenant (senior grade) Harold W. Parker, Jr., swung into swift routine action. He was neither perturbed nor excited. He had no way of knowing how serious the collision might be. It just never occurred to him that either ship might be in danger of sinking, and, as a matter of fact, the *Andrea Doria* never once during the night and morning hours sent the awful admission that she was sinking. To Lieutenant Parker, the first message was just one more among the 3,000 calls for aid received by the Coast Guard Rescue Center each year. But, as on each call, the action was complex, swift and sure.

On a large chart of the coastal waters, Lieutenant Parker spotted in an instant the location and availability of all Coast Guard vessels in the Third Coast Guard District extending from Rhode Island to Delaware. The district maintained three ships on rescue duty, alternating weekly in three conditions of readiness. In Status-A a ship has its full crew aboard, motors warmed, and is ready to put to sea on notice. Status-B was standby duty, followed by a number to indicate the hours it would take the crew to return to the ship and be under way. Status-C was off duty and not available.

A telephone call to the Sandy Hook Lifeboat Station in New York Harbor and a relay by voice radio put the 180-foot cutter *Tamaroa,* which was on Status-A, under way three minutes after the collision message reached Lieutenant Parker. The *Owasco,* on B-6 status in New London, Connecticut, was alerted via the East Moriches radio station. Lieutenant Parker next dispatched the cutters *Yakutat* and *Campbell* of the Coast Guard Cadet (training) squadron, anchored in Cape Cod Bay.

Picking up a telephone "hot line" open wire to the Coast Guard headquarters in Boston, he learned that Boston too had swung into action. The cutter *Evergreen,* returning to Boston from ice patrol duty off Newfoundland, had been diverted to the disaster scene 100 miles away; the *Hornbeam,* 90 miles away in Woods Hole and the *Legare* in New Bedford, both on B Status in Massachusetts ports, had been alerted. Every Coast Guard vessel available was dispatched in accordance with the Coast Guard policy that better a ship be sent out and not needed than not sent out at all. In fact, before Lieutenant Parker went off duty at seven o'clock the next morning, eleven Coast Guard vessels had been sent out of port. Three were recalled before reaching the scene.

136

Aircraft in New York and Boston were alerted to fly to the disaster area but the orders were canceled before the planes were aloft because of fog. Coast Guard stations up and down the coast, from the airfields in Bermuda to Argentina, were alerted and took cross radio bearings on the *Doria's* radio signals to pinpoint her position—just in case the position sent by the ship had been incorrect. As Lieutenant Parker worked through the night he came to realize that this was the biggest rescue operation of his ten-year career in the Coast Guard. In fact, he decided, it was the biggest since the sinking of the *Titanic* in 1912. But whatever its efforts, the Coast Guard was not equipped to be of much immediate help to a distressed ship so far beyond coastal waters.

Considerably closer to the scene was the 390-foot United Fruit Company cargo ship *Cape Ann*, returning empty from a chartered trip for the Isbrandsen Line to Bremerhaven, Germany. The twelve-year-old freighter carried a crew of forty-four and only one radioman and he, S. Charles Failla, had closed down the radio shack at 10 P.M., not failing, however, to set the radio's autoalarm on 500 kcs for distress calls. At 11:23 he was in bed, reading, in his cabin adjacent to the radio room when the alarm went off like a shrill alarm clock. Flinging his book aside, the radioman dashed to his radio receiver in time to catch the *Stockholm* message and SOS from the *Doria*. The strength and clarity of the radio signals told Failla, an experienced radioman, that the *Cape Ann* was close by the distress scene. To be certain of the collision location, Failla sent out, GIVE POSITION AGAIN. Back came a repetition of the SOS with the position. ROGER, Failla replied. STAND BY NOW.

The radioman found his captain on the bridge, close by the radar, where he had been for the past twelve hours

137

while the 6,600-ton freighter was plowing through thick fog. Captain Joseph A. Boyd for all his thirty-three years at sea was still a man who worried in fog. He had heard the auto-alarm go off in the radio shack but he wouldn't dare leave his radar for one unnecessary minute in a fog which obscured the bow of the *Cape Ann*. But receiving the news, he put his third mate, Robert Preston, on the radar and rapidly charted his own position and that of the *Andrea Doria*. The *Doria* was only fifteen and one-half miles to the southwest, a few degrees off his course to New York.

"Steer 248 degrees," he told the helmsman as he charged back into his wheelhouse. He telephoned the news to the engine room and demanded maximum speed possible and then sounded general quarters to alert his crew. As the *Cape Ann* pounded to the rescue, her speed gradually building up from fourteen to seventeen and a half knots, the realization slowly came to the lean, balding forty-nine-year-old Captain Boyd that the large ship he and his third mate had seen speeding by in the fog at about eight o'clock that night must have been the *Andrea Doria*.

Radioman Failla, tapping out Captain Boyd's message, thought the men on the Italian luxury liner would be happy to learn that the *Cape Ann* expected to be on the scene in about thirty minutes. But back came the query from the *Doria*: How MANY LIFEBOATS? Failla answered: Two, and the *Doria* radioed back: SOS DE ICEH—DANGER IMMEDIATE. NEED BOATS TO EVACUATE 1,000 PASSENGERS AND 500 CREW. WE NEED BOATS.

Other skippers turned their ships toward the *Doria*'s position and sent word that help was on the way. The Norwegian freighter *Lionne*, 150 miles away, asked the *Doria* whether she was needed. NEED IMMEDIATE ASSISTANCE, came the *Doria*

138

reply. The *Private William H. Thomas,* a Navy transport
returning to New York with troops and dependents from
Europe, was nineteen miles east of the *Doria,* engulfed in
fog, when she radioed: WE ARE SEVEN MILES SOUTH OF NAN-
TUCKET AND PROCEEDING YOUR POSITION. Forty-five miles
farther to the northeast churning through the same fog was
the Tidewater Oil Company tanker *Robert E. Hopkins,*
which had just left Boston on her return trip to Corpus
Christi, Texas. The tanker sent her position and said she was
coming full speed with her two lifeboats. Her captain, René
Blanc, was a man with nerves of steel. He not only navigated
the long, empty and unwieldy tanker through the pads of
fog, but he zigzagged full speed at fifteen knots through a
maze of small fishing boats off the Massachusetts coast
before he could reach the open sea.

To say that these men and the masters of the other ships
in the vicinity responded to the *Doria's* SOS without a
moment's hesitation would be untrue. But to their credit,
they responded readily, knowing only that the *Andrea Doria*
was in some sort of distress, but not that she was in danger
of sinking. The sense of responsibility of a ship's master and
the wear upon his nerves when he must decide to put caution
aside to risk the safety of his ship and passengers in diverting
his ship from course to speed through a thick fog in the hope
of aiding a sister ship in distress—this cannot be truly estimated or described by men ashore.

The burden of responsibility borne by the master of a
freighter, a tanker or a transport does not weigh as heavily
as it does upon the captain of a passenger liner, and the
single man who was probably most troubled by receiving the
SOS was the Baron Raoul de Beaudéan, vacation replacement master of the venerable French liner *Ile de France,*

carrying 940 passengers and a crew of 826 to Le Havre, France. He might well have told himself, upon receiving the news, "There but for the Grace of God . . ."

The *Ile*, a dowager in the society of luxury liners, had left New York at the same time as the *Stockholm*. As did the *Stockholm* behind her, the *Ile* enjoyed the advantages of a calm sea, a gentle wind from the southwest, and good visibility. Lunch and dinner that night introduced the passengers on the *Ile* to its sumptuous and unexcelled cuisine. The 44,500-ton ship, heavier than the more modern *Doria* and *Stockholm* together, had led a full and charmed life since she was launched in June, 1926. She was one of the largest and fastest ships in the world, and year after year the *Ile* maintained her renown as one of the most pleasant, comfortable and fun-loving ships afloat. She served six years through the second World War and carried 626,000 troops safely to all parts of a world torn by war. Returning for repairs after World War II to her original shipyard in St. Nazaire, France, she was completely overhauled and outfitted in 1949 and once again sailed as a testament to the French concept of gracious living.

Captain de Beaudéan, nobleman of fifty-three who surprised and charmed his passengers with his use of a monocle and Gallic wit, went to his bridge after dinner as usual on the night of July 25. He noticed the moon and stars overhead, the uneven soft swells of the ocean ahead of his ship and all the small details of the eight-to-midnight watch on the bridge. Then he went to his spacious cabin behind the wheelhouse for a perusal of the ship's papers and passenger list. He took no part the first night out in the ship's entertainment, high-lighted by a "cutting in" dance guaranteed to crack the social frost of any landlubber. At five minutes after

140

ten that night about eleven miles away from the Nantucket Lightship, the *Ile de France* suddenly encountered the fog and Captain Beaudéan was hastily summoned to the bridge.

The fog, as he later noted in his logbook, was of "exceptional intensity," and Captain de Beaudéan set the extra fog watch, put on the fog whistle, closed the watertight door, checked the radar and telephoned his Engine Room to take the "usual precautions." The usual precautions were not unlike those of the *Andrea Doria,* for the *Ile de France* also had a schedule to keep. Her speed through the fog was not much less than twenty-two knots. Captain de Beaudéan chain-smoked cigarettes down to quarter-inch stubs as he himself kept watch on the radar. Visibility was almost nil as the fog enveloped the bow of the French ship. He recalled the letter he had posted to his wife from New York describing the mental strain of navigating the giant *Ile* through fog on the voyage to New York.

The *Ile de France* steamed by the Nantucket Lightship at 10:34 P.M., passing six miles south of the lightship as viewed by radar, and then picked up Track Charlie, its regular route for the transatlantic crossing.

Captain de Beaudéan was at the radar when his radio officer, Pierre Allanet, burst into the quiet wheelhouse with news of the disaster. He had picked up an SOS from the *Andrea Doria* as relayed by an unidentified ship at 11:30 P.M., but he could hear nothing on 500 kcs from the *Doria* herself. Captain de Beaudéan looked at the message. SOS— HERE AT 0320 GMT LAT. 40-30 N, 69-53 W. NEED IMMEDIATE ASSISTANCE. Knowing he was not too far from the scene, he sent the radio officer back for more information and went into the chartroom to fix the position of his ship. Returning with more intercepted messages, the radioman told him that

141

the *Doria* had collided with the *Stockholm*, that several ships were rushing to the scene, including the *Cape Ann* and the *Thomas*.

Captain de Beaudéan pondered the worst dilemma of his thirty-five-year career: to go on to France or to turn back to the rescue. He could hardly believe that a modern liner like the *Andrea Doria* actually was sinking. Nothing in any of the radio messages mentioned sinking. Yet there was the SOS and the call for immediate assistance. He could not lightly dismiss the SOS as a mistake in judgment of a hysterical captain. He knew the sea too well for that. But the question was: Was the *Ile de France* herself needed for the rescue? He was under no rigid obligation to go to the rescue. The 1929 International Conference for Safety of Life at Sea, following the rescue fiasco involved in the *Titanic* disaster, made it mandatory for every ship hearing an SOS to proceed directly to the scene, unless specifically released from that obligation by the ship in distress. But that strict requirement was toned down in the 1948 Conference. Now, as long as other ships were known to be going to the aid of the distressed ship, it was left to the discretion of a ship's master whether or not to respond to an SOS.

Captain de Beaudéan was fully aware of the moral demands of the tradition of the sea, but he also realized the tremendous expense of turning back his fuel-hungry old ship. He would have a good deal of explaining to do to the French Line if he steamed back to the *Doria* and then found the *Ile* was not needed. Yet, if the *Ile* were needed, the French Line would never question his action. It was a complex decision but his alone to make. He was, after all, as the Merchant Marine Minister of France was later to say, the "Sole Master after God" of the *Ile de France*.

142

Captain de Beaudéan, knowing that other ship masters would understand his predicament, decided to ask the *Doria* directly if the *Ile* were needed. He sent his ship's position as of 11:40 and asked the *Doria:* DO YOU NEED ASSISTANCE? The *Doria* in reply repeated without hesitation its original distress message with the words: NEED IMMEDIATE ASSISTANCE. But the *Ile,* because of some quirk in radio communication, did not receive this message. Captain de Beaudéan turned to the *Stockholm* for advice and the *Stockholm* captain radioed back that he in good conscience could not send his lifeboats to the *Doria* until he was assured of the safety of the *Stockholm* passengers. Inspection of damage on the *Stockholm* had not been completed. The *Ile* monitored radio messages of other ships and it soon became clear the *Doria* needed lifeboats, as many lifeboats as she could get.

Once his decision was made, Captain de Beaudéan, who had taken command of the *Ile de France* only a month before, acted swiftly and surely. He swung the 793-foot ship around in a wide circle and set a direct course to the scene of the disaster forty-four miles away. At 11:54 that night, eleven minutes after his first message to the *Doria* was sent, he radioed: CAPTAIN ANDREA DORIA—I AM GOING TO ASSIST YOU. WILL REACH YOUR POSITION 5:35 GMT (1:35 A.M.). ARE YOU SINKING? WHAT KIND OF ASSISTANCE DO YOU NEED?— CAPTAIN.

From the *Doria,* no answer came. But radioman Failla on the *Cape Ann,* correctly surmising the difficulty, relayed: SOS MESSAGE—DORIA WANTS TO DISEMBARK 1,500 PASSENGERS AND CREW. SUGGEST STRONGLY YOU HAVE ALL YOUR LIFEBOATS READY TO ASSIST.

The captain telephoned to the Engine Room for full speed ahead and set about preparing for the rescue operation

143

ahead. He summoned the second-in-command, Staff Captain Christian Pettre, and gave orders for the preparation of lifeboats, the selecting of crews and the necessity for not alarming, if possible, the passengers on the *Ile*. Ship's Doctor Michel Delafon was advised to prepare the ship's hospital for an unknown number of injured. The stewards' department was sent scurrying for extra blankets. Chefs for all three classes were told to start preparing food and vats of hot coffee and bouillon. Captain de Beaudéan himself remained riveted at the radar, without which he would have been a man rushing through the night with his eyes shut. Alternately he cursed the fog which obscured the bow of his own ship and he prayed that God in his mercy would lift the fog before he reached the *Andrea Doria*. The captain was far more worried for the safety of his own ship and passengers as the *Ile* converged with other ships on position 40.30 N-69.53 W than he was for his crew's ability to carry out their orders to the credit of the ship and the French Line.

As the thirty-year-old *Ile de France* pounded through the sea and fog, her crew responded to the cry of distress with a spirit and enthusiasm akin perhaps to the first regiments who marched across France to the strains of the *Marseillaise*. News of the disaster spread by word of mouth throughout the crew's quarters in myriad forms of distortion and inaccuracy. But speculation only added fuel to the flames of spirit among the deckhands, cabin boys, engineers, chefs and stewards who rolled out of their bunks after a hard day's routine to take part in the emergency. This was the opportunity for the newest kitchen helper or office boy to prove he was above all a seaman. It was a chance once again to serve the tradition and legend of the sea and the glory of the best-loved ship of France. The veteran seamen aboard knew

144

the *Ile* as an old, uneconomical ship to operate, but they knew too of her record during the second World War, of her prewar glory, and of her postwar rescue missions to the British cargo ship *Chiswick* in distress in the mid-Atlantic in 1950 and the rescue of twenty-four men in a sixty-mile-an-hour gale from the foundering Liberian freighter *Greenville* eight hundred miles west of Land's End in 1953.

As the *Ile de France*, the *Cape Ann*, and the *Thomas* raced toward the stricken *Andrea Doria*, the Italian liner drifted sideways toward the nearby *Stockholm*. Captain Nordenson first noticed the change in position of the two ships in his radar, and then from the wing of his bridge he saw the lights of the Italian liner drawing closer and larger in the night. The *Doria* was drifting directly for the crushed bow of the *Stockholm*, as if seeking vengeance.

Captain Nordenson, wasting no time in trying to get out of the way, plunged the levers of the engine telegraph to FULL SPEED ASTERN and shouted to the helmsman for a hard starboard turn. Peder Larsen swung the helm and the ship began to vibrate as the engines started, but the ship did not turn and, as the men soon discovered, neither did she move. As the *Andrea Doria* came on, the bridge of the Stockholm was thrown into turmoil. The Engine Room was called, the helm was checked, the floodlights were beamed on the bow to determine if the anchors were down because of the collision. But the engines were operating normally, the wheel seemed undamaged, and the five-and-one-half-ton anchors were in place. Not only were they in place but they had been smashed into the wrecked side of the ship's bow.

Helpless, Captain Nordenson stared at the drifting *Doria*. His pink face changed to a deep red as his blood pressure rose. Then the *Doria* floated by. It passed the *Stockholm* bow

145

by less than one-third of a mile, drifting away out of control. When the danger of a second collision was past, Captain Nordenson sent word forward to the bow that he wanted an explanation why the *Stockholm* could not be moved. The explanation reported back to the bridge was simple enough. The chain locker, situated in front of the collision bulkhead, had been smashed open. The two anchor chains had unwound their full 700-foot length and apparently had tangled and caught on something on the ocean bed some 250 feet below the ship. The *Stockholm* was moored to the bottom of the ocean.

As the heavy anchor chains had unswirled, they carried with them the bodies of three teen-aged crewmen who disappeared without a trace from the two most forward cabins on A-Deck. It was only after Chief Purser Dawe completed his check of the crew roster that no doubt was left as to the fate of seventeen-year-old Kennth Jonasson and Sune Steen, one year older, in Cabin 1-A. John Hagstrom bore witness that his roommate, Evert Svensson, had been in Cabin 2-A, across the hall, at the time of the collision, repacking a suitcase of gifts he had purchased in New York for his mother and the girl in Sweden he hoped to marry. Hagstrom, to whom he displayed the gifts, had left the cabin for a breath of air on deck at 10:45.

Chief Officer Kallback directed the intensive work of a rescue team of five engineers, thirty various crewmen, the ship's doctor and senior nurse. The forward cabins had been smashed and compressed upon one another, their steel walls folded in and out like the bellows of an accordion. Entry was possible through narrow door openings to some cabins while others, sealed closed, had to be burned open. But before dawn every cabin had been entered and carefully

146

searched for survivors. Acetylene torches were used to cut through the steel walls while men stood by with emergency fire hoses to quell any outbreak of fire. The sprinkler system, which had burst and flooded the decks, had been shut down in the Engine Room. As injured crewmen were found by rescuers, either Dr. Ake Nessling or Nurse Karin Claesson was summoned to administer first-aid and to supervise the stretcher-bearing of the injured to the hospital.

In her cabin adjacent to the hospital, Nurse Claesson had been standing near a porthole, sipping from a cup of coffee, when the ship vibrated suddenly and she had looked out of the porthole in time to see the twinkling lights of another ship. Then came the crash. Her coffee cup flew from her hand as she stumbled backwards onto a settee. The slim, shy Miss Claesson, who had been a nurse on the *Stockholm* for three years, reacted instinctively. She tied a lifebelt over her nightgown and headed for the door. But with one hand on the doorknob, she stopped for a swift mental debate. Would it be better to present herself for service immediately, un-dressed as she was, or to spend several minutes dressing appropriately? Modesty triumphed and the young nurse changed into a fresh blue denim uniform and a white starched apron.

Rounding a corner to the A-Deck foyer, Nurse Claesson tripped and fell headlong into the river of water flowing down the corridor from the ruptured sprinkler system for-ward. She fell at the feet of the chief purser as he emerged from his office. "It's terrible," she exclaimed as Dawe helped her up. "We must have run into a big ship!"

"Oh, it might not be so bad," he replied in an even voice. The chief purser advised her to return to the hospital

147

where she could change her dripping clothes and be available for further orders.

Later the orders came and she went forward to the wrecked section of the bow to join Dr. Nessling. She gasped and trembled with shock at the sight of the first crewman she found lying crumpled on the deck of a cabin on Main Deck. The body in the light of a bare emergency bulb was a deathly bluish green. Nurse Claesson had never seen a traumatic death in her twenty-six round-trip voyages on the *Stockholm* but, steadying her own nerves, she knelt beside the body and felt for a pulse. The pulse was strong and even. Puzzled, the nurse dropped the crewman's wrist and then she noticed her own fingers. They were bluish green and sticky. It was paint! The unconscious form of pantry boy Sven Ahlm had been covered with paint splashed from the paint locker forward of his cabin, but his injuries were minor. Amid the wreckage, Nurse Claesson found Ahlm's roommate, Karl Elis Osterberg. He died of a fractured skull in the ship's hospital two hours later.

The engineers spent almost an hour burning a hole two feet wide through the wall of Cabin 5-A where rescuers found thirty-six-year-old Wilhelm Gustavsson unconscious, one leg broken and crumpled beneath him, his face covered with blood with one eye hanging from its socket by a shred of muscle tissue. Dr. Nessling replaced the eye in its socket and assigned one crewman to hold the eye in place with a gauze compress while Gustavsson was carried from his cabin to the ship's hospital. Lars Falk, a twenty-year-old pantry boy, presented an even more difficult transportation problem. He was found in another cabin with a crushed skull, a broken neck, blood running from his mouth. With his life hanging by a shred, his fellow crewmen somehow managed to carry

148

him successfully through the wreckage without jarring the vertebrae of his neck.

One of the most popular crew members of the *Stockholm* was found in his pajamas close to death. Fate had singled out Alf Johansson. He had postponed his vacation for this last voyage before marrying his childhood sweetheart. Only because his regular partner at a nightly bridge game which lasted to midnight was off the ship on vacation had the thirty-year-old Johansson gone to bed before eleven that night. In his cabin—4-M—the body of the husky blond seaman had been smashed like the splintered steel and wood around him. The nurse and doctor cut away his bloodied pajama pants to find compound fractures of both legs, the splintered bones jutting through the flesh. Worse, although not immediately suspected, his skull had been fractured. As Nurse Claesson administered morphine, Johansson whispered, "I think it is finished for me." She thought he smiled in comprehension of the irony of events.

Another seaman quartered in the bow undoubtedly owes his life to seasickness. Bernabe Polanco Garcia, a thirty-six-year-old Spaniard who had signed on the *Stockholm* in Gothenburg as a cleaning man in the crew's quarters, was a lonely man among the tightly knit crew of Scandinavians. A few minutes before eleven, just before the collision, he had been beset by a wave of nausea and had made his way about halfway up to the open deck for a breath of air when the collision sent him reeling. He dashed to the open deck in time to see the *Andrea Doria* veering away, and then through a babble of voices and noise, the seasick Spanish sailor heard the thin cry of a girl calling for her mother. It came from the wreckage on the open deck of the bow. He

149

followed the sound, crawling on hands and knees, until he came upon a young girl in torn yellow pajamas. She stared into the face of the thin seaman and amazed him by speaking her first words in Spanish: *"Dondé está Mamá?"*

"Was she here?" he asked, bewildered. Not since he had boarded this white, Nordic ship had anyone spoken to him in his native tongue.

"She was here with me," the girl answered, continuing the conversation in Spanish. "But who are you?"

"I am a man from Cádiz."

The conversation bordered on fantasy because what the girl in torn pajamas and the Spanish sailor on a Swedish ship were trying to comprehend was fantastic.

The girl was Linda Morgan, born fourteen years ago in Mexico and raised in Italy and Spain where the vicissitudes of journalism had taken her mother, father and stepfather. She was alive because the *Stockholm* bow miraculously had swooped beneath her bed and had catapulted her from Cabin 52 on the *Andrea Doria* to the bow of the *Stockholm*. She landed behind a curved sea breaker wall, two and one-half feet high, some eighty feet behind the peak of the bow. The wall, designed to deflect sea waves breaking over the bow from the ship's electrical equipment, had shielded Linda Morgan from flying fragments of wreckage. Linda's sister, eight-year-old Joan Cianfarra, sleeping on the inside bed of Cabin 52, perished beneath the crushing bow of the *Stockholm*.

Linda, whose last recollection was going to sleep on the *Doria*, cried "I want my mama" as she was extricated from the wreckage by the Spanish seaman and two Swedish sailors. Thinking Linda was a *Stockholm* passenger who had wandered to the ship's forecastle, off-limits for passengers, with her mother before the collision, the three crewmen scanned the wreckage of the bow for the girl's mother. About fifty feet away on the starboard edge of the deck, some thirty feet behind the peak, they caught sight of a human form. But they did not mention this to the weeping girl who cried repeatedly in pain, "I want my mama." The woman's body on the bow appeared beyond reach on the other side of a jumble of shattered steel and wood.

Carried in the arms of one of the Swedish sailors, Linda was intercepted en route to the hospital by Chief Purser Dawe emerging from his office for a second trip to the bridge. "What happened to the girl?" Dawe asked, and in Swedish the sailor gave the officer his conjectured account of the two *Stockholm* passengers on the bow at the time of the collision. The chief purser took from his pocket the passenger list for that voyage and asked: "What's your name?"

"Linda Morgan," she replied in English. "Where's my mother? Do you know where my mother is?"

"No, but I'll look for her," Dawe said.

The chief purser checked his list for the name Morgan and then for the name given him by the girl, Cianfarra. "Where do you come from?" he asked, perplexed at finding neither name.

"From Madrid," she said. And that didn't help.

Finally, observing her different surroundings, she said, "I was on the *Andrea Doria*. Where am I now?" and the mystery was solved.

The first patient to reach the hospital that night, Linda was put to bed on a small couch in the doctor's consulting room of the ship's hospital. Nurse Yvonne Magnusson administered a quarter per cent morphine sulphate to relieve her pain and she dozed in her tiny private room until the doctor, still tending to crewmen in the bow, returned. As the story of Linda Morgan circulated among the *Stockholm* crew she became known and is remembered to this day as the "miracle girl," the source of a modern sea legend.

On the open deck of the bow Valdemar Trasbo, a short lightweight officer of the Purser's Department, crept gingerly through the dangerous wreckage to recover the lifeless body of the woman seen perched precariously near the edge of the deck. The thirty-two-year-old assistant chief steward crept cautiously through the ruins on the *Stockholm* bow. When he reached his destination, he gazed upon the unclothed body of a heavy-set elderly woman, sitting upright and facing the ship in a pose that made him think of a gallant statue. Reddish-brown hair flowed down to her shoulders and on a finger of her outstretched left hand was a gold ring with a blue stone setting. Trasbo turned his head away for a moment to compose himself. He had two fears. If jostled, the body might fall over the edge and be lost in the black sea below. Worse, the section of mangled bow on which he was resting might break off and carry him with the dead woman to the sea below.

Keenly aware of the risk to his own safety, he crawled to the edge of the deck, grasped a lifeless arm and pulled. To his unforgettable horror, the arm came away from the body. He dropped it, appalled. After a moment of indecision, he made another attempt. He tried to pull the body toward him by the hair, but the hair came away in his hand. With that he abandoned his gruesome endeavor and crawled back

152

to safety. From his description, the woman later was identified as Mrs. Carlin of Cabin 46 on the *Andrea Doria*.

Meanwhile, Second Officer Senior Enestrom discovered a simple way of clearing the water that flowed from the ruptured sprinkler system through the A- and Main Decks. With the captain's approval, he and Second Officer Junior Abenius opened two large doors in the side of the ship on A-Deck. The water which did not flow off of its own accord was swept out the open doors with brooms.

Captain Nordenson, realizing that the pumping operations would never gain any headway against the sea flowing into No. 1 hold, told the Engine Room to empty the ship's forward fresh-water tanks. There was no need for a supply of fresh water, he reasoned; the *Stockholm* certainly wasn't going on to Sweden. As ninety tons of water was pumped out of No. 1 fresh-water tank, the ship's bow rose in the water, relieving the pressure of the sea on the second watertight bulkhead.

Chief Purser Dawe reported that his stewards and pursers had checked and accounted for all passengers. There were no serious injuries among passengers, he told the captain.

As the flow of messages to and from the bridge, handled by Carstens-Johannsen, dwindled, Captain Nordenson told his somewhat shaky third officer to take a position fix. Once again Carstens went to the radio direction finder, and this time he was so nervous in handling the instrument, he mislocated the *Stockholm's* position by some five miles.

It was shortly after midnight that Captain Nordenson, reasonably assured of the seaworthiness of the *Stockholm*, made his first announcement to his passengers. "Attention please," he said in English over the loudspeaker system to the whole ship. "This is the Captain speaking. We have collided with the Italian passenger ship *Andrea Doria*. But there is no danger. There is nothing to worry about."

The forthright announcement, delivered in a tone of voice so calm and deliberate, took the spark out of passenger speculation. Some passengers returned to their cabins but most were not to be denied their expectation of further excitement. There was little enough for any of them to observe on the *Stockholm* itself and the fog and mist obscured all but an occasional glimpse of the lights of the *Andrea Doria* in the distance. Except for the hurried movements of the crew flitting by, everything in the passengers' quarters appeared normal. The ship was well lighted, the slight list was barely noticeable, and the bow and crew's quarters forward were off-limits and guarded by sentinels of the crew.

One hour and five minutes after the collision, the *Stockholm* received an appeal from the *Andrea Doria* with all the earmarks of desperation. YOU ARE ONE MILE FROM US. PLEASE, IF POSSIBLE, COME IMMEDIATELY TO PICK UP OUR PASSENGERS— MASTER.

The radio message from the captain of the *Andrea Doria* posed a dilemma for the sixty-three-year-old master of the *Stockholm*. The urgent appeal indicated the *Doria* must be in imminent danger of sinking. But then, the captain reasoned, why didn't they launch their lifeboats? His first responsibility was for the safety of his own passengers and he could not send away his own lifeboats while the remotest possibility existed that the *Stockholm* might need them. Yet he could not refuse lifeboats to a sinking ship one mile away.

154

He radioed the *Doria:* HERE BADLY DAMAGED. THE WHOLE BOW CRUSHED. NO. ONE HOLD FILLED WITH WATER. HAVE TO STAY IN OUR PRESENT POSITION. IF YOU CAN LOWER YOUR BOATS, WE CAN PICK YOU UP—MASTER.

A minute later, at 12:21 A.M., the *Doria* replied: YOU HAVE TO ROW TO US. And a minute later, the *Stockholm* sent back: LOWER YOUR LIFEBOATS. WE CAN PICK YOU UP. This rather argumentative exchange, apparently between the respective radio officers of the two ships, then was referred to the two captains.

Thirteen minutes later, Captain Calamai sent an explanation with a renewed appeal. WE ARE BENDING [listing] TOO MUCH. IMPOSSIBLE TO PUT BOATS OVER SIDE. PLEASE SEND LIFEBOATS IMMEDIATELY.

Captain Nordenson, meanwhile, conferred with Chief Officer Kallback and Second Officer Enestrom who told him that they thought the *Stockholm* was out of danger of sinking. The second bulkhead was holding and would hold firm against the sea. The captain dispatched word to be radioed to the *Doria:* the *Stockholm* would send lifeboats in forty minutes. He ordered Kallback and Enestrom to see to the manning, equipping and launching of all of the *Stockholm's* three motor lifeboats and four of her eight hand-propelled craft. The other four lifeboats would remain aboard—just in case.

As Enestrom was leaving the bridge, the captain called him back. "Stand there," he said, indicating the wing of the bridge, "and listen to hear if the loudspeaker system is working properly." The captain switched on the system and announced to the passengers: "This is the Captain speaking. As I have said before, we have collided with another ship. Now we are going to launch our lifeboats. But they are not for us.

155

They are to pick up survivors from the other ship. There is no danger on the *Stockholm*."

Enestrom went down to help with the launching of the lifeboats, marveling that the "old man" thought of everything.

Chapter Eight

"I WANT TO SEE THE CAPTAIN"

MORE THAN HALF of the crew of the *Andrea Doria*, or about 300 men, swarmed over the starboard side of the ship in the furious effort to launch the eight lifeboats on the lower side. In an atmosphere tense with apprehension because of the list, the fear of capsizing and the useless portside lifeboats, the men scrambled onto the starboard boats and frantically tore away the bindings, hooks and blocks which secured the boats to the davits. This was done in remarkable privacy for a crowded ship. Few passengers actually witnessed the lowering of the boats. Instinctively, the passengers had sought the high and seemingly safer side of the canted ship, and those who did wander to the lower side were directed by crewmen to go to the high side. With the boats carried in davits high and away from the decks of the superstructure, there was no panicked stampede by passengers for the boats. But Captain Magagnini and the three officers working with him had other troubles.

Of the eight lifeboats hanging in a line, the first two were jammed in davits near the hole in the side of the ship, and the davits could not be lowered away from the ship. No. 1 boat was a small craft of 58-person capacity, used for emergencies such as to rescue a man overboard. No. 3 was a motorboat which carried a radio transmitter and receiver with a capacity for 70 persons. When the remaining six big boats, bearing consecutive odd numbers from 5 to 15, were lowered one by one from their davits, they swung in the night air far from the side of the listing ship. It was impossible to secure them to the side of the ship at the Promenade Deck to take aboard passengers. Captain Magagnini saw he would have to alter the *Andrea Doria*'s abandon-ship plan.

All vessels which carry passengers are required by law to have a pre-arranged plan for abandoning ship in emergency and that plan must be tested once on every voyage, just as the alarm bell and the watertight doors are tested once every day. The abandon-ship plan on the *Andrea Doria,* as a plan, was the simplest one possible. Passengers were merely to don lifejackets and assemble at four muster stations along the Promenade Deck: first-class passengers in the first-class lounge, cabin-class passengers in their grand ballroom and tourist-class passengers on the open deck of the bow and the open deck aft near their own swimming pool. That was all. From the muster stations, the crew would lead the way to waiting lifeboats, which had been lowered and secured to the sides of the ship on both sides of the Promenade Deck. It

158

was only a short walk to the lifeboats, and passengers, young or old, had only to take one step down from the deck into the lifeboats. The glass-enclosed Promenade Deck had a ceiling-to-floor sliding door at each lifeboat position which could be pulled open at the appropriate time. If the ship were filled to absolute capacity of 1,250 passengers and 575 crew, there was room enough for everyone to step into one of the sixteen lifeboats and be lowered away from the ship in about forty-five minutes—in theory. Only eight men would have to remain on board to operate the eight winches which controlled the descent of all sixteen boats.

The theory—once again—was based on the assumption that the ship would not list more than 7 degrees and all lifeboats would be available for the passengers. But the *Andrea Doria* had listed 18 and 19 and then 20 degrees immediately after the collision. Half the lifeboats could not be lowered and the other half hung too far from the ship. Captain Magagnini faced one more unfortunate problem: passengers' baggage, which had been piled high on the starboard side of the Promenade Deck that afternoon for unloading at the pier the following morning, made disembarkation from that deck unfeasible.

After consulting with Captain Calamai, the harried Captain Magagnini, still in his pajamas and bare feet, gave the signal to lower the lifeboats to the sea without passengers. The boat crews, made up of deckhands and trained stewards, swarmed into the lifeboats. There was no exact counting of the men. Those who crewed the portside lifeboats as well as those on the starboard side swarmed aboard the lifeboats being lowered. Captain Magagnini authorized five extra men for each of the boats, which normally called for a crew of twenty. The extra men were to help handle the lines and the more difficult task of taking passengers aboard at sea level instead of at the Promenade Deck. Jacob's ladders, shackled to the deck at each lifeboat position and stored folded inside each boat, unrolled automatically down the side of the ship as the starboard boats were lowered to the sea.

The lifeboats, operated by pumping hand levers back and forth which turned the propeller, were no sooner in the water than they were propelled beyond the danger of the inclining ship and out of sight in the fog. Captain Magagnini sent Second Officer Franchini in Boat No. 9 to round up the other lifeboats and to direct them back to the ship. The officers agreed that it would be best to concentrate the abandon-ship operation on the open decks of the stern, which were closer to the sea than the high Boat Deck. There were three decks which could be used at the stern: the Promenade Deck where the tourist-class passengers were mustered near the swimming pool, the Upper Deck fantail which extended beyond the Promenade Deck, and the small capstan deck with its open sides below the fantail. Captain Magagnini led his men back to the stern and set them to work finding all available ropes, fire hose pipes and hawsers by which passengers could climb down to the boats.

Purser Bertini led some fifty passengers from the muster station on the bow, which seemed to him the most dangerous spot on the ship, aft on the Promenade Deck just as Boats No. 1 and 3 were pushed free of their jammed davits. As Boat No. 3 bumped down alongside the ship, it was secured to the Promenade Deck by its stern and held fast by an entrapped line. It was the only boat loaded at the level of the Promenade Deck. When Boat No. 3 reached the water, however, its crew could not start the motor.

160

Peterson, the chiropractor from Upper Montclair, New Jersey, in his search for help first enlisted the aid of a twenty-five-year-old seminarian of Philadelphia named Raymond Waite. The slender clerical student followed Peterson back to the wreckage of Cabin 56 and together they tried to lift the rubble away from Mrs. Cianfarra. From the position of the two women it was obvious that Mrs. Cianfarra would have to be freed before they could get to Mrs. Peterson. But the combined strength of the two men was not enough to move the inert mass which entrapped the two women.

Peterson went off once again in search of help and this time he found a cabin-class waiter named Giovanni Rovelli who was busy on the Promenade Deck handing out the reserve lifejackets. Rovelli, a forty-eight-year-old Genoese, heard Peterson's frantic plea and decided to help this burly, distraught passenger whose wife was trapped with another woman. Little did he know then that he was embarking on a life-or-death struggle that was to take more than four hours.

Rovelli, a wiry thin little man, found he could wriggle about far more easily in the tangled wreckage of Cabin 56 than could the 200-pound Peterson. Rovelli worked furiously in the wreckage, tossing the lighter pieces of splintered wall partitions and furniture away from the women. But he realized he would need a jack or some similar tool to lift the heavier wreckage. Peterson meanwhile had left in search of a doctor for his wife and Mrs. Cianfarra. Rovelli carefully explained to the two women the need for a jack. He assured them repeatedly that he would not desert them; he would return with a jack and they would soon be free of all this. Then he left them alone.

On the high side of the Promenade Deck, near the forward door leading to the ship's Winter Garden, Peterson found

161

the ship's two doctors and five nurses. The whole medical staff was tending to the two hospital patients who were lying on the deck wrapped in blankets. Despite the blankets, Rosa Carola was shivering so violently that Dr. Tortori Donati feared she was about to expire. Peterson, wearing only a curtain he had ripped from a baggage closet around his waist, demanded medical help, specifically morphine.

The doctor's initial hesitation struck Peterson as the height of callousness. To the doctor, the half-naked passenger seemed no different from many of the hysterical passengers who had demanded his attention for what he considered exaggerated ailments. But Peterson did get through to the doctor finally that he needed morphine for two women trapped in Cabin 56. The doctor promised he would look in at Cabin 56 as soon as he could and that he would bring morphine from the hospital.

Thirteen-year-old Peter Thieriot had a worse time trying to find help. After he had fallen asleep again, he awoke with the irrepressible feeling that he was slipping out of bed. He tensed his body to stay in bed, but finally, unable to sleep, he got up and switched on his cabin light. To his amazement he saw that his bed, the floor and the whole cabin was tilted toward the porthole on the starboard side. The ceiling was split open from one end of the room to the other. The boy then realized that the ship's motors were quiet and he rushed to his porthole to see the ocean below, not far from the porthole. He had not heard the collision but he realized that the ship was in danger. He dressed quickly and headed for his parents' cabin without the slightest idea of what had wrecked the ship. Picking his way over the rubble in the foyer, he reached the continuation of the corridor on the other side

162

of the foyer but there a bulge in the smashed starboard wall blocked his way.

Seeking another route, he climbed two decks up and asked for help among the people on the Promenade Deck. He could not get the attention of any crewmen. The few stewards he met brushed by him, intent upon some other task. Passengers sympathized, urged him to find a lifejacket for himself and treated him like a boy half his age who was lost. He tried to explain that he was not lost, it was his mother and father who were lost, but everyone seemed too busy and distraught to make much sense to him. Peter did return to his cabin for his lifejacket. The Foyer Deck was covered with oil and water as he found his way to his cabin. He hoped to find his parents looking for him at his cabin, but the room was empty. Tying a lifejacket around him, he set out once again for Cabin 180 where he still hoped to find his mother and father.

Meanwhile, Peterson climbed to the bridge of the *Doria*. He wanted to see the captain about recruiting enough men for a concerted effort at clearing the wreckage away from his wife and Mrs. Cianfarra.

The chiropractor explained his plight to Captain Calamai and the captain, in a calm, modulated voice, promised that he would send a rescue team to Cabin 56. The captain even addressed Peterson by name, remembering him from a previous social visit and inspection of the ship's bridge.

Captain Calamai, it seemed, performed his duties as shipmaster almost by rote, one part of him stunned by the catastrophe and the other part carrying on against an avalanche of demands. There was only so much he could do in the face of those demands with the number of men on the bridge, and no sooner did a problem arise than he gave an order designed to solve it. Above all, he struggled to maintain the calm deliberateness that had marked his career, determined to set the mood for his fellow officers and crew. Many appeals for aid reached the bridge. Two women were trapped in Cabin 230 on A-Deck. Several people were drowning in oil on B-Deck in the ten cabins which abutted the garage in the compartment between frames 153 and 173, which had been smashed open in the collision. As the calls for help reached the bridge, Captain Calamai generally ordered the man closest to him to organize a rescue squad and see what could be done.

Shortly after Peterson had left the bridge, Chief Engineer Chiappori reached the captain after a long, arduous climb from the Engine Room. He had more bad news. At 12:15 the ship's main electrical plant in the Generator Room had been abandoned. The pumps were still suctioning water but could not keep pace with the tons of sea flowing freely through the tunnel of the deep-tank compartment into the Generator Room. One by one the first four dynamos had been switched off as the water level approached the electrical parts. The sea water was waist high in the room when it had reached the fourth generator, and then the engineers had given up. The final two diesel motor generators had been closed down and the essential electrical load had been transferred to the emergency 250-kilowatt generator aft on A-Deck and to the two turbine-operated dynamos of 1,000 kilowatts each in the Main Engine Room. With the steady loss of electrical power, the ship's ventilation system had been sacrificed, the telephones were dead, the radio transmitter and receivers had to be switched to emergency battery power. The ship's remaining electrical power was circuited to the operation of pumps and to maintaining the ship's lights.

With the pumps available, the chief engineer explained, he was doing everything possible to correct the list of the ship, but the situation was hopeless. He was even taking the drastic measure of emptying the three large double-bottom tanks beneath the starboard sides of the Generator and Boiler Rooms. From the starboard outboard tank beneath the Generator Room, he was transferring oil to the wing tanks on the opposite side of the ship. Tanks 15 and 17 beneath the Boiler Room were being emptied into the sea. Captain Calamai listened to the bad news stolidly like a man bearing the whiplash. He neither offered advice nor issued orders to the chief engineer although it is well known, as the captain himself later admitted in court proceedings, that the emptying of lowside tanks tends to decrease the stability of a ship and increases the risk of capsizing. Decreasing the weight on the lower side of a listing ship was tantamount to lifting the ship's center of gravity, like shortening the pendulum on a grandfather clock.

There was no way of calculating exactly how long the ship would last. It had been impossible to take soundings because of the list. Yet, it seemed that the ship would not capsize as soon as Captain Calamai had at first feared. She seemed to have found a new equilibrium after her quick list to 25 degrees. Now, at 12:30 A.M., the list had increased only to 28 degrees. Rope guidelines had been strung by Third Officer Giannini across the wheelhouse so that the captain and men could walk from one wing of the bridge to the other. The radar set, tuned to the eight-mile range, showed two rescue ships closing in on the *Doria*. The ships, the *Cape Ann* and the *Thomas*, radioed a request that the *Doria* fire rockets to indicate her position. Giannini and another officer climbed to the roof of the wheelhouse where they fired two red rockets of distress into the night. Chiappori, before leaving

165

the bridge, pledged to Captain Calamai that his men would fight on in the Engine Room to the very last moment.

The rescue squad, sent to Cabin 230 where women were reported trapped, was intercepted at nearby Cabin 236 by Mrs. Wells, who implored them to free her daughter trapped between her bed and the wall. The men went to work and in fifteen minutes lifted the bed away from the wall, freeing the small, wailing girl. The men helped the mother and her small children along the flooded A-Deck to a stairway and up to the Promenade Deck muster station. Cabin 230 was forgotten. No one would ever know whether the three women behind its jammed door were dead or alive.

Dr. Tortori Donati, accompanied by Nurse Coretti, returned to the hospital for a supply of morphine and hypodermic syringes and then plodded to Cabin 56-58. There was no reason for them to stop in again in the men's ward where Robert Hudson, the American sailor, still was sleeping blissfully. In Cabin 58, the doctor found Peterson, Waite and a night watchman. Steward Rovelli at the time was off searching for a jack. Dr. Tortori Donati, profoundly shocked at the sight of the wreckage which filled the entire left side of Cabin 58, handed over the syringe and a phial of morphine to Peterson when the chiropractor explained that he was a doctor. The ship's physician could not see how the women, whose voices he could plainly hear, could be reached. He sent his nurse back to the hospital for an amputation saw and a cast saw. The night watchman he told to try to find an ax. He himself crawled into the smashed and narrowed hallway of Cabin 56, where he came upon the body of Cianfarra. He confirmed that the man was dead, and then crawled into the dark cabin. He tried to lift off some wreckage, but found it too heavy. The night watchman, returning with an ax, tried

166

to chop through the wall connecting the two cabins, but the veneered plywood attached to the ceiling merely vibrated with the blows, dislodging debris over the two women. Peterson meanwhile climbed beneath the wall partition and injected all of the morphine into the arms of his wife and Mrs. Cianfarra. Both women were in considerable pain.

Rovelli returned, unable to find a jack anywhere, and joined Peterson amid the wreckage. Together, the fifty-seven-year-old chiropractor of Upper Montclair, a wealthy suburban community in New Jersey, and the forty-eight-year-old waiter from Genoa, worked as equals in the single endeavor to move wreckage away from Mrs. Cianfarra, who had to be freed before there could be any hope for Mrs. Peterson. The two men had never met before, nor did they stop for introductions during their struggle. They succeeded finally in freeing Mrs. Cianfarra's right leg. Her other leg remained entrapped in twisted bedsprings. The men decided they needed tools: scissors or a knife to cut away a cumbersome mattress, pliers or wire cutters to snip the bedsprings, and a jack to lift a wall section and heavy beams.

Both women again pleaded with the men to leave them to die in the wreckage. They implored Peterson and Rovelli to save themselves before the ship sank. But on that subject both men were of the same mind: they would not leave the ship until both women were freed. As Peterson tried to bolster the spirits of his wife, Rovelli took it upon himself to encourage Mrs. Cianfarra. As the night wore on he made her his own special responsibility. Over and over again he reassured her, "Don't worry, lady, I will get you out of here." Personal identity seemed to mean nothing to the forty-eight-year-old steward who was risking his life for a woman he had never seen before. When Mrs. Cianfarra asked him his name, he said, "My name, what does it matter? Don't worry, I won't leave you."

Dr. Tortori Donati in the meantime had left in response to an appeal that men were needed to rescue several people drowning in oil on B-Deck. This time he took with him Dr. Giannini and the two males nurses. A single narrow stairway with three flights of steps was the only access from A-Deck to the latitudinal corridor of B-Deck adjacent to the garage which had been torn open by the collision. Descending the stairway to the dark corridor of the ship below the level of the sea was frightening. The screams of several women could be heard at the top of the stairway.

Two engineering officers and two seamen at the lowest stairway platform above the corridor deck explained the situation to the doctor's party. Four persons already had been pulled out, but high on the port side of the corridor three women were too terrorized to try to reach the stairway in the middle of the corridor. The sea water mixed with fuel oil was waist high at the center stairway and was slowly flooding the corridor. The starboard side was under water. The doctor by playing the beam of a flashlight down the narrow corridor could see three forms crouching at the end of the corridor. All his coaxing was futile. The women seemed not to hear him because of their own continuous wailing.

Repeatedly the men tried throwing a rope to the hysterical women, but each time one reached for the line she would slip and go under the oily water. The black slimy water sloshed back and forth in the corridor as the listing ship rolled in the sea. After the two engineers had left to return to their other duties, Dr. Tortori Donati as senior officer decided the only way to save the women, all Italian emigrants, was for the men to go in after them. The prospect was harrowing, but it was

equally harrowing just to be on the stairway watching the
black water rise, suspecting that the ship might sink at any
moment. One crewman, with a rope tied about his waist,
plunged into the water and struggled to the women. He
coaxed but he could not convince them to pull themselves
along the rope to the stairway and safety. Another crewman
had to venture into the corridor to force the women one by
one along the rope. One of the women clutched a satchel in
one hand, leaving only one other hand by which to hold on
to the rope. "Throw the bag away," the crewman screamed at
her. "You will lose your life for that bag." But she held on to
it as if it were life itself.

The three women reached the stairway in a state of shock,
hysteria and emotional collapse, but otherwise the doctor
found them uninjured. The third woman to reach the stairway
refused to climb to the deck above. "I have no clothes on,"
she wailed. The exasperated doctor argued with her at length,
convincing her finally that smeared from head to foot with
thick black oil, she was as decently covered as were the other
two women in their drenched nightgowns. He left the three
with the crewmen and two male nurses to be brought to the
Promenade Deck, and headed with Dr. Giannini aft on
A-Deck to the hospital to pick up more supplies.

Later, while the doctors were on Upper Deck during their
climb from the hospital to the Promenade Deck, they learned
that one of the two women in Cabin 56 had been extricated.
The first surgeon sent Giannini on to tend to the patients on
the Promenade Deck while he himself went to Cabin 56. He
found Mrs. Cianfarra wrapped in a blanket, lying quietly on
the floor in the hallway of Cabin 58. Her face was cut and
her hair matted with blood. She had been freed finally, some
two hours after the collision, by Peterson cutting through the

169

twisted bedsprings with pliers found in the radio shack and by Rovelli hacking away a mattress with a vicious-looking carving knife taken from a kitchen galley.

Mrs. Cianfarra was lifted in the blanket to be carried topside. She cried out as she was jostled. It was the first scream or sign of tears since her ordeal began. "I think my leg and arm are broken," she said in a quiet voice by way of explanation to the doctor.

The doctor bent toward her and said, "You are a very brave woman. We will take care of you now." Mrs. Cianfarra, numbed by shock and morphine, was carried in the blanket to the high side of the Promenade Deck.

Most of the passengers had sought the high side of the ship, trying to get as far away as possible from the prospect of the ship rolling over on them. Some headed directly for the muster stations in the interior of the Promenade Deck while others first went to their cabins for lifejackets and valuables. But once having arrived on the high side of the ship, there the people stayed, mostly in isolated groups. The angle of the decks made it nearly impossible to move around. For those with families, there seemed no place to go, no place safer than the high side of the ship.

The only thing to do, it seemed, was to stay put and wait for some responsible word of what had happened and what would happen next. That word never came. For many, the sheer waiting and the uncertainty of the first two hours after the collision was the worst agony of the night. The loudspeakers strategically placed about the Promenade Deck, the lounges and the Boat Deck were visible but silent. Passengers waited, knowing nothing. They speculated upon conflicting stories, rumors and theories, but it was easier to believe that the Engine Room boilers had exploded than that

170

the *Andrea Doria* had collided with another ship in the middle of the ocean.

Those who congregated on the port side of the ship had no way of knowing that the lifeboats on the other side had been lowered away. Excitement spread sporadically each time a group of crewmen climbed aboard a portside lifeboat and attempted to launch the boat. Occasionally passengers climbed aboard a deserted lifeboat as it hung in its davit, waited for something, anything, to happen, and then climbed out again in disgust or despair.

There was no way for the passengers to accurately estimate the danger. They speculated but did not know whether the ship would sink or sail on to New York. Few people knew or believed there had been a collision. Certainly no one knew the *Andrea Doria* had collided with another passenger liner, the *Stockholm*.

While the passengers waited in ignorance, news of the collision and the *Andrea Doria*'s appeal for lifeboats to evacuate its passengers was flashed around the world by the press wire services, radio and television. Amateur radio operators up and down the east coast of the United States picked up the distress messages which crackled across the air waves, and notified various news outlets.

Ironically, the collision had interrupted a rather wistful conversation in the bar next to the Cabin-Class Ballroom on the possibility of an engine breakdown which would stretch the pleasurable voyage another day or so. George Krendell, a New York insurance broker, and Sylvan Hendler, an importer-exporter, agreed they would not mind the day. But Christine Grassier and Marguerite Lilley, although thoroughly pleased with the ocean trip, said they were anxious to see the United States. Christine Grassier, a black-haired petite woman of

171

French-Indo-Chinese extraction, made her home in Menton, France, near the Italian border, where she had met Marguerite Lilley, whose parents lived in the little town. Mrs. Lilley was married to an English businessman and lived in London.

Krendell, facing a porthole, saw the lights of the *Stockholm* as it slid by after the collision. In stunned silence the four looked at one another, and then Krendell leaped to his feet. "Stay there, I'll be right back," he shouted. He ran to the nearby corridor and flung open two doors leading to the Promenade Deck. When he opened the first door leading to a small cubicle, the ship lurched on her starboard list and Krendell was thrown through the second door toward a ten-to-fifteen-foot hole in the glass side of the Promenade, ripped by the *Stockholm* sliding by. Baggage stacked on the deck began tumbling through the hole. He looked about to find his own luggage and noticed with some surprise that his three cases of liqueurs and a carton of perfumes purchased in Paris also had been brought up on deck from the hold. The deck was loaded obviously not only with cabin luggage but also baggage stored in the ship's hold.

While Krendell was out on deck, his friend Hendler excused himself from the ladies and made straightaway for the vault in the Purser's Office, where he had deposited for safekeeping $16,000 in cash, and several exotic jewelry items bought in Italy.

Krendell, who fancied he knew something of ships since he sailed his own boat at East Hampton, New York, advised the girls to stay put while he fetched their lifejackets. But the two women insisted on accompanying him. The three set out on a tortuous route to their cabins one deck below and toward the stern. The nearest stairway, when they reached it, was

172

jammed with people and the corridors on Upper Deck, although less crowded, were more difficult to navigate. A stream of water, most probably from a ruptured water pipe, flowed along the downward side of the starboard corridor about twelve inches deep. Krendell and his two women companions had to grasp and struggle around each person going in the opposite direction since everyone was trying to walk beyond the reaches of the water, holding on to the starboard wall with one outstretched arm. As the ship rolled, there were intermittent cries, "We're sinking, we're sinking." But more often men and women in nightclothes demanded of those fully dressed, "What happened?" "What shall we do?" "Are we sinking?"

Krendell's Cabin 114 was opposite that of the girls' in a narrow passageway off the main corridor. The proximity had led to their meeting soon after they had all boarded the ship in Cannes. Krendell, a slender, fair-complexioned man more than six feet tall, quickly gathered up the two lifejackets in his cabin, his passport and papers, and then went to the other cabin. "Hurry, hurry," he shouted impatiently. It occurred to him that women did not relinquish their prerogative to keep men waiting even on a sinking ship. The two girls finally emerged from their small cabin, Marguerite clutching a small overnight bag which Krendell carried for her.

Upon reaching the Promenade Deck, an officer directed them to the port side of the ship, explaining that they must help counterbalance the list. At the moment, it seemed perfectly logical, and the three joined a crowd of passengers milling about on the port side of the Promenade Deck. After a while they climbed one deck up to the open Boat Deck, where again they stood about with the crowd until Hendler appeared, carrying a ship's life preserver with him. The Purser's Office had been locked and deserted, he told them, and he saw no sense in waiting there for his $16,000.

They remained on the port side of the misty, damp deck, speculating with others and complaining about the lack of information. At about midnight there was a brief announcement over the loudspeaker in Italian. But the words were indistinguishable, even to Marguerite Lilley, who had been previously married to an Italian count and spoke the language fluently. Virtually everyone on deck was gathered toward the stern, holding on to a railing or a stanchion or seated on the deck.

Sylvan Hendler suggested they move forward toward the lifeboats in the center of the ship, where the deck was almost deserted. They made their way forward slowly, grasping the railing along the superstructure wall, and crawling across areas where there was no railing for support. Krendell suggested they try the starboard side, but Hendler thought it best to be prepared to leap overboard from the port side in case the ship rolled over. Anyone on the low side of the ship would be sucked under and lost if the ship went down, he argued. But Krendell, after a glance over the port side, said it would be suicide to try to jump that distance. "I want to know what's going on on the other side," he insisted.

Krendell deposited the overnight case he had been carrying with Hendler and the two women, who had accumulated besides their lifejackets two round life preservers. Leaving them at an agreed-upon spot where they would wait for him, Krendell found a through corridor to the starboard side which seemed like a steep slushy ski slope. He made his way down one-quarter of the corridor when his feet skidded from under him and he slid on his back, feet first, swiftly toward the door

174

at the low end of the corridor. "I've got to twist over," he told himself. "If I hit that wall and break a leg, I'll never be rescued." Grasping at the wet, slippery deck, he managed to turn his body about and he struck the wall with his shoulders and back.

He picked himself up unhurt and went out to the starboard side of the Boat Deck. His heart sank then and it occurred to him for the first time that he might not be saved after all. The starboard side appeared weirdly deserted. The davits were empty, the lifeboats gone. He looked over the side and saw the ocean strewn with debris and oil and surprisingly close to the deck. From a distance beyond the thick padding of fog he heard the foghorn of another ship echoing the continuous throaty blasts of the *Doria's* horn. After a few moments Krendell noticed a series of ladders over the side. Down along the deck he saw several groups of crewmen, and he realized that it was from the starboard side that the *Andrea Doria* was being abandoned.

He set out to get his friends on the high side of the ship but he reached only the halfway mark of the corridor, pulling himself on a railing along the wet, inclining deck, when he again slipped to the floor. This time he could not lift himself to the waist-high hand railing. He felt rather foolish and doltish, struggling on the slippery floor but try as he might he could not get to his feet. He estimated his chances of sliding back down to the starboard side and beginning over again when Marguerite Lilley appeared of a sudden at the door of the high side, and, seeing his predicament, eased herself down the corridor to his side. While she grasped the hand railing, Krendell pulled himself up like a cripple, clutching at her legs and body for support.

Back on the port side they convinced Hendler and Christine Grassier that their best hope for getting off the ship was from the other side. But this time they avoided the slippery corridor. They slowly dragged themselves along the handrails around the forward end of the superstructure to the low side of the ship and aft along the deck until they reached the first rope ladder. Four crewmen were there, one of them hanging over the railing and shouting to someone in the water below.

An overhanging lamp at each boat position from the Lido Deck above cast a diffused light over the Boat Deck and the side of the ship. Below, they saw a stout woman in a life-jacket floating in the water, moaning and crying. Holding her to the side of the ship was a crewman at the bottom of the ladder. He held the woman with one hand and the ladder with the other while keeping one foot on a rung of the ladder and the other on a small four-by-four-foot raft. All the while he kept up a shouting argument in Italian with the man leaning over the railing. The man on deck, apparently a petty officer in charge at the ladder, kept repeating, "You stay there and hold her!" From the bottom of the ladder, the crewman shouted back, "I can't, I can't hold her any more." Suddenly the crewman scampered up the ladder and swung himself over the railing, dripping wet. The petty officer, still berating him, vehemently ordered another man over the side, and a second sailor went down to hold on to the woman, who was too heavy to lift out of the water.

Krendell remained at the ladder about fifteen or twenty minutes and despite Marguerite Lilley's attempts in Italian they could learn nothing from the seamen about chances for their rescue. Krendell, an individualist not to be outdone, decided to see the captain.

He climbed a narrow flight of slippery steel steps to the Lido Deck and another flight to the Sun Deck, taking one

176

step each time the ship wallowed in the waves. When he thrust his head and shoulders above the railing of the bridge wing, Krendell saw two men peering into the fog, one with binoculars. The smaller, younger man, apparently an officer cadet, noticed him and ran to bar his way. "You can't come up here," he said.

"I want to see the captain," Krendell demanded.

"You can't come up. It is not allowed."

"Well, I'm coming up," said Krendell as he swung open the gate to the bridge wing, pushing the smaller man aside. As he headed for the door of the wheelhouse, the officer with the binoculars tried to stop him. They argued at the wheelhouse door and Krendell purposely raised his voice so that if the captain were inside, he would hear him. He could distinguish the shapes of several men moving about rapidly in the wheelhouse, giving him the impression of confusion. "I want to see the captain," Krendell shouted. "I want to know what's going on."

From inside the wheelhouse, a man whom Krendell assumed was Captain Calamai came to the door and said to the officer who was blocking the passenger's entrance to the wheelhouse, "You tell the gentleman what he wants to know." So gentle was the tone of voice in contrast to Krendell's temperament at the moment that he relented and retreated from the wheelhouse.

"No, we will not sink," the officer told him in answer to his question. "There is no danger, no danger. The ship must list 40 degrees before she will turn over, and she will not do that. There is no danger. . . . The list is now only 20 degrees."

This statement, Krendell did not believe. The list was closer to 30 degrees, he thought. The officer insisted that ships were on their way to the rescue and he pointed out the sound

177

of a ship's fog whistle in the distance, but to Krendell it sounded like the foghorn of the ship he had heard before and at the same distance from the *Doria*. He left the bridge exasperated, not knowing what to believe or what to do.

Back on the Boat Deck, he lost track of time as he and his friends waited, until suddenly out of the fog there appeared a lifeboat, quite near the ship and only half filled. It seemed that the men in the boat were lost and had come upon the ship by mistake. The men, seeing the *Doria*, reversed the lifeboat's direction and began pulling away from the ship. The petty officer at the ladder became positively furious. Earlier, he had called in vain for two crewmen to return to the ship but they had paddled away on individual life rafts. Now he yelled, cursed, and demanded that the lifeboat come back to the ship. As the lifeboat started away from the ship, he threw several metal flare cylinders at the lifeboat, shouting, "I will accuse you . . . I promise . . . I will accuse you."

The lifeboat was turned around again and, after a wobbly start, headed directly for the ladder and the woman still floating in the water. At the very last moment, the man at the foot of the ladder kicked the now-unconscious woman away from the ship as the lifeboat banged into the side of the ship. The crewman then jumped into the boat and with the help of others the heavy-set woman was lifted into the boat.

The petty officer then turned to the four passengers and told them to climb down to the lifeboat. Both women were afraid to climb over the side. Neither would go first. After some discussion, Hendler descended to the lifeboat, followed by Christine Grassier and then Marguerite Lilley. A rope was tied around the waist of each in case of a mishap on the narrow ladder. The crewman who pulled up the rope after
178

Marguerite Lilley then began to knot it around his own waist, announcing, "I go now."

"No, you not go," said the petty officer.

"Yes, I go; the ship is sinking now," he cried, clutching the rope.

A swift shove by the petty officer sent the crewman stumbling some fifteen feet down the sloping deck. The petty officer told Krendell, "You go now. You don't need the rope. Just hold the ladder and do not look down."

"I've got this case," Krendell said, holding up the overnight bag Marguerite Lilley had given him.

"Never mind the case," the petty officer said. "You don't have much time."

The men in the lifeboat were shouting that they intended to leave and other passengers, seeing the activity at the ladder, began drifting forward. Krendell set the case on the deck and quickly climbed down the ladder. When he reached the boat without the case, Marguerite Lilley called up to the deck, "Throw down my case. Throw down my jewels." Krendell had not realized what was in the case. The petty officer called back it was too dangerous to drop the case into the boat; someone might be hurt, and by that time the lifeboat crew released the ladder and pulled away from the ship. A girl about fourteen years old was left hanging one-third of the way down the ladder. While the petty officer renewed his screams, the lifeboat glided away from the ship on a long, meandering route through the fog to the *Stockholm*. All the cajoling of Marguerite Lilley did not convince the lifeboat crew to return to the ship which they were positive was about to sink.

Somewhat earlier than 2 A.M., after the lifeboat had seemed to be going aimlessly in circles in search of the distant foghorn, they arrived at the quiet white ship that was the *Stockholm*. The seaman in charge of the lifeboat called out to a man framed in the side door of the *Stockholm:* Was it safe to come aboard? Was the ship sinking? What ship was it?

From the *Stockholm*, the man at the door shouted the answers and beckoned the lifeboat to draw near and allow the passengers to come aboard.

Krendell and the others were thankful when they set their feet upon the solid deck of the *Stockholm*. Crewmen lined the corridor near the door, offering help and directions. The seriously injured were to go to the nearby hospital. Those in need of first-aid would be escorted to the Tourist-Class Dining Room, where tables had been pushed together and covered with blankets to serve as temporary beds. All others were directed to the large Tourist-Class Lounge, which had been converted to a reception room where coffee and sandwiches were served buffet style.

When the two men and two women reached the lounge, the sight surprised them. They had thought they were among the very first to escape from the *Andrea Doria*. But before them, they stared at a crowded room. As they looked about in wonderment, they soon realized the room was crowded with crewmen from the ship they had just left. Looking around for other passengers, they saw only a few they could recognize as fellow travelers. Estimating by eye, it seemed there were about two hundred crewmen from the *Doria* who had arrived at the *Stockholm* before them. They were attired for the most part in the white jackets and attire of stewards, waiters and kitchen help. The room seemed noisy and filled with Italian crewmen, who had formed a long line leading to the food on the buffet table. Some, Krendell and his friends noted, were coming around for second helpings of food and cigarettes.

Later, a request for volunteers from the Italian crew to help out in the kitchen was announced. But there were no volunteers and before long, Swedish officers made the rounds of the crewmen in the room and selected men who were ordered to help serve food and wash dishes.

Still later, Krendell chanced to meet his own dining room waiter of the *Doria* who accepted the offered tip which Krendell had expected to give him the following morning on the *Doria* in New York. The waiter, expressing surprise that the four companions had not reached the *Stockholm* earlier, blandly explained that he had come aboard at about 12:30 A.M.

Chapter Nine

"SEND DOWN A LADDER"

THE FIRST SURVIVORS from the *Andrea Doria*
reached the *Stockholm* sometime between 12:30 and 1 A.M.,
most probably at about 12:45. No one on either ship, of
course, held a timepiece to the events which followed the
collision. The stark events of the night stood out amid a
jumble of impressions, but the exact hour or minute and sometimes the sequence were lost in the chaos and excitement.
To some, minutes seemed like hours, and to others the night
passed like five minutes. The first survivors to reach the
Stockholm came in three lifeboats close upon one another.
They were sighted by a lookout on the bridge of the *Stockholm*, who focused a bright spotlight upon them.

Chief Officer Kallback rushed to an open side door on

Main Deck near the stern, which the lifeboats were approaching. The first boat had just come alongside when the chief officer waved all three boats farther ahead toward the lower door midships on A-Deck. The A-Deck door on the port side of the ship, not far from the Purser's Office, was only six feet above the sea. The anxious Swedish welcoming party standing at the door was considerably surprised to see that the large white lifeboats of 146-person capacity were each less than half filled. The boats came swiftly alongside the open door of the *Stockholm* and there followed a ferocious scramble in each boat as the survivors rushed to board the Swedish ship. It seemed to the Swedish crewmen that the last ones who remained in the lifeboat would constitute the crew who returned the lifeboat to the *Doria*. As the survivors came aboard, the initial surprise of the Swedish crew changed to chagrin tinged with dismay because, with few exceptions, the survivors were all men, the vast majority of them wearing the gray kapok lifejackets of crew personnel and the white starched jackets of the steward department.

With a grasp of the arm and a heave, they were pulled aboard one swiftly after another. The men of the *Stockholm* felt inwardly hurt at this turn of events. The abandoning of the *Doria* by her crew before the passengers cast a reflection not only upon the *Andrea Doria* but upon seamen everywhere who for generations had lived and died upholding the tradition of the sea that says "women and children first." The only mitigating explanation offered was that these men who forsook their ship in mistaken fear were for the most part not sailors in the maritime sense of the word, but rather waiters, dishwashers and kitchen workers ashore who happened to ship out to sea to eke out a living.

184

The launching of the *Stockholm* lifeboats began a few minutes after 1 A.M. Second Officer Enestrom took the first one, lifeboat No. 7, down and away from the *Stockholm* with one engineer and three crewmen aboard. He headed the motorboat toward the lights of the *Andrea Doria* and within a few minutes passed two more Italian lifeboats approaching the *Stockholm*. Junior Second Officer Abenius followed in the second motorboat, lifeboat No. 8. When the two officers had received their orders, Carstens, who had not left the bridge since the collision, approached Captain Nordenson sheepishly, unsure of his commanding officer's feelings toward him. He had explained the radar bearings and his sighting of the other ship before collision and Captain Nordenson, his stern eagle face expressionless, had listened carefully and then had said nothing. He told Carstens merely to write down his observations before he forgot them.

The young officer, rattled but anxious to take a lifeboat out to the *Doria*, rushed into the chartroom, took up a pencil, and on a small scratch pad scribbled what is probably the briefest description of a major ship collision in history.

At 2300 [11 P.M.] discovered the echo in radar. On 1.8′–1.9′ [miles] distance saw two top lights and weak red light. Turn then starboard to clearly show [*Stockholm*] red light. The lookout called down and reported light[s] on port. Ordered "starboard" "Midships" "Steady so." The turn about 20°. Went back to the bridge wing and saw then green light [of *Doria*]. Ordered then hard starboard and ordered stop and full astern. At the moment of collision the "Andria Dora" blew. The signal was not identifiable because of the collision.

At 2309 the moment of collision.

The visibility was at the time good on starboard but fog patch developed rapidly wherefore the "Andria Dora" could not be seen until distance 1.8–1.9 [miles].

After composing his account of the collision, with its misspellings and omissions, Carstens approached his commanding officer again. "Captain," he said, "I would like to take out Boat No. 1."

Boat No. 1 was the last of the *Stockholm's* three motor lifeboats. Captain Nordenson hesitated for a moment, scanning young Carsten's face, and then said, "Yes, all right."

Carstens turned in an instant and dashed from the bridge, determined to reach the motor lifeboat before it was dispatched from the ship.

Meanwhile, as the *Cape Ann*, the *Thomas* and the *Ile de France* drew nearer to the *Andrea Doria*, the radio signal of the Italian liner grew weaker and weaker. Radioman Failla on the *Cape Ann*, who had received messages from the *Doria* earlier without any trouble, feared the ship might be going down at that moment. But the trouble actually was a grounded antenna on the *Andrea Doria*. At 12:15 A.M., with the loss of power from the Generator Room, the *Doria* radiomen had switched to their auxiliary transmitter and emergency battery power. But the signal from these sources was so weak that it was distinct only to the nearby *Stockholm*.

The radar antenna rotating around the mast, which was tilted toward the sea, scanned an elliptical horizon which included more sky than surface area. On the bridge, Captain Calamai could not be sure of what his radar was showing him. Second Officer Badano, nervously awaiting the arrival of rescue ships which had radioed they were on their way, began to doubt the accuracy of the position which he had calculated. The rescue ships seemed an awfully long time in coming. When the *Doria* lifeboats had left the ship, a dead stillness had descended upon the bridge. Except for a few

186

seamen remaining as lookouts, the bridge was virtually deserted. Everyone was away carrying out orders of Captain Calamai which had been issued soon after the collision. Badano was disturbed by a recurring recollection of one small Italian freight ship that had sunk with all hands aboard only thirty miles west of Genoa because it had sent out a wrong position (through a simple error) that had sent rescue ships to a point thirty miles east of Genoa.

A mistake of one degree in the position of the *Doria* in that latitude meant sixty miles, enough for every rescue ship to miss the disaster location. Badano, knowing he would not be at ease until he rechecked the position for which he was responsible, returned to the chartroom, where the loran was still flashing its electronic waves on its small screen. He carefully laid off the position of his ship again and noting the position on a scrap of paper went into the Radio Room to make certain that the correct position had been sent. He compared his latest position with the one sent out and was reassured. He had made no mistake. It was only a matter of time and waiting for the rescue ships to arrive.

The *Cape Ann* was the first to arrive. Captain Boyd cautiously steered the freighter by radar between the *Andrea Doria* and the *Stockholm*. It was 12:45 and he knew he had arrived, but he could not determine in the fog which ship was which. Failla in the radio shack tried to contact both ships for information. The *Stockholm* gave its position and from that, Captain Boyd knew the *Andrea Doria* was to the left of his ship, engulfed in the thick fog. He gave the direction to his first lifeboat, which had been lowered to the water. Ten minutes later his second and last lifeboat was lowered to the sea and disappeared in the fog as its crew pulled on their sixteen-foot oars.

At 1:23 A.M. the Navy transport *Thomas* arrived on the scene and quickly sent off her two motorboats. One boat was equipped with radio by which Captain John O'Shea hoped to maintain a contact with the *Andrea Doria*, relaying all messages to the Coast Guard in Boston. Captain O'Shea, a heavy-set man with a florid face and a shock of white hair, kept six lifeboats aboard the *Thomas*—just in case.

At about the same time, the first lifeboat from the *Stockholm* reached the *Doria*. Second Officer Enestrom steered his craft around the spoon-shaped stern of the mammoth listing liner and "tied up" at a pair of heavy hemp mooring lines hanging from the low side of the ship's stern. Actually, the lifeboat was secured in place only by two of its four crewmen hanging on to the ends of the hanging ropes.

"Send down a ladder," the sinewy Swedish officer shouted to the ship above. A face appeared over the railing of the deck. "A ladder," Enestrom yelled, "lower a ladder." He was still calling for a ladder when the man above, in a moment, swung himself over the railing and expertly, hand-over-hand, came swiftly down the rope to the lifeboat. The man, wearing the white jacket of a steward or kitchen worker, scampered to a seat and without a word to anyone sat stolidly down, burying his face in his hands.

Enestrom's boat was quickly filled as crewmen, men passengers and a few women came down the two rope lines leading to the boat. It was not difficult to tell them apart. The crewmen climbed down hand-over-hand; the men passengers descended more slowly; and the women slid down in apparent agony, allowing the rough rope to slide through their clenched hands. His boat was about half filled when Enestrom glanced overhead and saw a man, shouting in Italian, poised to drop a small child over the side of the ship.

188

"No, no, no, wait," he yelled up to the man and waved his arms as if to push the child back. "He's out of his mind," the Swedish officer exclaimed as he hastily told four men to spread a blanket. The child, dropped from a height of about twenty feet, emitted a long, shrill scream that sounded like the whistle of a bomb before he landed safely in the blanket. Four other children followed this aerial route. One, a small girl of about two years, missed the blanket. Luckily, she missed the boat, too. A crewman fished her from the water, wet and weeping, but safe.

The second lifeboat arriving from the *Stockholm* was spotted from the stern deck of the *Andrea Doria* before it reached the ship, and a drove of anxiety-ridden passengers, having waited for two hours for some sign of rescue, stampeded to the starboard railing and leaped overboard. The short and sudden human hailstorm from the heights of the listing ship had a nightmarish effect upon the five-man crew of the *Stockholm*'s lifeboat No. 8. But as those in the water swam and thrashed their way to the lifeboat, it proved to be a surprisingly easy and swift way for the lifeboat crew to take aboard survivors. The bright orange lifejackets pinpointed the swimmers in the dark sea. In short order, the 64-person-capacity lifeboat was filled, and headed back to its mother ship.

The second trip of lifeboat No. 8 to the *Andrea Doria* was not so easy. The fog had begun to lift somewhat but the list of the stricken ship had become even more ominous, and the swells of the sea had increased the danger of the small lifeboats smashing against the side of the rocking ship. So busy were the men of lifeboat No. 8 in handling the lines as survivors came down, they failed to notice the harried Italian father who dropped his four-year-old daughter from the deck

189

some eighteen feet above. Fearing that if his only child fell into the sea she would drown, Tullio Di Sandro, a stocky, almost bald Milanese, aimed for the lifeboat below and let his daughter fall from his arms. She fell headlong, striking the railing edge of the lifeboat. Second Officer Abenius whirled around at the thudding sound behind him and saw at the bottom of his boat the inert form of a small, thin, dark-haired girl in a nightgown. The twenty-seven-year-old officer glanced upwards in time to stop others from dropping children over the side until he had set up a large double blanket as a rescue net. In the dim light of the lifeboat, a sailor sprinkled cold sea water upon the face of the unconscious child. A woman in the boat knelt by the seaman's side to help. When they could not revive the little girl, she was wrapped in a blanket and carried to a sheltered part of the lifeboat.

Abenius assumed that the woman who stayed with the child was her mother, but he was wrong. For some reason, neither parent on the deck above followed the child into the lifeboat. They were not to see her again until two days later in the U.S. Public Health Service's Brighton Marine Hospital in Boston, where she died of a fractured cranium without ever having regained consciousness.

News of the lifeboat with the large blanket must have spread on the stern decks of the *Andrea Doria*. Some twenty to twenty-five other children were caught successfully in the double blanket which had been stored in the lifeboat as an emergency sail.

The lifeboat almost capsized at one point when a stout woman, unable to support her weight on a rope, crashed into the boat. Throughout the early morning hours of the rescue, women continued to fall from the ropes, many suffering broken, sprained or wrenched limbs. And many of those who

190

did not fall burned and ripped the skin from their hands and thighs as they slid down the coarse rescue lines. Not only was it psychologically terrifying, but it was physically next to impossible for the older passengers to climb down a rope from the height of a two-story building. But, short of jumping the distance, it was the only way off the ship for the passengers on the open stern decks of the *Andrea Doria*. One fifty-three-year-old Pennsylvania woman, Mrs. Julia Greco, broke her back when she struck a lifeboat. She lingered in agony in a hospital for six months before she became the fifty-first fatality of the disaster.

Other passengers, both men and women, were petrified with fright while on the ropes and, unable to go either up or down, hung there until their strength ebbed away and they fell. Trasbo, the assistant chief steward of the *Stockholm*, in lifeboat No. 8, climbed up to help down one middle-aged woman who had frozen in terror midway on a rope. When he had eased her down on his shoulders safely into the lifeboat, the terrified woman, who had not uttered a sound, broke into racking sobs. She flung her heavy arms around the neck of the short, slight steward and smothered him with kisses and wet tears. He fought to free himself. The woman, thanking him in Italian which he did not understand, pressed upon him her rosary beads as a token of her appreciation. But just as firmly as she made the offer, Trasbo, a devout Lutheran, declined.

The night at this first stage of the rescue was filled with cries and screams and chaos. Among the hundreds of passengers and crewmen on the open fantail of the ship the rule was not "women and children first" but "survival of the fittest" and "the strongest go first." Women were shoved aside in the dash for each of the first lifeboats reaching the

191

ship. Men with children in their arms were brushed out of the way as the strongest stumbled, groped and crawled about the deck. Many crewmen did try to bring order to the scene, but they were hopelessly outnumbered and ineffectual in trying to round up terrified and hysterical passengers. The loudspeakers blared: "*Stati calmi, stati calmi,*" but people did not remain calm when a lifeboat was sighted in the water below.

A half-mile away on the bridge of the *Cape Ann*, Captain Boyd heard a wail of cries from the listing ship that rose and died away and rose again in repetitive crescendos which unnerved his stomach. Never in his thirty-three years at sea had he witnessed such a sight. Through his binoculars he saw people crawling madly about the decks of the ocean liner which blazed with lights. He expected to see the *Andrea Doria* keel over and go under at any minute. He feared for his lifeboats which had made one trip back and had returned to the *Doria*. At one point, the *Cape Ann* had drifted more than a mile away from the Italian ship and with one of his own lifeboats and one of the *Doria*'s boats hanging on, he had maneuvered the freighter closer to the Italian ship. But he dared not approach closer than a half-mile for fear of striking people in the water.

Captain O'Shea on the *Thomas,* gazing upon the evacuation of the ship, shared one thought with many of the other experienced men of the sea who witnessed the scene. If this had been the winter, or even four months later, it would have been total catastrophe. Few of those whom he could see leaping from the ship would survive if the sea were rough. In a rough sea, he thought, the *Doria* would have gone down long before the *Thomas* or any other ship had arrived. Luckily, the sea was calm, almost smooth, with long, modulating swells. In fact, never had any of the men viewing the *Andrea*

192

Doria from the decks of their ships seen a vessel list at such an angle and long survive. The *Andrea Doria* was at that time listing about 30 degrees, although from afar it appeared to be more. The *Lusitania,* blasted open by a torpedo, listed 25 degrees before she sank. The *Titanic,* with five of her watertight compartments ripped open by an iceberg, hardly listed at all before she plunged, bow first, to her final grave.

Carstens took out lifeboat No. 1 as the last of the four hand-powered lifeboats left the *Stockholm.* His small motorboat reached the *Andrea Doria,* of course, long before the other boats which had to be pumped by hand levers. He tied up at the extreme end of the starboard side of the listing ship. If either his engineer or the three sailors in the lifeboat realized he had been in command of the bridge at the time of the collision, they said nothing. Once his lifeboat was observed from the decks above, men and women passengers and Italian stewards in white jackets seemed to pounce upon the boat from everywhere. The small boat bobbed and drifted alongside the black hull of the *Andrea Doria.* Carstens noticed that the bottom of the overhanging hull was several feet out of the water, indicating the ship was down by the bow. He pushed his boat away from the large ship as it came dangerously close to smashing against its side.

The young officer, who had felt no fright at the time of the collision, was scared out of his wits when a woman passenger, hanging on to a swinging rope, smashed into his shoulder and knocked him toward the edge of his lifeboat. He grabbed on to the gunnel of the lifeboat to avoid being pitched overboard and he ducked as the woman swung back past him and fell into the water. She was picked up a moment later. While confusion reigned, the lifeboat was borne up on a wave be-

193

neath the overhanging stern of the *Andrea Doria*. Carstens whirled around at the sound of the crash and saw the unmanned tiller of his lifeboat smash against the *Doria*, break off and fall into the sea.

His small lifeboat was crowded with forty survivors when he pushed off from the *Doria*. An emergency oar was fitted into the empty tiller socket at the stern. The lifeboat was steered back to the *Stockholm* as two men handled the awkward makeshift tiller. After dispatching his passengers at a side port, Carstens brought his boat under the *Stockholm* bridge and reported his mishap. He was ordered to secure the boat and report to the bridge. His rescue efforts for the night were ended.

Far from the *Andrea Doria* a dissonant chorale of screams and wailing could be heard on the ships nearby, but on the decks of the Italian ship itself, though there were individual outbursts, there was no mass hysteria. Those weeping in fear were far outnumbered by Italian immigrants who, having climbed to the open deck, fell to their knees in prayers of thanksgiving for their deliverance. These prayers generally were followed by more prayers and beseeching of patron saints for personal safety and the safety of the listing ship. The more fervent the prayers, the more loudly did the Italian Catholics, as is their custom, literally cry out for their saints in heaven to hear them. Adding to the general bedlam were those calling at the tops of their voices not to their saints but to lost kin.

Crewmen distributed spare lifejackets from the reserve boxes on deck and tried to muster passengers on the port side of the ship. It proved impossible to keep people on one side of the deck while so much activity was going on on the op-

194

posite side. Some passengers joined the crewmen in helping other passengers climb over the rail to the hanging ropes. Some passengers worked by themselves doing crewmen's work. Klaus Dorneich, a twenty-five-year-old German automobile salesman en route to Mexico, joined with four Austrian Fulbright students in lowering older passengers from the deck of the ship with a rope tied about their waists. The students had found several short lengths of rope and tied them together so that they had one line which reached the lifeboats below. A seventy-two-year-old blind shoemaker from Brooklyn, New York, Joseph Maggio, hysterically balked at the idea of trusting his life to a rope. So the young men forcibly bound the screaming old man in a net and lowered him away. Mrs. Lilian Dooner, who climbed topside from C-Deck with her two-year-old daughter Maria on her back, fended for herself leaving the ship. She found a rope, tied it about her little girl and lowered away. But the rope broke. The twenty-four-year-old mother hesitated not a moment. Following her daughter over the side, she plunged into the ocean and came up with Maria. A few minutes later mother and daughter were hauled into a lifeboat.

John Vali, a twenty-seven-year-old former New York waiter returning from an extended vacation in Italy, leaped overboard to save a pretty nineteen-year-old girl he had had his eye on throughout the voyage. Melanie Ansuini, emigrating to the United States with her family from the lovely Italian town of Perugia, had lost her grip on a stern rope and had been knocked unconscious in her fall into the water. Vali leaped in after her, saved her life and eight months later was rewarded with her hand in marriage.

Giuseppe Pomilio, an Italian bridegroom emigrating to join his seventeen-year-old wife in the United States, stripped off his shirt for a woman he found shivering on deck in only her pajama bottoms. Giovanni D'Elia, his wife and their three sons all leaped from the deck in preference to chancing a rope descent.

The chaos during the first two hours following the collision was confined almost exclusively to the stern decks of the ship where the tourist-class passengers gathered. The other two-thirds of the ship was relatively calm and quiet. In the cabin and first-class quarters of the Promenade and Boat Decks, passengers did not even know the ship was being abandoned. Once having reached the muster stations and the port side of the ship, people settled down to wait for word of what to do and what to expect. The waiting was agony, for no word came. Speculation and rumors were rampant: there had been an explosion ... a collision ... a submerged wreck had been struck ... the ship was sinking ... the ship could not possibly sink ... rescue ships were on the way ... the *Doria* would soon continue on its way to New York. ...

People clung to the handrails, stanchions and to other people; they sat on the floor of the lounges and on the deck chairs along the port Promenade Deck and on the deck of Boat Deck, leaning against the wall of the superstructure. Some complained bitterly that they were told nothing. Others went about comforting those who were weeping and those in fear. In the first- and cabin-class lounges, children were stretched out on the floor everywhere, asleep, their heads cushioned in the lap of a parent. Italian immigrants who had come to the first- and cabin-class quarters from the decks below, covered with black oil, were in most need of comfort.

196

There was a pattern to the fears of the immigrants. Firstly, they feared they would be drowned; they feared rescue by a ship which would return them to Italy, and then, if they were taken to their new chosen land, they feared the United States Government would not admit them without their passports which they had lost. Many priests, nuns and seminarians returning from summer visits to Rome helped to comfort passengers. Monsignor Sebastian Natta, the ship's chaplain, had taken the Holy Eucharist from the altar of the chapel after the collision. Breaking the sacramental wafers into the smallest bits possible, he went about the ship giving consolation and communion to those who knelt before him. *"Corpus domini nostri Jesu Christi custodiat animam tuam in vitam aeternam."* (May the body of our Lord, Jesus Christ, preserve your soul into life everlasting.) But he refused to give general absolution. For that there was no need, he insisted—there was no imminent danger of death.

In another part of the ship, however, Father Thomas Kelly, a young priest from Chicago, gave general absolution to other passengers in the belief there was an actual danger of sudden death. In the Cabin-Class Ballroom, two members of the band led passengers in song to pass the time, while nearby a small group of middle-aged Americans caroled the old favorites of 1920 vintage to bolster their courage. Many first-class passengers congregated in small groups and passed the time with conversation. One thoughtful crew member supplied a group on the Boat Deck with a bottle of Scotch to keep up their spirits. Other crewmen tended to their own spirits.

And so they waited for one, two and almost three hours without knowing what had happened to the ship nor what was going to happen to it until shortly before two o'clock in

197

the morning. Then the hundreds of passengers on the port side of the Promenade and Boat Decks of the *Andrea Doria* all saw at approximately the same time the glorious sight of a huge ship. Large block letters in white lights blazoned her name across the night—ILE DE FRANCE. "Praise the Lord," and "Thank God," said hundreds of men and women in one form or another. Everyone, or almost everyone, smiled or sighed in relief and some began to sing and some applauded.

Chapter Ten

"TELL THEM I DID EVERYTHING I COULD"

THE ARRIVAL OF THE *Ile de France* turned the emotional tide of the night. Word of the arrival spread throughout the *Andrea Doria* and changed despair to hope and hope to certainty: rescue was at hand. The *Ile de France* was the single, stanch reinforcement which in battle changes chaotic retreat into advance and victory.

For the *Ile de France*, it was a night of glory. So many things could have gone wrong and all of them worried Captain de Beaudéan, for this was his first sea rescue. But all went right for the French ship. Everything was ready before arrival: the lifeboats, food, blankets, spare rooms, hospital beds. At 1:15 A.M., Captain de Beaudéan saw in his radar scope the cluster of ships at the scene fifteen miles away. Twenty-two minutes later and eight miles away, he reduced his 22-knots speed for a safe approach and he prayed silently and fervently for the fog to lift. And eight minutes later, at 1:45 A.M., the weather complied. The fog broke into patches and disappeared, unveiling a summer night resplendent with a million stars, full moon and a calm sea. Two miles away, Captain de Beaudéan left his radar scope and with his own eyes picked out the *Andrea Doria* among the four ships ahead of him. Her list was unmistakable.

"Turn on the lights, all the lights, and let them know we are here," he told Pettre, his chief mate, as he maneuvered the *Ile* toward the listing ship. Floodlights on the Sun Deck spotlighted the vivid orange and black colors of the ship's two funnels. Stretching between the funnels in ten-foot-high block letters the name *Ile de France* was lighted like a white marquee against a black background, proclaiming the arrival of the ship that symbolizes France on the high seas.

Despite his many years at sea, the sight of the *Andrea Doria* caught Captain de Beaudéan emotionally unprepared. The Italian ship appeared still so beautiful, her modern, rounded lines unimpaired as far as the eye could see. She was lustrous in the night, her many deck lights glittering along the length of the ship and the two powerful spotlights on her angled mast casting a bright shimmering reflection on the oily water.

Captain de Beaudéan had an impulse to do something histrionic. He wanted to comfort those waiting on the *Andrea Doria*, to call out into the night, "Patience! I am here . . . the *Ile de France* is here," but, of course, he remained silent, gazing through his binoculars at the listing ship. The starboard decks seemed empty and the *Doria* appeared deserted

200

although he could hear occasional cries from the direction of the ship. Beyond the dying ship, Captain de Beaudéan saw the reflected whiteness of a ship gleaming in the moonlight and he knew it to be the *Stockholm*.

Captain de Beaudéan, a shipmaster whose experience had taught him courage as well as caution, maneuvered his 44,500-ton ship closer to the starboard side of the listing ship. When he was as near as he dared to go, he cut his motors and the *Ile* drifted to a stop alongside the *Andrea Doria*. Only 400 yards separated the two ocean liners. With the *Ile* shielding the *Doria* from the direction of the waves, the water between the two ships was converted to a lagoon, a calm harbor heavy with oil slicks and perfect for the operation of the lifeboats. Captain de Beaudéan reasoned, rightly, that the *Ile* would be safe as long as she drifted at the same rate as the *Doria*. Only once during the night did he have to start up his motors and back away when currents set the *Doria* too close to the *Ile*. Otherwise the two mammoth ships maintained the same relative position side by side through the night.

It was 2 A.M. when the *Ile de France* came to a stop in the lee of the *Andrea Doria*. Five minutes later the first French lifeboat was in the water and heading for the stricken ship. Ten other lifeboats hit the oil-slick water in rapid succession. Captain de Beaudéan kept seventeen lifeboats aboard for the safety of his own passengers, reasoning that along with the boats of the other ships, eleven *Ile* lifeboats, each with a capacity of ninety persons, would be sufficient to evacuate the *Andrea Doria* in one or two trips.

Captain de Beaudéan nervously chain-smoked cigarettes as he watched his lifeboats draw up beneath the listing ship and begin to take on passengers. With an electrically powered megaphone, he called to his men, "Be careful," and yet he

201

realized they had little if any control over their own safety. If the *Andrea Doria* capsized, the lifeboats at her starboard side would be crushed and thrust under the sea by the huge ship. He prayed that the Italian ship would remain afloat at least for one more hour, or perhaps two.

Seven minutes after the *Ile* had arrived, the first *Andrea Doria* lifeboat tied up at her side. Its passengers were taken aboard through a C-Deck door and up ladders to the port side of the ship, which faced the *Doria*. The starboard side door facing the open ocean was shut because of choppy waters. The sea off Nantucket was true to form: when the weather cleared, the sea became rough. The long undulating swells changed to short, choppy waves which increased the hazard of lifeboats being wrecked against the side of the large ship. While the motorboats generally continued to bring survivors to the mother ship, the hand-propelled boats headed for the *Ile de France*, which was the nearest ship to the *Andrea Doria*. The four non-motor boats of the *Stockholm* made one trip back to the white ship two miles away, but after 2 A.M. they headed for the nearby *Ile*.

Enestrom in an advantageous location near the stern of the *Doria* worked out a plan with the crew of a French lifeboat by means of sign language. *Ile* lifeboats tied up alongside his boat, and passengers who slid down the ropes to the Swedish boat stepped into the French boat to be taken to the *Ile*. A spirit of co-operation and unity spread amongst the lifeboat crews as the men went to extremes to accomplish the task before them. Men pumped the levers of the hand-driven lifeboats until their swollen hands bled. They climbed ladders and ropes to help people down. As the night drew on, some even climbed up to the decks of the *Doria* to search out more survivors. Each boat seemed to develop its own self-appointed

202

swimming expert to rescue survivors from the water. Jean-Pierre Guillou, a fifteen-year-old messboy on the *Ile*, dove in to rescue a small child, and Armando Gallo left the security of an *Andrea Doria* lifeboat to leap into the sea after fireman Fortunato Spina, a 300-pound crewman whose girth equaled his height.

With the eleven additional boats and the quick turn-around provided by the *Ile de France*, lifeboats became plentiful along the starboard side of the *Andrea Doria*. There were in all twenty-eight lifeboats, more than enough for the eight ladders and the rope lines over the ship's side. There might have been thirty lifeboats except that two *Doria* boats made only a single trip to the *Stockholm*. One boat as the last crewman scrambled aboard was kicked away and set adrift. The *Stockholm* crew refused to allow aboard the crew who tried to desert a second lifeboat. But the men who had laboriously rowed Boat No. 3, whose motor could not be fixed, had no intention of rowing two miles back to the *Andrea Doria* with just two emergency oars. They waited alongside the *Stockholm* until a fellow crewman from the *Doria* threw them a line and led the lifeboat to the stern of the Swedish ship, where it remained tied through the night.

It was Boat No. 3, which, before it left the *Doria*, took aboard Richard Roman Hall, the three-and-one-half-year-old son of actress Ruth Roman. The actress had slid across the ship from the port to starboard side in a safe, sitting position, splitting her party dress as she explained later "right up to my fanny." She handed her son to Officer Cadet Giuliano Pirelli, a twenty-three-year-old lad who was serving as a children's elevator at one of the rope ladders. The boy was tied to the young cadet and was carried piggy-back down the

203

steps of the ladder to lifeboat No. 3, which, during its long, wallowing stay beneath the ship, had been filled with about 120 persons. Pirelli climbed back up to the Boat Deck and Miss Roman started over the rail to the ladder, when the lifeboat pulled away from the ship. The distraught actress screamed for the lifeboat to return, and her young son in the boat wailed, but such were the vicissitudes of rescue.

Peter Thieriot, continuing his search for his parents, made three separate attempts to reach their cabin. When he found the direct route blocked, he circled ahead of the collision area and tried another stairway. But again he found his way blocked. No one had seen either his mother or father. Again and again he was told, "They must be around somewhere." The boy was glum when he repeated his inquiry to Morris Keil, a New Orleans antique dealer with whom Peter had made friends during the voyage. Keil, his wife, daughter and the daughter's hometown friend, Gay Barton, were among a group of first-class passengers waiting patiently for some word of what to do. "How about some ping pong?" the unknowing antique dealer suggested, trying to cheer the boy up. "No, thank you," Peter said politely as he walked on. "I'll just continue to look."

He made his way along the Boat Deck to the bow of the ship and then down to the Foyer Deck and the corridor which would lead to Cabin 180. The Foyer Deck, when he reached it, was flooded with water above his ankles. He sloshed through the deserted corridor to a point where he could see at an angle a section of his parents' cabin. A heavy girder and smaller wreckage blocked the doorway. Beyond, he thought he saw the night air where the outboard wall of the cabin should have been. Yet, to this thirteen-year-old boy, this was not proof that his parents were dead. The idea, if it entered his confused mind at all, did not register. He had no way of knowing whether his parents had left the cabin or not, and so he continued his search on the decks above crowded with people.

With lifeboats lining up at the stern and at the side ladders, word was passed to the muster stations for the first time for the abandoning of the ship, children first, the disabled and elderly next, then women and finally men. Many tourist-class passengers already had left the ship, but those who had been mustered in the Tourist-Class Dining Room, where the movie had been shown, and those herded on the port side of the Promenade Deck, were led to the starboard-side ropes and were helped in a more or less orderly fashion off the ship. Crewmen linked hands to form a chain around the fantail railing to prevent any further leaping from the deck. Other crewmen lined the way from the Promenade Deck down to the Upper Deck fantail, helping to support passengers on the decks now sloping at a thirty-degree angle.

In the First-Class Lounge, where calm prevailed generally, men passengers and crew helped women, children and those of advanced age. Passengers were passed from hand to hand to the high side of the Promenade Deck and helped up a ladder to the Boat Deck. Each person was then seated and pushed off for a 45-foot slide across the deck into the arms of a waiting crewman on the low side of the ship and from there led to one of the ladders. Walking without support was impossible. Safety ropes were tied about the waist of most passengers, particularly the women, for the descent down the rope ladder. Children were carried down piggy-back. Infants, perhaps the most difficult to get off the ship, were in many cases balanced precariously across the forearms of men climbing down ladders. Jerome Reinert, a twenty-one-year-old engineer returning from a European vacation celebrating his college graduation, volunteered his services and took turns on one ladder with three other young men traveling first class. There was weeping and wailing, mostly from Italian mothers when they were forced to hand over their children for the descent down the ladders, but by and large, a sense of direction and relative calm characterized the abandoning of the ship from the First-Class Lounge.

When instructions to abandon ship from the starboard side reached Drs. Tortori Donati and Giannini, who were camped with their patients and nurses forward of the First-Class Lounge, it set off a rush by the thirty-odd passengers who had gathered there. But the two doctors quickly gained control. "No, no, no," shouted Dr. Tortori Donati, "the sick and wounded must go first . . . there is plenty of time . . . the ship will not sink . . . the calmer you are the better you are. . . ."

His words, and perhaps the authority of his uniform, as oil-besmirched as it was, checked the incipient rush. Passengers were quite willing to heed authority once it was exercised, and they waited while the doctors and nurses carried their six patients in blankets across the ship to the first glass door on the starboard side of the Promenade Deck. The first passengers who followed slipped and fell on the linoleum floor which had been splattered with oil dripping from the three women passengers rescued from B-Deck. Dr. Tortori Donati, who had himself fallen and bruised a leg, convinced the passengers to slide in a sitting position across the ship as slowly as possible, using the heel of one foot to brake their speed.

Getting from the port to the starboard side of the ship was

one thing, not too difficult once one learned the knack, but getting a lifeboat to come alongside was another. A small section of the Promenade Deck was cleared of baggage. But the one door available on that deck was almost directly over the gaping collision hole in the ship. For about a half-hour the two physicians and some passengers shouted to lifeboats passing by, heading for the midsection and stern of the ship. None responded. The lifeboat crews either did not hear the calls in the welter of cries and noise that came from the ship, or, more likely, they preferred not to approach the vicinity of the ominous black hole in the side of the ship which appeared large enough to suck in any of the lifeboats.

One lifeboat which had been alongside the ship farther astern finally maneuvered forward beneath the open glass door of the Promenade Deck. Once again the passengers who had waited with growing despair surged forward and once again the two doctors ordered them to wait their turn. Meanwhile, Steward Rovelli, on another search for the much-needed jack, happened on the waiting crowd and offered his services again to Mrs. Cianfarra, whom he had adopted as his special responsibility.

Mrs. Cianfarra hung on Rovelli's back with one arm around his neck as he carried her down to the waiting lifeboat. The deck of the increasingly listing ship was only about nine feet above the waiting boat. With his ward safely in the boat, Rovelli climbed back on deck and continued his determined search for a jack.

Dr. Tortori Donati, having established his authority over the passengers near him, saw to it that his patients left the ship first. He himself handed Rose Carola, his heart patient, down to a seaman in the lifeboat as the boat rose to the crest of a wave. A male nurse held the end of a rope looped under

the old woman's arms lest she fall. Mary Onder, whose fractured right leg could sustain no weight, was lowered next in
the same manner. The three oil-slick Italian women, their
blankets tucked in around them, zoomed down the rope without any help, lubricating the rescue line as they went. The
rope here was not like the coarse hemp lines used on the
stern. It was smooth, bound in red plastic-like cloth, and was
ordinarily used as a safety guide line in a public room during
stormy weather.

When the three women had reached the lifeboat below,
Dr. Tortori Donati turned to Joseph Onder and motioned for
him to join his wife. Because his patients were his primary
concern, the doctor next sent four of his five nurses in the
first boat with the patients. He then selected the women
among the passengers nearby, according to their ages, to
follow into the boat. Many of the women needed considerable
coaxing before they would venture over the side of the ship
by way of a rope, and ten young New England seminarians,
returning from a pilgrimage to the Holy City, aided in comforting those whose courage wavered during the ordeal. The
young men came forward only when their help was needed,
preferring to stand back and out of the way while Dr. Tortori
Donati supervised the order of abandoning ship. They themselves refused to leave the ship until all others had left.

Instructions on abandoning the ship made the rounds of the
Andrea Doria by word of mouth. The last group to be notified
were the cabin-class passengers who had calmly remained in
the vicinity of their muster station midships on the port side.
Their muster station had been the responsibility of Third Officer Giannini, who had been busily employed on the bridge
from the time of the collision until 2:30 in the morning. Then,
as the sight of lifeboats lining up like taxis along the side of

the ship relieved the tension on the bridge, Captain Calamai's concern shifted from the problem of lifeboats to the need for ways to speed the abandoning of the *Doria*. As Giannini was about to set out for his muster station, Captain Calamai instructed him to lead the passengers to the stern and, once there, to locate some of the ship's cargo nets and string them over the side of the ship. The captain recalled the practice of using nets to debark troops from transport ships in wartime.

Third Officer Giannini, who was no relation to the ship's second doctor, Renzo Giannini, scampered down from the ship's bridge on Sun Deck to waiting passengers on the Promenade Deck.

The young blond officer, who earlier had discarded his shoes and socks, impetuously cast aside his lifejacket which he had found too cumbersome for the work he had at hand. Personal fears were forgotten in the fury of work to be done. He was besieged by the anxious passengers when he arrived in his uniform. The questions flew fast. "Are there lifeboats?"

"Are we getting off now?"

"What shall we do? Where are the lifeboats?"

Giannini called for everyone to follow him. But some women and some men, who had waited so long, just couldn't believe lifeboats actually were anywhere about. "There are plenty of lifeboats . . . Plenty of lifeboats," Giannini repeated in English and in Italian. Passengers struggled awkwardly to their feet, and Giannini arranged them in a sort of line, instructing them to hold hands and to help one another as they followed him to the starboard side of the stern where, he assured them, lifeboats truly were waiting. Hearing voices from the deck above, Giannini leaned out through one of the several opened glass doors and shouted for those on the Boat

209

Deck above to come down and join the line which he was going to lead to the lifeboats.

He led the way across the slippery tilted deck to the last doorway on the Promenade Deck, down one flight of stairs, and then across to the starboard side of the fantail on Upper Deck. The third officer ordered a bos'n's mate to find cargo nets, but the mate balked. The nets, said the bos'n, were locked away in the cargo holds and it was too dangerous to try to fetch them at this point. One net was found, however, the one used to cover the Tourist-Class Swimming Pool. That was put over the side. But middle-aged tourists proved not to be as agile as trained combat troops and many became entangled in the spidery net which dangled away from the side of the listing ship.

On the bridge, some measure of relief was felt. Utter catastrophe had been avoided. The ship, the pride of Italy, which had seemed about to capsize immediately after the collision, was remaining afloat after all, heroically struggling against death, it seemed, as each minute ticked away. The ship, as shown on the inclinometer, was now hovering at 33 degrees. It was impossible to walk without holding to the guide lines strung across the bridge. But the rescue ships— the *Cape Ann,* the Navy ship *Thomas,* and especially the *Ile de France*—had arrived and their boats were at work. From the port bridge wing, Captain Calamai could see the high side of the ship emptying, and from the starboard wing he watched the progress of the little dark figures, each a person, climbing over the side and down to the boats. Screams and cries still pierced the air, but now they were only occasional. He could hear the splashes of those leaping from the ship into the oily, debris-laden water off the starboard side, but these too were less frequent than before. The respite gave him time to think, but to think clearly he had to struggle against a deep sadness which was overwhelming him. Could the ship after all be saved? There was perhaps a glimmer of hope, and he hastily penned a message to the Coast Guard.

At 2:38 A.M., the *Doria* radioed the *Stockholm* the captain's message to be transmitted to the Coast Guard: IN POSITION 40.30N 69.53W COLLISION. WE NEED IMMEDIATELY TUGBOATS FOR ASSISTANCE—MASTER. The Navy ship *Thomas* broke in to say: WE "ARE" CONNECTION WITH U.S.C.G. STATION IN BOSTON. WILL FORWARD YOUR MESSAGE. At 3:08 A.M. the *Thomas* relayed the Coast Guard's reply to the *Doria*: ADVISE THAT THE CG CUTTER EVERGREEN WILL ARRIVE THIS POSITION WITHIN 4 to 5 HOURS. The *Evergreen*, like the other Coast Guard cutters already on the way, was equipped with a towing hook on the fantail for emergency towing. The question then became: Could the *Doria* survive until the arrival of the tugboats?

In the Engine Room of the *Andrea Doria*, the men faced the irony of having too much water on the starboard side and not enough water on the port side of the ship. The list had brought the ship's sea intake valves on the high side out of the ocean. When that happened, the circulation pump which cooled the port turbo-dynamo sucked in air instead of cold sea water and consequently overheated and stopped. The engineers, most of them stripped to their trousers and dripping perspiration in the steam-filled Main Engine Room, tried to use fire pumps to feed cool water to the port dynamo, but the pumps were insufficient for the job. As a last resort, they tried to cool both the port and starboard dynamos from the sea water intake on the starboard side, but that too failed. The overheated port dynamo came to a final coughing stop.

211

At the same time, as the ship's list increased, the bilge water beneath the Engine Room began to overflow on the starboard side. Before long, and before the engineers became aware of it, water touched the electrical parts of the turbo-dynamo near the starboard wall of the Main Engine Room. A violent short circuit crackled ominously and that dynamo stopped. The engineers got to work on this new problem. The electrical circuit and the starboard dynamo were started again, while pumps were put to work on the rising water. The starboard sea intake was closed because it wasn't needed and cooling water was pumped from the flooded bilges instead of from the sea. But with the increasing list, the flooding of the starboard side of the Main Engine Room continued. It soon covered the circulation pump of the starboard dynamo and in fear of another short circuit, the starboard dynamo was stopped. All the electrical power of the ship, except for the 250 kilowatts supplied by the emergency generator on A-Deck, was lost. With the steady loss of electrical power, the boilers one by one had to be shut down as it became impossible to pump water to cool them. The main electrical and mechanical plant of the huge ship, as intricately interwoven and interdependent as the organs of the human body, broke down and ceased to function.

The engineering officers conferred and agreed: there was nothing more to be done. The list was 33 degrees, the room was filling with steam, sea water hissed in contact with hot pipes, the men were exhausted, it was impossible to walk and difficult even to crawl, there was nothing they could do if they remained. So, battening down the hatches behind them, the men abandoned the three rooms of the Engine Department. It was fifteen minutes before three in the morning.

The last of the engineers in the Engine Room, officers and

men, climbed the escape ladders to A-Deck and headed aft to the ship's one remaining electrical plant. The emergency generator, powered by batteries, produced only enough electricity to maintain the ship's lights and one sealed emergency pump suctioning water from the flooded Generator Room. Chief Engineer Chiappori struggled wearily to the bridge to report personally the final sad news to the captain.

At about the same time, Thure Peterson was besieging the bridge again, pleading for help to free his wife. He asked again and again for a jack, but Captain Calamai, whose knowledge of English was limited, could not comprehend the word "jack." When the captain finally did realize that Peterson was demanding a "lever," he promised to do what he could. He ordered a nearby officer to accompany the distressed passenger back to his cabin and to see what could be done.

There were times of deathly lull in the wheelhouse when everyone was away from the nerve center of the ship, carrying out the captain's orders. Captain Calamai never was at a loss giving orders, but there were only relatively few men qualified to perform the many tasks that demanded attention during the emergency. There was only one ship's carpenter who could take soundings. Only a few men were trained to use the signal lamps. It became abundantly clear during the night that the *Andrea Doria* was designed and manned as a luxury liner. It had an overabundance of waiters and stewards, chefs and dishwashers, but it did not have a crew trained for multiple emergency actions.

During the lulls, Captain Calamai often stared out upon the rescue scene, lost in thought. Once, at about 3 A.M., he approached Second Officer Badano, took him by the arm and said softly, "If you are saved, maybe you can reach Genoa

213

and see my family. . . . Tell them I did everything I could."

Badano, an ingenuous young man, did not comprehend the meaning of the older man's words. "Look," he said, pointing to the nearby *Ile de France,* "we will be saved. We've lost the ship, yes, but I am sure if they can save one they can save two." Captain Calamai said nothing. "If I can be saved, you too can be saved, isn't that right?" Badano asked.

The captain nodded sadly and walked away.

Chapter Eleven

"MY SCHEDULE IS IMPERATIVE"

ON THE *Stockholm,* Captain Nordenson began to consider how he would get his damaged ship back to New York. The *Stockholm's* role in the rescue operation diminished considerably after 2 A.M. She had taken on board by that hour about 425 survivors, but with the arrival of the other rescue vessels, the lifeboats preferred to bring survivors to the closer ships. The white ghostlike *Stockholm* sat silent in the water, anchored by her tangled anchor chains, some two miles away from the *Andrea Doria* and cluster of rescue ships. Captain Nordenson from the wing of his bridge could see the busy activity of the lifeboats plying between the glittering Italian liner and the nearby *Ile de France, Cape Ann* and *Thomas.*

Aboard the *Stockholm* everything was going smoothly. The dining room, converted to a first-aid station, was adequately handling survivors with minor injuries. The ship's hospital was a scene of feverish activity. It had been expanded to seven adjoining cabins vacated by the ship's petty officers, and there was no shortage of medical help. Among the *Stockholm*'s passengers, two surgeons and five registered nurses volunteered their services. An Italian physician among the *Doria* survivors joined the team of three doctors—the ship's doctor and two *Stockholm* passengers—who were operating, setting broken limbs and caring for the injured in the ship's hospital. The Italian doctor moreover helped with the translating necessary for consulting with most of the patients. The ship's kitchen was keeping up a steady supply of sandwiches and spaghetti along with soft drinks and hot coffee. All intoxicating beverages had been locked up directly after the collision.

With the damage to the *Stockholm* brought under control, Captain Nordenson felt his ship was sufficiently seaworthy to make it back to New York at a slow speed. However, he wanted some ship to follow him back as an escort in the event that he might have to disembark his passengers for safety's sake. At 2:30 A.M. he sent a personal request to the *Ile de France:* COMMANDER, ILE DE FRANCE—OUR FORESHIP DAMAGED AND NUMBER ONE HOLD FLOODED. OTHERWISE SHIP TIGHT. WILL TRY TO PROCEED TO NEW YORK WITH SLOW SPEED. IF YOU ARE GOING THERE WITH PASSENGERS FROM ANDREA DORIA COULD WE AS A PRECAUTION KEEP COMPANY?—NORDENSON, MASTER MS STOCKHOLM.

The message put Captain de Beaudéan on the spot. The French captain, worried over the high cost of operating the thirty-year-old *Ile de France,* correctly estimated that this

216

rescue operation, delaying his ship thirty-six hours, would cost the French Line in the neighborhood of $50,000. His answer went back to the *Stockholm:* MASTER STOCKHOLM—WILL PRO-CEED NEW YORK FULL SPEED WHEN ALL MEN RESCUED. PLEASE ASK ANOTHER SHIP. MY SCHEDULE IS IMPERATIVE.

At three o'clock, Captain Nordenson did just that. ALL SHIPS—OUR FORESHIP DAMAGED AND NUMBER ONE HOLD FLOODED. OTHERWISE SHIP TIGHT. WILL TRY TO PROCEED TO NEW YORK WITH SLOW SPEED. AS A PRECAUTION WE WANT A SHIP TO KEEP US COMPANY TO NEW YORK. PLEASE INDICATE—MASTER.

No offer came immediately, but shortly afterwards a message came from Captain Calamai, who as master of the ship in distress was commander of the distress area. FROM CAP-TAIN TO SS STOCKHOLM—IF YOU ARE IN BAD CONDITION, YOU CAN PROCEED TO NEW YORK AND MANY THANKS FOR ASSISTANCE. OTHER SHIPS STAY HERE AND ONE SHOULD KEEP WATCH FOR ME 500 KC/S. NOW SPARING BATTERIES.

The *Stockholm,* despite Captain Nordenson's hopes, was not nearly ready to start back to New York. Her lifeboats were away at the *Doria* and she was still moored to the collision scene by her tangled anchor chains. Dr. Ake Nessling, the ship's doctor, informed the captain that the lives of four crewmen and the unidentified little Italian girl depended upon early hospital care, and at 3:50 A.M. the captain radioed the Coast Guard in Boston for helicopters to remove the five critical casualties.

Aboard the *Ile de France,* the traffic of survivors continued unabated. Exhausted crewmen gave up their places in lifeboats to seamen anxious to replace them. More than 160 crewmen manned the *Ile*'s eleven lifeboats through the night and more than twice that number worked zealously to supply hot

217

food and drinks and blankets to those coming aboard. Yet, with all the turmoil of this activity, the venerable *Ile* was so large that most of its own passengers slept undisturbed through the night. Arising for breakfast the next morning, they never saw the *Andrea Doria* at all.

Hans Hinrichs, a sport fisherman, author and veteran traveler, was one of those who did awaken to the sounds of the lowering of the lifeboats. He left his cabin to investigate and remained on deck to watch the rescue operation from start to finish. In fact, he persuaded his deck steward, Marius, to sneak him into the restricted area of the main gangplank where most survivors were coming aboard. As each lifeboat came alongside, Hinrichs waved a red sports shirt and for hours shouted, "Emie, Emie," seeking his old friend, Mrs. Walter Lamp of Milwaukee, whom he knew to be aboard the *Doria*. He had sent her shortly after dinner that night a radiogram from the *Ile:* So NEAR AND YET SO FAR! SHIPS THAT PASS IN THE NIGHT. HAPPY LANDING. He never did find his friend because she landed happily on the *Thomas*.

As the hours slowly slipped by, the scene on the *Andrea Doria* gradually changed. The rush to escape from the ship flagged to a general reluctance toward leaving the ship at all. Women hung back, insisting that men go first. Crewmen had to cajole, coerce and physically force reluctant passengers, some men as well as women, to trust their lives to a ladder, a rope or a cargo net. From various lifeboats, sailors climbed up to the decks of the sinking ship to round up survivors.

Peter Thieriot was persuaded finally to leave the ship with the Passantes. The Denver couple told the boy that his mother and father must have left the ship earlier. Peter

218

doubted that his parents would leave without him, but his mind could not fathom the alternative. Only later in a lifeboat on the way to the *Ile de France* did Peter Thieriot look back at the *Andrea Doria* and see the true location of the point of collision. He realized then he would never again see his mother or father.

Steward Rovelli waited on an almost deserted deck for an American officer he had met on the deck of the *Doria* who had promised that he would get a jack from his ship. Peterson found Rovelli looking out to sea and there together they waited, almost without hope, until a voice from a lifeboat below was heard. "Are you the fellow who was looking for a jack?" They never did discover which rescue ship delivered the jack.

A line was thrown up to the deck and slowly Rovelli and Peterson hauled up a 150-pound jack with a six-foot-long handle. Even more arduously they lugged their massive prize along the sloping deck, down a flight of stairs to Cabin 58 where they sat for a while, exhausted. Then they hauled the jack under the wall partition and set it up in the wreckage. They encouraged Mrs. Peterson to "hang on," while they placed the jack against the wall of the elevator shaft to lift the wreckage from her body. But the handle was too long to operate in the confined space. This was a minor difficulty after what these men had been through. Peterson soon found an ax which had been left in Cabin 58 and chopped a section of a towel-rack bar which served as a short jack handle.

While Peterson held the base of the jack in place, Rovelli started to pump the handle. He began to feel weight upon the jack and then the wreckage began to move. Suddenly, Mrs. Peterson exclaimed, "Oh, I think I'm going . . ." Rovelli turned to look and saw blood hemorrhaging from her mouth.

219

"Doctor," he said softly to Peterson after a moment, "I think your wife's dead."

Peterson crawled to her side and confirmed that the struggle was over. Kneeling there amid the wreckage, he made his farewell to his wife, and then he and Rovelli covered the small, frail body with cushions and left Cabin 56-58 and the *Andrea Doria*. It was close to 4:30 A.M.

Dr. Tortori Donati never left his self-appointed post at the first glass door of the Promenade Deck, where he helped passengers over the side to the lifeboats through the morning hours. Dr. Giannini made one trip into the cabin-class quarters when the ship doctors had received word of a woman with a broken leg in need of aid. But the slim, nervous second doctor had been unable to locate the woman. When the Promenade Deck was cleared of passengers, the two doctors followed the ten New England clergymen, who had waited until last, down into a lifeboat. At the *Ile de France*, Dr. Tortori Donati sent his colleague aboard with the last of the passengers. He told the lifeboat crew to take him back to the *Doria*, where he suspected he might be needed by the crew still on board.

The abandoning of the *Andrea Doria* had been swift since the 2 A.M. arrival of the *Ile de France*. At about 3:30 A.M. there had been fewer than one hundred passengers left on the ship. Shortly after 4 A.M., Captain Magagnini passed the word to the bridge that the decks were clear—all passengers were off the ship. Captain Calamai then issued the order for the crew to abandon ship, asking for volunteers to remain on board until the arrival of the Coast Guard tugboats. It was his first authorization that night for crewmen to leave the ship, excepting the lifeboat crews. Captain Calamai also radioed the Navy transport *Thomas* to stand by to assist the *Doria,* if necessary.

With the crew gone, except for some forty volunteers who remained aboard, the *Andrea Doria* became as still as an empty graveyard at night. The long, graceful ship glistening under the lights which reflected on the wet surface of her decks was still beautiful. Looking down upon the ship from the bridge wing, there was no sign of damage. Yet a sense of limpness pervaded the deserted ship leaning wearily on her side in the dark ocean. The forty aboard dwindled to twenty as some of the men were authorized to join the boat crews of three *Doria* lifeboats which were standing by.

At the last, twelve men remained on the *Andrea Doria.* The senior officers, including Staff Captain Magagnini, Chief Officer Oneto, First Officer Kirn, held their final conference on the bridge. The younger men—among them Third Officers Donato and Giannini and the two officer cadets, Mario Marraci and John Conte—sat at a respectful distance from the senior officers. With the younger men were several seamen. Quiet prevailed. The bridge clock showed the time to be almost five in the morning. The list was close to 40 degrees. The final conference was conducted in low, soft voices, hardly breaking the aura of silence on the deserted, dying ship.

The senior officers reviewed the situation: the extent of flooding below decks, the list, the expected Coast Guard tugboats, how much time was left, the abandoning of ship. Captain Magagnini reported that all passengers were off the ship, and that all accessible cabins had been searched. In this, he was relaying information from the purser officers who in turn were relaying reports from various stewards who had made various checks. But there had been no systematic

221

search. Some stewards had looked into the cabins at their stations; others had not.

Probably at the very same moment the staff captain was reporting to Captain Calamai that all cabins had been searched, Robert Lee Hudson awoke alone in the pitch-black hospital room. He had the odd sensation that he had been sleeping on the wall. It was like the start of a weird, vivid dream. He climbed uphill across his bed, easing himself off the bed until his feet touched the floor. The floor sloped parallel to his bed. He groped his way to the corridor and looked down the long, empty hallway. All was still and deserted and it took several moments for him to realize where he was and what must have happened. He was alone on an empty, sinking ship. Water was rising in the cross corridors to the high side of A-Deck. The low side of A-Deck was under water. Hudson looked down at his body clad in white pajamas and seriously wondered whether he was dreaming or had actually awakened to this. He seemed to be awake and yet it seemed impossible that he was alone on the luxury liner which was listing at an incredible angle for no reason that he could discern.

"Is anybody here?" Hudson screamed, and he heard his voice travel down the empty, silent corridor. "Help!" he called at the top of his voice, but there was no answer. He stumbled down the corridor with the sensation that he was walking more on the walls than on the floor. He groped his way up the stairs to the open deck and breathed deeply of the salty early-morning air. From the empty high side of the stern, he slid down the deck to the starboard side. But the last of the crew already had gone forward to the bridge. Hudson saw the empty ropes and cargo net over the side of the ship. In the distance, he noticed several lifeboats. The night was lovely with the soft yellow glow of the moon and the stars and the calm sea. There was no indication of any disaster other than the incredible list of the *Andrea Doria*. Hudson's mind was unclear and confused.

For some reason, he climbed down the cargo net, became entangled and dangled there until a lifeboat from the Tidewater Oil Company tanker *Robert E. Hopkins,* which had arrived on the scene not too long before, came beneath the net. The tanker's chief mate, Eugene Swift, in command of the lifeboat, reached up and grabbed the limp body of Hudson, who seemed to be in a state of shock. The American sailor was the last passenger to leave the *Andrea Doria*. He was the only survivor taken aboard the tanker which had sped fifty miles to the disaster scene. As far as Swift could see, the decks of the listing Italian ship were deserted.

In the wheelhouse of the *Andrea Doria,* quite unaware of the activity on the stern, the officers expressed their opinion to Captain Calamai that the ship had to be abandoned. The captain wished to remain until the arrival of the tugs. The discussion went back and forth over the same points as it seemed apparent to all that the ship, then listing almost 40 degrees, could not survive another four hours.

"There is nothing more to be done," Captain Magagnini concluded. "It is senseless to stay aboard, *Commandante,* a senseless risk of life. We can wait for the tugs in the lifeboats."

The officers, each holding on to something for support, silently waited for their commander's decision. It was their prerogative to suggest, his to decide.

"You go," he said gently. "I will stay."

They protested but they understood: he wanted to go down with his ship. Monsignor Natta, who was the captain's confessor, spoke a few words to him. The chaplain had come to

223

the bridge after the ship had been emptied of passengers. The captain listened to his spiritual advisor and to his officers who interjected suggestions. But it was his friend Magagnini who forced the issue when he said firmly, "It is useless, but if you stay, we will stay with you."

To those men who saw him at this time, Captain Calamai seemed to have aged ten years in the six hours since the collision. His broad chest, straight back and determined mien had sagged as if he himself were as near death as his own ship. His spirit was gone, his voice hardly audible, and in his gray eyes his men saw a sadness so terrible that for decency's sake each averted his gaze from the captain's face. There is nothing so tragic, these men of the sea knew, as a shipmaster losing his ship, whatever the cause.

Captain Calamai, somewhat weak and unsteady upon his feet, was led down to the Boat Deck and to the ladder midships at the position of lifeboat No. 7. Just as the sun peeked over the horizon, bringing the first silvery rays of dawn at 5:30 A.M., the men climbed over the side and down the Jacob's ladder to lifeboat No. 11. They left the ship in reverse order of rank. Staff Captain Magagnini, second-in-command, reached the lifeboat last and looked up to see Captain Calamai leaning against the deck railing, alone on the vast ship. The old man—and now he literally looked like an old man—seemed as if he were about to topple over the side because of the angle of the deck upon which he stood. He made no move to leave the ship.

"Come down," the staff captain shouted.

Captain Calamai waved his hand as if to brush away the lifeboat. "Go, go away. I remain."

"Either you come down or we'll all come up."

224

"Go," said the captain again. "I'll wait for the tugs. If need be, I'll swim out to you. Go. . . ."

Captain Magagnini climbed up the swaying rope ladder to the deck and told Captain Calamai that the men in the lifeboat all would return aboard the ship unless the commander came down. The master of the *Andrea Doria* at last nodded his assent. Captain Magagnini again went down the ladder so that the captain could be the last man to leave his ship. This time Captain Calamai followed him.

It was shortly after 5:30 A.M. The light of the new day was breaking fast. The *Andrea Doria* was abandoned.

Chapter Twelve

"SEAWORTHINESS NIL"

AS THE LIFEBOATS were being hoisted and secured aboard the *Ile de France*, Hans Hinrichs, the writer, reflected upon thoughts which must have occupied the minds of the hundreds of travelers gazing safely from the decks of the rescue ships upon the silent, dying Italian liner. The *Andrea Doria* never could have been more beautiful than she was then in the blue-gray light of the early dawn. The tiles of her three swimming pools sparkled as the sun, red and fiery, rose and overpowered the soft yellow of the moon at the opposite end of the sky. Hinrichs felt transfixed by the cyclorama of color and beauty as he stared at the graceful lines of the *Andrea Doria* against the vastness of the ocean which surrounded her. "If her doom is decreed," he told himself, "this is the time when she should sink into her briny grave."

Captain de Beaudéan obtained his release from the *Andrea Doria* a few minutes before 5 A.M. as soon as his lifeboats returned empty, indicating there were no more passengers to be rescued. "You may go—thank you," said the *Andrea Doria* by signal lamp. Captain de Beaudéan then radioed the *Stockholm,* implicitly asking her permission: MASTER STOCKHOLM —ALL PASSENGERS RESCUED. PROCEEDING TO NEW YORK FULL SPEED. US W H THOMAS STANDING BY ANDREA DORIA. NO MORE HELP NEEDED—MASTER ILE DE FRANCE.

At five minutes past six, the last boat was aboard and secured and ten minutes later the *Ile de France* was under way, bound for New York. The leviathan ship moved slowly in a wide circle, circumnavigating the sad *Andrea Doria,* and as the French ship took her leave the Tricolor of France was raised and dipped three times while at the same time Captain de Beaudéan sounded three prolonged blasts on her steam whistle. It was a farewell salute to one of the youngest and fairest maidens in the society of luxury liners.

The mournful salute had a tremendous emotional impact upon the exhausted men in the three *Andrea Doria* lifeboats which bobbed in the choppy sea as the wind rose with the new day. Some men wept openly.

In lifeboat No. 11, Captain Calamai sat up forward with Captain Magagnini. The twenty-six other men in the boat kept a respectful distance from their commander. Little was said. It was a time for each of them to think over what had taken place the night before. The activity of the rescue was past, leaving their minds clear for sad and unpleasant contemplation. In the whole world, at that moment, there could not be a man more tragic than this shipmaster who had lost

228

his ship. The men understood that. There was no use trying to console the silent Captain Calamai. The captain brushed aside the offer of medical help from Dr. Tortori Donati. Only when the lifeboat drifted too far from the ship did he murmur to the staff captain who, in turn, indicated to Second Officer Badano at the tiller to steer the lifeboat closer to the ship. The abandoned *Andrea Doria* would be a salvage prize for anyone who could board her and take her to safety. Although this was hardly likely, Captain Calamai certainly wasn't ready even to risk the possibility of anyone getting closer than himself to his ship. The prospect of salvage has always been the reason behind the tradition of shipmasters remaining with their sinking ships until the very last moment.

The wait for the Coast Guard tugboats stretched into an eternity for the men in the lifeboats, in contrast to the press of action aboard the *Andrea Doria* which had preceded it. The lifeboats, designed to carry 146, were virtually empty with twenty-odd passengers in each and bobbed like corks on the choppy sea. In Boat No. 11, the officers relieved the weary crew at pumping the Flemming levers which propelled the boat. The sun beyond the bow of the *Andrea Doria* rose slowly, turning the dim morning into a bright, sunny and white summer day. It seemed incongruous and cruel that the day should be so sunny and cloudless after so foggy a night had brought ruin to the beautiful ship that had been their home.

The *Andrea Doria*, slipping farther and farther onto her side, seemed stark and pitiful, dying nakedly in the light of day before the eyes of strangers staring from the decks of nearby ships. Dr. Tortori Donati was reminded of the vigil he had stood at the bedside of his dying father, who lingered in

229

agony from eight in the morning until 3:30 in the afternoon. Many of the doctor's fellow officers were torn between the slight hope of towing the *Andrea Doria* to safety and the wish that the senseless agony be ended swiftly.

Daybreak brought in endless succession small airplanes, most of them chartered by the news media. They swooped down upon the *Andrea Doria* as photographers, cameramen and reporters recorded the scene in perhaps the finest photographs, newsreels and written descriptions of a marine disaster in history. The *Doria* men in the lifeboats, however, saw the planes as vultures pecking away at a helpless carcass. It seemed somehow indecent in broad daylight.

No one at the scene knew at that time that the listing ship had been abandoned. The *Thomas,* which was the only United States Government ship at the scene, reported to the Coast Guard at 7:40 A.M.: No COMMUNICATION WITH THE ANDREA DORIA. HAS 45 DEGREE STARBOARD LIST. LARGE GASH BELOW STARBOARD BRIDGE WING. LIST INCREASING. SEAWORTHINESS NIL. LAST REPORT CAPTAIN AND 11 CREW STILL ON BOARD. No PASSENGERS. In fact it was believed and reported for some time that the captain and eleven men had leaped from the ship only moments before she sank.

From the decks of the *Stockholm* the sky was scanned constantly for a sign of helicopters requested to evacuate the five critical casualties who had been brought up to the ship's fantail. Captain Nordenson, at the urging of the *Stockholm's* doctor, had sent messages repeatedly for helicopters, each one more urgent than the last. At 7:30, two were sighted in the sky, a large Air Force craft and a smaller Coast Guard helicopter, escorted by a Coast Guard PBY Albatross seaplane from Nantucket.

The helicopters swooped down for a look at the deserted *Andrea Doria* and then came on toward the *Stockholm*. It was 7:40 A.M. They had been dispatched at dawn from their bases in Massachusetts—the Air Force helicopter from the Otis Air Force Base and the Coast Guard craft from Salem, both stopping at Nantucket to pick up doctors. The smaller Coast Guard helicopter made the first try to settle cautiously down on a 55-foot diameter rolling plot which was the *Stockholm's* fantail. As a landing field, fenced in by a four-foot railing, it was just five feet smaller than the minimum desired, and the morning wind had whipped up to some fifteen miles an hour. Chief Petty Officer James W. Keiffer, piloting the craft, decided against landing. This did not deter Lieutenant Claude Hess from making a stab at the *Stockholm* deck with his larger Air Force helicopter, but to no avail.

The men in the two flying beetles then went to work on their specialty, the delicate operation devised in the second World War and perfected in the Korean conflict of lowering a stretcher basket to ground or sea level while hovering in the air above. The Coast Guard helicopter, throbbing in one spot some twenty feet above the *Stockholm* deck, took aboard the most seriously injured. Norma Di Sandro, still in a deep coma, was the first strapped into the basket and hoisted to the waiting physician in the helicopter. Her identity was still unknown. Dr. Nessling on the *Stockholm* had attached to her nightgown an identification tag which said only: *Italian child born—is recommended treatment at nearest surgical clinic— consequence of fractured cranium.*

Alf Johansson was hoisted from the ship next. The good-natured seaman had appeared to have recovered from the initial shock of the collision. He had joshed his nurses on the ship about his condition, "Maybe I'm not going to die after

231

all." But a half-hour before the helicopters arrived, he lapsed into a coma. Shortly after the helicopter landed on Nantucket Island, he expired.

One by one, the other three crewmen were lifted to the Air Force helicopter: Lars Falk with his broken neck and fractured skull, Wilhelm Gustavsson bereft of his left eye, and Arne Smedberg with a brain concussion and shattered right leg.

By 8:30 in the morning, fifty minutes after they had come, the two helicopters and the lumbering Albatross roared away, leaving the men of the *Stockholm* to cope with the bedeviling anchor chains. Since 5:30 in the morning, when he had become aware that the rescue operation at the *Andrea Doria* was finished, Captain Nordenson had concentrated on trying to free his ship from its underwater mooring. He drove the ship full speed back and forth but he could not tear loose from the tangled grip of the anchor chains on the bottom of the sea. By 6:30 A.M. all seven lifeboats which had gone to the *Doria* had returned and were secured in their davits, except Boat No. 7. An acetylene torch and equipment had been lowered to Second Officer Enestrom with orders for him to try to burn through the heavy steel links of both anchor chains. Each link weighed seventy-five pounds.

But when Enestrom maneuvered to the port chain, he found his small boat so close to the jagged raw edges of the splintered steel bow that he and his crew were in danger of being slashed as their boat rose and fell in the choppy sea. The starboard side was no better and the thirty-year-old officer had the sensation that the bow was about to crash down upon him. Although the men on the ship could not discern it because of the piles of wreckage, the bow was indeed hanging by a few interior strands of steel. Bringing the lifeboat

232

back under the wing of the bridge, Enestrom called up to his captain that the task assigned to him was impossible, and he was given permission to secure his boat.

In the light of day, the crew made as careful a search as possible of the bow. A good part of it turned into souvenir hunting. They found intact a small red autograph book belonging to Linda Morgan which had lain on the bureau next to her bed on the *Andrea Doria*. Chief Purser Dawe found a glass cocktail shaker, marked *Made in Milan,* which was in perfect condition.

Chief Officer Kallback and Chief Bosun Ivar Eliasson, supervising the burning of the anchor chains at the windlass on the bow, were more successful than Enestrom. The starboard chain, once cut through, roared down its hawser pipe and into the sea. Its detached anchor remained in place, stove into the side of the ship. The other anchor chain, however, when burned through, fell limply on the deck. It apparently was jammed in the wreckage of the bow in the interior of the ship. The ship was maneuvered back and forth again but the heavy anchor chain could not be dislodged.

Chief Officer Kallback led a contingent of engineers doggedly down to the Main Deck of the forecastle for the arduous job of burning through the hawser pipe which protected the anchor chain in the body of the ship. It was a task that was to take the better part of an hour.

Meanwhile, the scene had come to look like an international convention of ships at the Times Square of the Atlantic, as the waters off Nantucket have been popularly known. The *Ile de France* and the freighter *Cape Ann* had departed, but there remained the transport *Thomas* and the tanker *Hopkins* (which had arrived in time to help in the rescue), the Navy transport *Sgt. Jonah E. Kelley,* the Hondurian freighter *Manaqui,* the Danish cargo ship *Laura Maersk,* the British freighter *Tarantia* and the Norwegian freighter *Free State.*

The Coast Guard cutter *Evergreen,* the first of eleven cutters to take part in the disaster, arrived at 8:06 A.M. and immediately assumed command of the disaster area. Coast Guard headquarters in New York and Boston had dispatched all available craft through the night until a few minutes after 6 A.M., when the cutter *Humboldt* left Boston. The *Thomas,* then the United States command ship at the scene, radioed: PLENTY SHIPS NOW. NO FURTHER ASSISTANCE NEEDED. The *Humboldt,* which would have arrived at about 6 P.M., was recalled.

The *Andrea Doria,* meanwhile, leaned farther into the sea. Only the upper edge of the huge hole in her side was visible above the water as the sea seemed to be reaching up to engulf the glass walls of her Promenade Deck. From the air, to those who looked down upon the ship from airplanes, she looked unmarred with none of her wound showing. But from her lifeboats, to the men who had sailed her, she looked ghastly, her night deck lights glowing in day, her red-painted underside showing above water on the port side and the steady gush of water, being suctioned from her Generator Room by a sealed emergency pump, still flowing from the portside vent, splashing into the sea. She would soon roll over on her starboard side, the men in the lifeboats knew.

The rest of the world, of course, did not know. Maritime experts were giving their opinion to the public, some guardedly, that the modern Italian liner, constructed in conformity with the standards of the International Conference of 1948, would not sink. In the house of Lloyd's of London, where the clocks were five hours ahead of eastern time, the maritime insurance men worked through the day in a funereal atmosphere, checking the news tickers regularly, knowing full well that this sea disaster would undermine a sea safety record of a generation and that, if the *Andrea Doria* did sink, it would equally undermine the trust in all the international standards of ship stability.

In Italy, where news of the collision reached the streets early in the morning and the fate of the *Andrea Doria* hung in the balance throughout the day, people feared the worst. The disaster spread profound shock through the leading seafaring nation of the Mediterranean. To the people of Italy, the *Andrea Doria* meant more than any ship ever meant to the people of the United States. The Italian liner had been recognized throughout Italy as representative of that nation's renaissance as a seafaring nation. With more than half of her ships destroyed in World War II, Italy had rebuilt steadily so that by 1955 she had regained a position second only to Britain's Cunard Line in carrying the most passengers across the North Atlantic, from Europe to New York and back again. The Italian Line carried more than 100,000 passengers a year in 1955 and again in 1956 and again (despite the loss of the *Doria*) in 1957. It was the *Andrea Doria* which represented this success at sea for the people of Italy. The *Andrea Doria* among all the ships of Italy, in short, was held in a special love, like the first-born son of an Italian family.

In Genoa, the home port of the *Andrea Doria*, shocked and silent citizens filled the Piazza de Ferrari to wait the day long before the large white building in the square which housed the home office of the Italian Line. The news that came forth from the building was sparse.

Mrs. Calamai learned of the disaster from a glance at a banner headline across the front page of a newspaper's extra edition while she was out doing her morning shopping. She headed for her home in a run, her eyes burning with tears. A small crowd had gathered at her front door, but she burst through them, hardly aware of the people, and locked herself in the sanctity of her home. Her younger daughter, Sylvia, who was sixteen, screamed out in anguish but then took to comforting her mother.

The following day, this warm and gentle woman told Michael Chinigo, a reporter for the now defunct International News Service, of the hours she had spent following radio reports on the fate of her husband and his ship.

"I had to gather my strength to inform my husband's aged mother. I did so, and told a white lie when I assured her he was safe. My heart kept coming up in my throat because I wasn't sure at all. I spent five hours of torture, minute by minute, as I followed the succession of events by radio and frequent calls to the offices of the Italia company.

"I alternated frantic calls with prayer. I don't remember how many prayers I offered and how many supplications I made. I do remember invoking God's intercession to avoid loss of life and spare my Piero. I knew my husband's temperament and his dedication to the navy code of honor. I knew he would go down into the sea with his ship unless he were ordered to leave it by someone high up.

"I mentally went down with him a hundred times until I learned that top officials of the Italian Line had asked the Merchant Marine Minister to order my husband to abandon ship."

She couldn't know of course that the order had been radioed to the scene too late to reach Captain Calamai, who had been persuaded to leave his ship by the insistence of his fellow officers. But she did ask the reporter to get word to

236

her husband that their elder daughter, Marina, who he knew was traveling to London, had arrived safely. "Please tell Piero," she said, "we are well but will continue to worry until we hear from him directly. Tell him to telephone."

Captain Calamai expressed his thanks but declined the invitation to board the destroyer escort *Allen* which came alongside his lifeboat at about 8:30 A.M. He preferred, he told the United States warship, to wait for the promised Coast Guard tugboats. The destroyer escort, returning from a training cruise for Navy reservists off St. John's, Newfoundland, had reached the scene before daybreak but after the rescue operation had been completed.

Captain Calamai's torturous vigil came to an end five minutes before nine in the morning when he sighted a squat, black-hulled craft with white superstructure advancing slowly toward him from the north. The small boat turned out to be the Coast Guard cutter *Hornbeam*, bearing the designation W394 on her hull, which had left Woods Hole, Massachusetts, seven hours before. The cutter, equipped with towing bit and equipment, rounded the sagging bow of the *Andrea Doria* and came alongside lifeboat No. 11. A spark of life fluttered in the haggard face of Piero Calamai when he recognized the small craft as the long-awaited tugboat. Helped aboard the cutter, Captain Calamai climbed directly to the pilothouse of the small boat to take up the problem of towing with the young lieutenant, Roger F. Erdman, who commanded the *Hornbeam*. The other men in lifeboat 11 and from lifeboat No. 5 also climbed aboard and were happy to accept steaming hot coffee from the Coast Guard crew. Thirty-one men in the third lifeboat accepted the hospitality of the Navy's destroyer escort *Allen*, while waiting for word of the outcome of the conference in the pilothouse of the cutter.

The cutter *Evergreen,* maintaining direct radio contact with the Boston Coast Guard, sent word to its headquarters at 9:20 A.M.: HORNBEAM STANDING BY SS ANDREA DORIA. PICKING UP 45 CREW MEMBERS FROM LIFEBOATS, INCLUDING MASTER. WILL ADVISE POSSIBILITIES TOWING VESSEL.

Back came prompt orders from Boston: HORNBEAM SHOULD NOT ATTEMPT TOW. ITALIAN LINE CONTACTING MERRITT, CHAPMAN AND SCOTT AND MORAN TOWING AND ASSISTANCE FROM EITHER OR BOTH BELIEVED FORTHCOMING.

The order was hardly necessary. The *Doria*'s list was about 50 degrees. Her Promenade Deck was in the water and her bow was sagging heavily. Towing was out of the question. Captain Calamai heard the words which constituted the decision of the young Coast Guard lieutenant and he could not dispute them. He looked out at the sea glistening in the sunlight and saw his ship sinking. The sinking itself began at 9:45 A.M., when the ship lurched over on her side at somewhat less than a right angle to the water. Captain Calamai could look down the black interior of his ship's funnel as the elliptical stack faced him, hovering just above the water line. The ship might have gone at that moment but instead she hovered there, high out of the water and over on her side.

In truth, she was not sinking at that moment; she was capsizing. So the marine engineer would view it technically, and to him there would be a world of difference. For any ship filled with sufficient amount of water will sink of the weight. Modern ships are designed that they may sink, yes, but not capsize. Compartmentalization, cross flooding and all of the engineering progress in the design of major ships through the years were aimed at preventing a ship from rolling over, and

238

all of these engineering feats were incorporated into international law as enunciated in detail in the various maritime conferences. To the marine engineer, it indicated that there was something unstable or unseaworthy about the *Andrea Doria* or there was something wrong with international standards and the approved design of ships. Just where this fault lay was not to be known until later, but the very fact that the *Doria* hung for eleven hours after the collision with her port side high out of the water indicated that she was not sinking because of the weight of water entering her hull; she was rolling over, capsizing. It was a terrible fate for so beautiful a ship. For Captain Calamai, it was heartbreaking.

At 10 A.M., the sea lapped over the bow, covering it for an instant and then washing away, only to surge up over the bow again. Two minutes later, the ship's single funnel bearing the red, white and green colors of Italy dipped beneath the waves and the sea flowed in. The *Andrea Doria* was then completely on her side at a 90-degree angle to the sea, the water flowing fast into the giant ship along her entire length. One more minute and the ship was cut in half along her length, the starboard side of the ship gone beneath the waves. The three swimming pools in a row began taking in water. The eight lifeboats on the port side hung rigidly and undisturbed. The ship hovered there and then the bow plunged under, leaving a white wake in its place while the round stern thrust up and out of the water, indecently uncovering the ship's rudder and twin propellers. She hung there in a final hesitation and then she went down.

Some of the portside lifeboats, but not all, tore free from the ship at the last and floated away with the long trail of debris that stretched upon the water. Some of the lifeboats, in which the crew had not released the falls, went down with the ship. The *Andrea Doria* plunged beneath the waves on her right side, bow first. Her stern rose higher in the air and then was gone, sending a small fountain spray of sea water up toward the sky. The *Andrea Doria* disappeared from sight at 10:09 on the morning of July 26, 1956, two miles southeast of where she and the *Stockholm* had collided exactly eleven hours earlier. The dark sea was marked with bright green effervescence 700 feet long. The violent bubbling continued for fifteen minutes as the remaining air escaped from the luxurious interior of the dead ship settling to rest on the sandy bottom 225 feet beneath the surface of the North Atlantic.

Ten minutes later the *Evergreen* radioed a report on the over-all situation:

> SS ANDREA DORIA SANK IN 225 FEET OF WATER AT 261409Z IN POSITION 40.29.4 NORTH 69.50.5 WEST. EVERGREEN WILL SEARCH DEBRIS. HORNBEAM HAS REMAINING SURVIVORS ABOARD. LEGARE RETRIEVING A BODY ALONGSIDE STOCKHOLM. OWASCO STANDING BY TO ESCORT STOCKHOLM TO NEW YORK. SUGGEST OTHER COAST GUARD UNITS EXCEPT TAMAROA AND THOSE ON SCENE BE RECALLED.

The final death throes of the *Andrea Doria*, which had been a home and a way of life for the men who sailed her, was observed for the most part in a silence of sadness and awe by her crew from the decks of the *Stockholm*, the *Hornbeam* and the *Allen*. Death points up one's aloneness in this world. Some men wept; others just watched. In the silence aboard the *Allen*, the Italian crewmen began to empty their pockets of articles belonging to the *Andrea Doria* and they rendered

240

them, keys, flashlights and similar items, to the sea which had taken the mother ship. They paid their tribute to the silent sea. They wanted no memento of an unlucky ship.

The Coast Guard cutter *Tamaroa* was on the way from New York to join the cutter *Owasco* in escorting the *Stockholm* back to New York. The persistent grip of the remaining anchor chain finally gave way when the engineers burned through the links at the Main Deck level and Captain Nordenson had again raced the *Stockholm* violently back and forth, pushing and pulling on the entrapped chain. Chief Officer Kallback and Chief Bosun Eliasson, standing near the anchor windlass, felt the deck crunching and falling away under their feet. They leaped toward the sea breaker wall just as 69 feet of the smashed bow crashed to the sea, taking with it the $100,000 anchor windlass, the entrapped anchor chain and the body of the woman, which could not be freed from the wreckage. It was just a few minutes after 10 A.M.

The cutter *Legare,* informed of the body by radio, immediately searched the water near the *Stockholm,* but only two sharks could be seen. Captain Nordenson maneuvered the *Stockholm* gently through the water, testing its seaworthiness, and at 10:15 set his course due west, heading back to New York at a speed of 8.4 knots, with the *Owasco* as escort, to be joined later by the cutter *Tamaroa.*

Captain Calamai and his men rested aboard the small and strange Coast Guard cutter *Hornbeam* while arrangements were worked out for their transport to New York. Exhaustion took hold on the men after their twenty-seven hours without sleep and more than twelve hours without food. The nervous energy which they had spent through the night left them limp and melancholy. The sea, flowing over the sunken *Andrea Doria,* sparkled in glistening innocence under a bright

241

sun. Captain Calamai, in contrast, looked like an old, tired man. The stubble of beard on his unshaven face was white.

Taking advantage of the lull in radio communications, the Coast Guard in Boston asked for some details on the collision and extent of damage to the *Andrea Doria*. The inquiry was routed to the *Hornbeam* via the *Evergreen,* and Captain Calamai obliged his host by answering, for the message came back to Boston: MASTER STATED RUPTURE JUST AFT OF BRIDGE IN RELATION TO HULL. PENETRATION ONE-THIRD OF SHIP. LENGTH 40 FEET. VESSEL TOOK 25° LIST IMMEDIATELY AFTER COLLISION. DRAFT NOT KNOWN.

Such information, which may appear innocuous to the layman, could constitute vital data pertaining to the stability of a ship. Attorneys for the Italian Line, fully cognizant of the lawsuits which would follow, no sooner learned of this divulgence of information than they put a stop to it via the Coast Guard Commandant of the Eastern Area in New York, who radioed to the scene: PASS TO MASTER OF THE SS ANDREA DORIA—ITALIAN LINE REQUESTS UNDER NO CIRCUMSTANCES DISCUSS CASE UNTIL ARRIVAL NEW YORK. REFER ALL INQUIRIES TO ITALIAN LINE OFFICE.

Attorneys for the Swedish-American Line, with the same concept of self-preservation in mind, sent similar directions to Captain Nordenson on the *Stockholm.*

It was after eleven in the morning when Captain Calamai and his men boarded their lifeboats and pulled away from the *Hornbeam*. The sea was empty as the two lifeboats containing forty-six men approached the destroyer escort *Allen*. Summer sailors in the Naval Reserve, lining the deck railings, watched the approach of the lifeboats and presently noticed a shark skimming the water close behind the last lifeboat. The shark seemed intent upon one stout crewman who was sprawled in the stern of the boat, his arms oustretched on the boat's gunnels and his body leaning outside the boat. It seemed as if the shark needed only to reach up to seize either of the arms. The men on the *Allen* shouted and screamed at the Italian crewman but he, apparently lost in thought, did not hear them. When after several moments he did turn and look at the monster behind him, he leaped to the center of the boat.

The *Allen* was the final ship to leave the scene carrying survivors of the *Andrea Doria* to New York. Captain Calamai and his officers retired to the seclusion of the captain's quarters aboard the American ship, where they began to prepare their report on the disaster. Captain Calamai realized no doubt what lay ahead of him: he would have to account for all his actions in the worst sea collision in history.

Passengers of the *Andrea Doria,* returning to New York on five other ships, for the most part smarted with recollections of their treatment on the *Andrea Doria* following the collision. Although first-class passengers generally had only praise for the liner's crew, many survivors were indignant over the lack of information, instructions and help afforded them. The passengers all vehemently denied that they received any instructions or information over the loudspeaker system.

On the *Cape Ann,* eighty-seven survivors, almost all tourist-class passengers, signed a petition complaining of the lack of instructions at the ship's lifeboat drill before the collision and the absence of an alarm, instructions and organized help from the crew after the collision. But the most serious charge which became public when the survivors reached New York was that so many of the crew abandoned the ship before the passengers.

The charge cast a stigma upon the integrity of not only the *Andrea Doria* crew and the Italian Line but the seamen everywhere. One of the sea's finest traditions had been violated, if the charge were true, and the crew of the *Stockholm* who had seen the arrival of the first five *Andrea Doria* lifeboats spoke of it reluctantly. The Italian Line vehemently denied it. No one certainly had kept a check on each one leaving the *Andrea Doria* or arriving at the *Stockholm*. Yet the unfortunate truth was to be found in the distribution of passengers and crew aboard the five rescue ships carrying survivors to New York.

The simple fact was that the *Stockholm*, which received the bulk of her survivors before the arrival of the other ships, had more of the Italian crew than any other vessel. During the early phase of the rescue, those leaving the *Andrea Doria* sought the *Stockholm* when she was the only other ship at the scene. Later, however, the Swedish ship, moored by her anchor chains two miles from the *Doria*, became the farthest and least desirable of the rescue ships at the scene. At the end of the rescue operation, limping back to New York, the *Stockholm* had on board 234 of the 572 crew and officers of the *Andrea Doria* in addition to 311 passenger survivors.

The *Ile de France*, the last ship to arrive, returned to New York with 177 crew and 576 passengers from the *Doria*. Captain Calamai and 76 of his crew returned on the destroyer escort *Allen*, while the rest of his crew were divided between the *Cape Ann*, which had received 129 survivors, and the Navy transport *Thomas* with 158 passengers and crew. And, of course, there was the Tidewater tanker *Hopkins*, as gallant a rescue ship as the others, which brought back one survivor: Robert Hudson, the lucky sailor from New Orleans.

244

In terms of numbers, it was the grandest, most successful rescue operation in maritime history. Of the 1,706 passengers and crew who had been aboard the luxurious *Andrea Doria,* 1,662 were rescued from the stricken ship. One of these survivors, Carl Watres, a jolly businessman who had become popular on the Italian liner by playing the piano and singing, succumbed to a heart attack while returning to New York aboard the *Stockholm.* One woman, Mrs. Julia Greco, died six months later of a broken back suffered in abandoning the *Doria.* One child was fatally injured in the rescue operation itself, Norma Di Sandro, who had been thrown into a lifeboat by her father. Forty-three persons went down with the ship —all of them, as far as is known, killed in the collision area of the *Andrea Doria.*

Six Coast Guard cutters remained at the scene for the mopping-up operation. Debris from the lost *Andrea Doria* had drifted over a nine-mile area. The final and hopeless search was made for survivors and bodies. But, possibly because of the sharks in the area, no bodies ever were found. For weeks afterwards, though, residents along the coast of Massachusetts, particularly the islands of Nantucket and Martha's Vineyard, collected souvenirs, including paintings and other works of art, which had floated up from the sunken ship. The *Doria's* eight lifeboats, drifting free in the area, were dutifully picked up by the Coast Guard cutters. The *Yeaton* towed three boats back to New London, Connecticut; the *Legare* took three others to New Bedford; and the *Hornbeam* picked up two for its journey back to Woods Hole, Massachusetts. The cadet squadron of the *Campbell* and *Yakutat* gave their young trainees gunnery practice in order to sink the overturned and splintered portside lifeboats which had survived. The *Evergreen* stayed until there was nothing

245

more to be done, and at 3:15 P.M., July 26, it anchored a bright yellow 50-gallon drum at latitude 40-29.30 North, longitude 69-50.36 West. Thus the ocean grave of the *Andrea Doria* was marked by a yellow buoy, a reminder for all who pass the scene afterwards.

Chapter Thirteen

"I'M ALSO WONDERING ABOUT THAT"

THE COLLISION of the *Andrea Doria* and *Stockholm* was one of those great news events which people mark in their lifetime by remembering what they were doing when they first heard of it. In the maritime section of Lloyd's of London, the venerable insurance firm whose corporate life is tied to shipping, men worked silently through the day fervently hoping that the traditional office bell would not toll the death of the *Andrea Doria*. When in the late afternoon, the bell did toll its knell as it has sounded the sinking of ships for hundreds of years, the men of Lloyd's of London noted with awe the passing of a great modern ocean liner. The sinking of the *Andrea Doria* was voted by American newspaper editors high among the ten most important news stories of 1956, in the company of the bloody Hungarian revolt against Communist rule and the re-election of President Dwight D. Eisenhower as President of the United States. A picture of the sinking won the Pulitzer Prize as the best news photograph of the year. Press coverage was overwhelming from start to finish. The first news reports of the collision had been flashed around the world even before the passengers of the *Andrea Doria* learned what had happened.

How it had happened, however, was another matter. Attorneys for the Swedish and Italian lines took charge once the crews reached New York. While the lawyers themselves worked to discover the cause of the disaster, they gave the officers and crews of each ship the age-old legal advice: Anything you say may be held against you; therefore, say nothing.

Even before the surviving *Stockholm* reached New York, the Italian Line suggested to the Swedish-American Line that the case be settled immediately, out of court, so as to avoid any "washing of dirty linen in public." The lawyers knew that a public trial would lay bare the sins and secrets of the entire maritime industry and that no steamship company could help but be hurt by the publicity. But the Italian Line price tag—to share equally the losses without affixing blame for the disaster—was too high. It would cost the Swedish-American Line $15,000,000 to pay half the value of the lost *Andrea Doria*, not counting passenger, baggage and freight claims. The offer to settle out of court was rejected.

A gentleman's agreement to avoid public counterincriminations against one another could not be kept because of the barrage of press demands. Captain Calamai arrived in

Brooklyn on the *Allen* late Thursday night, his nerves shattered and his body fatigued from his ordeal, and was forced to read a prepared statement twice to satisfy the press. Captain Nordenson, arriving the next day on the *Stockholm*, granted a press conference aboard his ship. The serious charges of neglect voiced by *Doria* passengers forced Giussepe Ali, the manager of the Italian Line, and Captain Calamai to call a press conference to defend the crew of the *Andrea Doria*. But throughout this unavoidable publicity, and despite the demands of the press and public for information, neither captain would say a word on how the collision had occurred.

This vacuum was soon filled by speculation and rumor. The first reaction to the collision was incredulity. As one morning newspaper reported, "Experts on radar said today they could not explain how the collision between the *Andrea Doria* and *Stockholm* could have taken place because both vessels were equipped with radar." It was explained to a public whose curiosity had been aroused that radar permits men of the sea to see through fog for distances up to forty or fifty miles, hence ample time to avoid collisions.

But this initial theory—or lack of theory—soon gave way to more dire hypotheses: some captains never use their radar sets in fog; some sail with broken radar sets, some men suffer a sort of "radar hypnosis" by staring into the small screens; one so-called "expert" said radar beams bounce off thick fog banks and are reflected like a mirror; one meteorologist reported a sunspot cluster 100,000 miles in diameter that night which he suggested might have deflected the radar beams of the two ships.

In fact, in the first weeks that followed the collision, it is highly unlikely that either the Swedish or Italian Lines, their lawyers or the captain and crews of both ships knew precisely how and why the collision occurred. The captain and crew members could report only what they knew and that was only one side of the story. If someone with perfect eyesight and memory or with a telescopic camera had hovered overhead in a helicopter during the half hour that the two ships approached one another, an explanation would have been a simple and clear matter. Lacking that, the admiralty lawyers could attempt only to reconstruct the disaster in court with the exchanging of documentary evidence and testimony, much in the manner of detectives seeking out and correctly interpreting clues.

Court action was swift. The Italian Line filed suit against the Swedish Line for $25,000,000, which was later raised to $30,000,000, for the loss of the *Andrea Doria*. The Italian Line said in effect that it was blameless: the two ships were on a parallel and opposite course and would have passed safely starboard-to-starboard, or right side to right side, if the *Stockholm* had not turned to her right and crashed into the *Andrea Doria;* the *Doria*, a fully seaworthy ship manned by an experienced and licensed crew, sank as a result of the collision; hence, the Italian Line wanted $30,000,000, the full value of its luxury ship.

The Swedish Line sued the Italian Line for $2,000,000, half to cover the repairs for a new bow for the *Stockholm* and the other half to cover the loss of business during the repairs. The Swedish Line said the two ships would have passed safely port-to-port, or left side to left side, if the *Doria* had not caused the collision by making an illegal left turn and crossing the *Stockholm's* bow. Further, the Swedish Line claimed, no matter which ship caused the collision, the *Doria* sank not because of the collision but because the ship was not seaworthy and /or was not manned by a competent crew.

Each line, claiming innocence, filed for exoneration from liability and, if that were denied, limitation of liability. They agreed only to the principle of consolidating their suits and those of all passengers and shippers of cargo into one court action in the United States District Court for the Southern District of New York. Of almost equal importance with their plea of complete innocence were the applications of both lines to limit the extent of their liability if found guilty. Maritime law, recognizing the inherent risk of setting a ship upon the sea, differentiates among three basic causes for all ship disasters.

An "act of God" such as a stroke of lightning or violent storm can sink a seaworthy ship, for which no man can be held responsible. Secondly, negligence of the crew beyond the knowledge or power of the shipowners can cause the loss of a ship, in which case the shipowners cannot be held liable for damages beyond the value of the ship plus pending freight charges *at the end of that voyage.* Otherwise a shipowner would be forced to risk his full fleet upon the vicissitudes of a single ship. Thirdly, however, the law holds a shipowner or company fully responsible for damages if a ship is lost because it is unseaworthy or if the owner knowingly allows his ship to be handled in a negligent or illegal manner.

Since neither the Italians nor the Swedes could claim an "act of God" caused the collision, both did petition for the right to limit their liability. The Swedish Line put up a fund of $4,000,000 representing the appraised value of the *Stockholm* at the end of that voyage, which was $5,000,000 minus her $1,000,000 bow which had been shorn off in the collision.

The Italian Line stated simply that the *Andrea Doria* at the end of her voyage was worth nothing. However, it posted a fund of $1,800,000 to pay death and personal injury claims of her passengers. This passenger fund of $60-a-ton had been written into international law after the families of the 134 persons killed in the burning of the *Morro Castle* in 1934 found themselves without recourse to collect damages.

With speed uncommon for the modern wheels of justice, the parties found themselves in court, ready to go, on September 19, less than two months after the collision. Carstens-Johannsen, sitting next to Captain Nordenson on the starboard side of the courtroom in the second row of crowded spectator benches, was to be the first witness. Attired in a new, shiny blue uniform, he looked like a young adolescent who wanted to bite his fingernails but did not dare. On the port side of the large, wood-paneled Room 1506 of the federal court sat Captain Calamai, his emotions masked in a funereal expression which he did not alter for the stares of those who recognized him.

This, in terms of law, was a "discovery" proceeding before trial. It was based upon the legal theory that, despite all fictitious trials to the contrary, a court trial is not a battle of wits and surprises by opposing counsel but rather an effort to arrive at truth and justice. Thus each side was permitted before trial to inspect all pertinent documentary evidence of the opposing side and to question under oath all opposing witnesses who might not be available for the actual trial. Practically, it allowed opposing sides in a civil litigation to discover enough information to convince each other to settle their controversy out of court.

The "discovery" proceeding for the *Andrea Doria–Stockholm* collision developed, however, all the fanfare of a full-fledged trial. More than forty newspaper, magazine and television reporters crowded the first row of benches. Ap-

252

proximately sixty attorneys jammed into the forward half of the large courtroom to represent the two ship lines and the 1,200 passengers and cargo shippers who were suing both lines for damages which eventually totaled more than $116,-000,000. Lawrence E. Walsh, the federal court judge assigned to the case, appointed and swore in four eminent attorneys to preside alternately as special masters at the pre-trial hearings. They were Simond H. Rifkind, a former federal judge who left the bench to return to private law practice; Louis M. Loeb, president of the Bar Association of the City of New York; Benjamin A. Matthews, president of the New York County Lawyers Association, and Mark W. MacLay, a specialist in admiralty law who had often served as a special court referee.

The special masters were not vested with the full authority of the court. Their rulings were not binding and could be (and were) appealed to Judge Walsh. The job of the special masters was to maintain order at the hearings and to compile a record of the pertinent facts as to how and why the collision occurred. This in itself was a major task in that so many lawyers were at cross purposes in the courtroom, each with an equal right to cross-examine the witnesses and to object to questions of the other attorneys.

While the two ship lines were in effect pleading not guilty or, if guilty, only to the extent of the value of the ships involved in the collision, attorneys for the passengers sought to prove two things. One, that both ships were to blame for the collision, and two, that they were operated negligently with the prior knowledge of the owners, hence fully liable and not entitled to any limitation of liability. The passengers, being innocent parties to the collision, were suing both ships for damages. If both ships were found guilty, there would be that much more money for the passengers to collect in death, personal injury and baggage claims.

Despite the many lawyers involved, the case became a courtroom battle between the two attorneys for the Italian and Swedish companies who, of course, had most at stake. Both attorneys had top reputations earned through more than thirty years' experience. Yet each was as different in personality and approach as two maritime attorneys could be. Charles S. Haight, who represented the Swedish Line, was a tall, soft-spoken, controlled man of impeccable manners whose dogged persistence in research and thorough questioning of witnesses was matched only by his extreme politeness in the courtroom. Representing the Italian Line, Eugene Underwood was a stocky, forceful lawyer whose rapid-fire cross-examination was often punctuated by a rapier wit. Both lawyers were accomplished experts in admiralty law and courtroom tactics and neither let pass without a fight the slightest nuance which might entrap his witness or reflect unfavorably upon his client. The hearing as a result was replete with objections and counter-objections and protracted legal arguments.

In accordance with the arrangements made with Judge Walsh, the first witness of the hearing was Carstens-Johannsen. Perched erectly in the solitary witness box beneath the raised judge's bench and facing the long and wide courtroom filled with lawyers, the press and spectators, the young officer looked to be as nervous and unsure of himself as would a longshoreman in the House of Lords.

Haight, standing at the left end of the first long table in front of the judge's bench, led the *Stockholm* officer as gently and swiftly as possible over the pertinent events leading up to the collision. This direct testimony put the events

254

The next morning, less than an hour before the *Andrea Doria* sank, her captain boarded the Coast Guard tug *Hornbeam*.

The final hour of the ANDREA DORIA *is dramatically recorded in this and the following ten pictures taken by news photographers aboard a Coast Guard plane and by Harry Trask, 28-year-old photographer for the Boston* TRAVELER, *in a private plane. Trask arrived just nine minutes before the end. As his plane swooped 75 feet over the sinking ship, he fought off air sickness to snap the pictures which won him the Pulitzer Prize for the year's best news photography.*

The starboard side: note the ladders and ropes over the side and the jammed position of the davits for Lifeboat No. 3.

The portside: note the eight lifeboats still in place, the Promenade Deck doors open and the flow of water still being pumped out of the abandoned ship.

The starboard side dips under . . .

. . . going down by the bow . . .

. . . the bow gone . . . half under . . .

. . . the portside lifeboats rigidly in place . . .

This photograph of the port lifeboats being torn from the *Andrea Doria* by the sea was cited as the key picture in the sequence which earned Trask the Pulitzer Prize.

Above: Harry Trask saw and recorded the end . . .

© Harry Trask Collection/The Mariners' Museum, Newport News, VA

. . . half a name left . . .

© Harry Trask Collection/The Mariners' Museum, Newport News, VA

. . . gone from sight . . .

... Then Trask photographed the *Stockholm* leaving the scene: note the door, through which survivors had been taken aboard, is still open.

The *Stockholm* reached New York. Compare her bow now with that on the first page of photographs.

Second Officer Lars Enestrom views the smashed bow in drydock at the Bethlehem Steel Company Shipbuilding Division in Brooklyn, N.Y. Repairs cost $1,000,000.

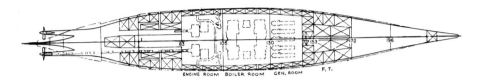

ENGINE ROOM BOILER ROOM GEN. ROOM F. T.

The bottom deck of the *Andrea Doria*: water flowed through the tunnel in the fuel tank compartment into the Generator Room. Watertight doors should have protected the Boiler Room and Engine Room from the direct flow of the sea.

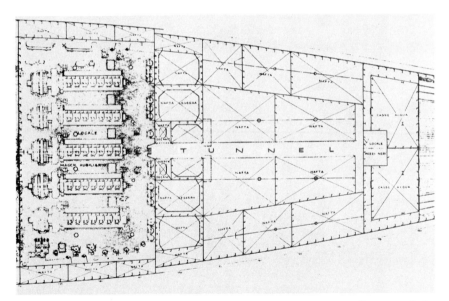

Close-up of the five empty starboard tanks flooded by the collision and the tunnel leading to the Generator Room.

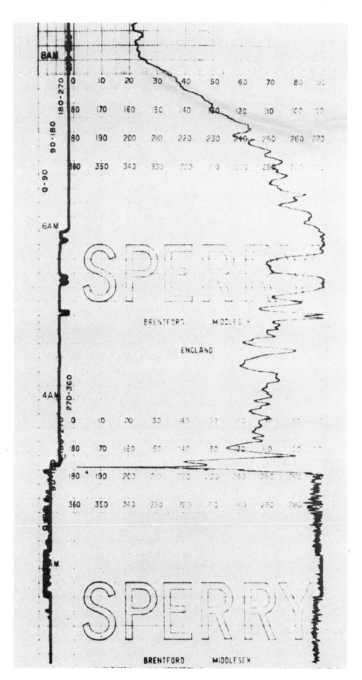

The course recorder graph of the *Stockholm* shows the lack of concentration of the helmsman, then the two starboard turns, the point of collision at 132° and the incredible swing directly afterwards. The pen line on the left margin tells what quadrant of the compass to read.

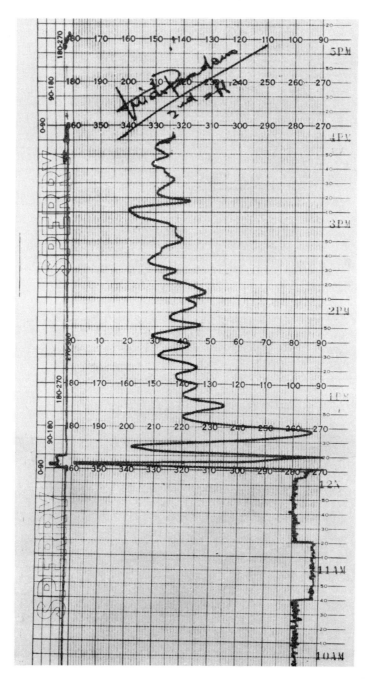

The graph of the *Andrea Doria* shows the approach to the Nantucket Lightship, a veering to the left and then a hard left turn, but it does not show the point of collision. The zigzagging line above merely indicates the drifting of a ship out of control.

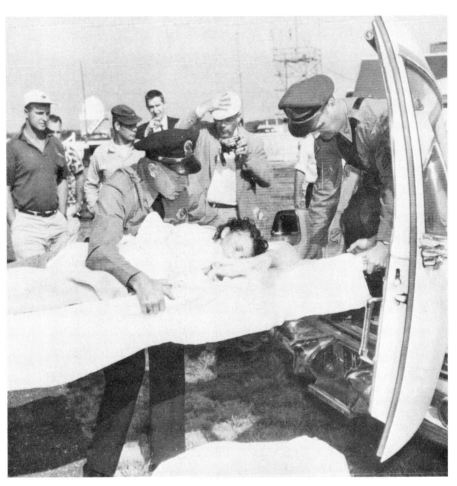

Norma Di Sandro, the youngest casualty of the night, one of five flown by helicopter from the *Stockholm* to Nantucket, here being transferred to an ambulance.

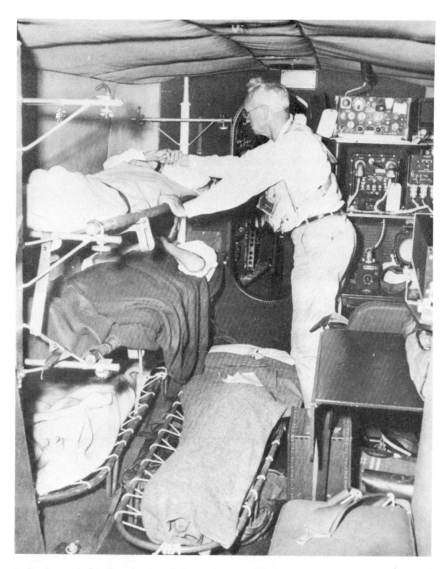

Only four of the five removed from the *Stockholm* survived to make the trip from Nantucket to Boston in this Coast Guard amphibian plane. Norma Di Sandro is on the stretcher on the floor. Three *Stockholm* crewmen are in the bunks.

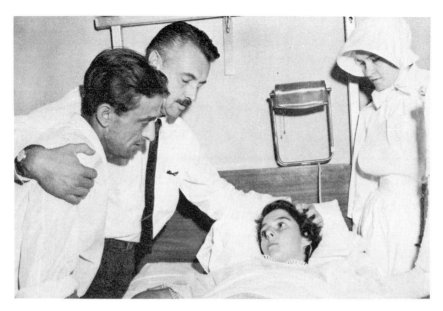

Linda Morgan, the "miracle girl" who was catapulted from one ship to another, being comforted by her father who has his arm around the "man from Cadiz."

Mayor Richardson Dilworth of Philadelphia and Mrs. Dilworth, who bumped into a swinging door.

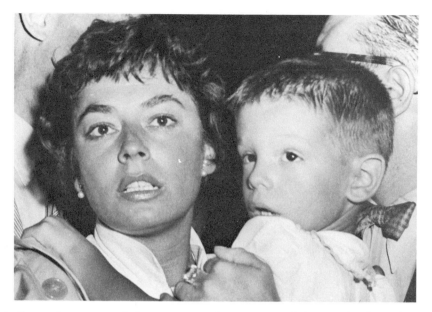

Hollywood actress Ruth Roman reunited at a pier with her son Dickie, whom she had lost while trying to board a lifeboat.

Mrs. Emma Ponzi, of Newark, N. J., reunited with her son Antonio, one of two who survived where 26 died in the collision section of C-Deck.

Captain Calamai, some 24 hours after the collision, being escorted ashore at the Brooklyn Army Base in New York.

in chronological order and that is about all. This was, after all, a "discovery" proceeding and the Swedish Line attorney, having reviewed the case with the officer for weeks before the trial, had nothing he wished to "discover."

Carstens testified to his schooling, training and experience before signing aboard the *Stockholm* on Whitsunday, the 19th of May, 1956. On the night of the collision, July 25, he had come on watch at 8:30 P.M., the sky was overcast and hazy, visibility was five to six miles, the wind was slight from the southwest. At 9:40 P.M., the captain ordered a change of course from 90° to 87° true.

At 10:04, 10:30 and about 11 P.M., he took radio direction finder bearings to fix the position of the *Stockholm* and found her slightly to the north of the course line set by his captain. On the latter two occasions, he turned the ship southward two degrees to compensate for the northerly currents and tides. At "about 11 P.M." he looked into his radar and saw a pip of a ship twelve miles away bearing slightly to the left. He waited until the ship was ten miles away and then he plotted the pip as being two degrees to the left. At six miles distance, he plotted the ship four degrees to the left. Then he connected the two marks with a straight ruled line and estimated the two ships would pass each other left-to-left at a distance of between a half mile to a full mile apart.

Aware of his captain's standing orders never to allow a ship to come within one mile of the *Stockholm,* he waited until he could see the lights of the ship before taking any action. He followed the course of the other ship on radar until he first saw her masthead lights 1.8 to 1.9 miles ahead of him, bearing 20° to his left. He ordered a turn to starboard to widen the passing distance, which was two points on the mariner's compass, or about 22°. He went inside the wheelhouse to answer a telephone call, in which his crow's-nest lookout reported the lights. When he returned to the wing of the bridge, the other ship had cut across his bow. Seeing that the ships were about to collide, he ordered a hard starboard rudder and put the engine telegraph on FULL SPEED ASTERN for both engines. He felt the ship vibrate as at least one engine went astern. Prior to this he had heard no signal from the other ship, but just before the collision he did hear something from afar which he could not distinguish because of the noise around him. And then came the collision. . . .

Haight concluded his direct examination, saying "Thank you, Mr. Carstens-Johannsen. That is all the questions I have."

The young officer pushed himself up from the witness chair and had slipped halfway out of the witness box when Special Master Rifkind, presiding the first day, commanded, "Stay where you are!"

Carstens sank back into the chair, little realizing then that he would be undergoing two full weeks of cross-examination by other, less friendly, lawyers.

Eugene Underwood, with years of courtroom experience and technique behind him, stood behind the second table in the front of the courtroom, and stared at the young witness for a moment protracted in the silence of the courtroom. Carstens fidgeted but he managed to meet the stare of the man facing him. The Italian Line attorney, wasting no time on preliminaries, launched his cross-examination with an attack.

"Is it correct that you did not sound any whistle signal before the collision?"

"Yes," replied the witness in an even voice.

"No fog signal?"

"No."

"No passing signal?"

"No."

"No signal to indicate a change of course?"

"No."

"When you went to nautical school, did they teach you the Rules of the Road?" The sarcasm hung in the air as the Swedish interpreter translated the question for the young third officer. Carstens was testifying in Swedish, except when he became excited and blurted an answer in English.

"Yes," he replied.

The Italian Line attorney, poised with the thumb of one hand hooked in his trousers' belt behind his back, quizzed the Swedish officer on the Rules of the Road and what he had been taught at nautical school.

But Carstens no doubt had been prepared for his appearance in court. He explained that he knew that Rule 28 called for a one-blast signal to indicate a turn to starboard. But that was only true when a risk of collision existed, he said. When he turned the *Stockholm* starboard, or to the right, it was only to widen an already safe passing distance from the *Doria* which was off to his left. There was no danger of collision and hence no need for a whistle signal.

The following day, Underwood quizzed the third officer on his duties and instructions as a watch officer on the *Stockholm*. Under the prodding of the attorney, Carstens ticked them off one by one. . . .

"Never to pass a ship closer than one mile . . . In case of mist, fog, snow or sleet or any other similar thing, immediately advise the captain . . . In case of greater [than normal] drift, the captain should be notified . . . Never to leave the bridge without a man as a lookout . . . Not to use the auto

257

[matic] pilot at night or when it is fog or looks to be fog . . . Always when it looks to be foggy, put the engine telegraph on standby, advise the captain and put the helmsman at the wheel . . . If there is a possibility, always check the position with the echo sounder and other aids to navigation [such as] radar and the radio direction finder . . . To check the lookout continually . . . See that the [masthead and side] lights are burning bright, properly . . ."

Carstens strained to think as Underwood asked, "Any other instructions?"

"Oh, yes," he remembered. "If there is anything unusual that we aren't used to, immediately advise the master, any time of the day . . . any time, day or night."

When he could remember no other instructions, Underwood suggested he had to check the steering of the helmsman. Carstens agreed to that. The lawyer suggested further that he had also to check the course recorder, which mechanically recorded even the slightest changes in heading of the ship, in order to see if the helmsman was steering a tight course. But Carstens would not accept this. The course recorder was in the chartroom and he did not leave the wheelhouse or bridge wings any more often than he had to. He checked the helmsman's steering simply by looking over his shoulder at the gyrocompass.

How often did he check the helmsman? It varied according to the man on the helm, Carstens said. Bjorkman, the first man at the wheel during his watch, he checked about three times during his eighty minutes at the wheel.

What about Peter Larsen, the wheelman at the time of the collision? The question seemed to flow in the normal stream of inquiry but the answer took the courtroom by surprise.

"I have to check him very often," Carstens blurted, stopping to correct himself, "rather often . . . when I pass by [him] every third or fourth time."

"At about what intervals of time?" Underwood demanded. Carstens stared ahead, his face blank. One could not tell if he was thinking, daydreaming or in a momentary trance. "Two minutes?" the lawyer suggested sarcastically. "Five minutes? Ten minutes? You tell me. You were there."

The witness replied in a low voice, "I can't say exactly. One time two minutes, another, ten minutes, another five minutes."

"Why did you have to check him often?" came the next incisive question. Carstens fumbled with the answer and Underwood said, "Please speak up."

Unable to control the modulation of his voice, the witness seemed to shout his answer. "He is more interested in the surrounding things than in the compass."

"You mean, he is not a good wheelsman, don't you?" the lawyer shouted across the courtroom.

"He is when he wants to be," retorted Carstens petulantly.

This was the first break in the witness' armor and the Italian Line attorney hammered away at it. Carstens conceded that he had been obliged that night to keep a close eye on his helmsman, but he insisted at the same time that Larsen did not allow the ship to yaw more than two or three degrees from the set course. It was indicative of the verbal battle which raged for more than four full court days between the twenty-six-year-old junior officer and the sixty-three-year-old experienced maritime lawyer.

They clashed on the subject of the weather. "It was variable cloudiness," said Carstens.

"Where was the cloudiness?" asked Underwood.

"It is hard to say."

"I appreciate that it may be difficult for you to say," Underwood asserted, "but you were there and I would like you to tell us."

"They changed all over the sky. It was changing cloudiness."

The lawyer posed question after question for further details and Carstens said the right side of his ship was brightly lighted for some six or seven miles by an almost full moon which cast a long beam of yellow light on the water. To the left of his ship, all was black. No, it was not fog, it was just the black of nighttime.

Why then, the lawyer demanded, did he not see the lights of the other ship? Masthead lights should be seen at least five miles off. "What do you think obscured her lights?" the lawyer asked.

"I'm also wondering about that," came the ingenuous answer.

"Do you know that it was fog?"

"There was no fog around me," Carstens insisted.

"What do you think was around her [the *Andrea Doria*] that obscured her lights until she got so close that she was less than two miles away?"

"Well," said Carstens, "it could have been a patch of fog that was laying over on the port side." But, he added, he did not think of that at the time because of the apparent speed of the other ship, which he judged from his radar. He didn't expect a ship going that fast to be in fog.

"Were you not worried at that time as to why you did not see the vessel's lights?" asked Underwood.

"There are many ship lights you don't see before four or five miles," Carstens said, adding that he did begin to worry when the other ship came within four miles but "I was sure that I would see her soon enough to have maneuverability from the port side."

The Italian Line lawyer sought to prove that the *Stockholm* was approaching fog, that the watch officer should have been aware of it, and he should have reduced the speed of the *Stockholm.*

But Carstens insisted there might have been a small patch of fog to his port but there was no sign of general fog around his ship. He had looked up at his masthead lights for signs of fog or mist about the lights, but saw none. He explained again and again that the *Stockholm* could be maneuvered or stopped dead in the water in less than a mile and so he waited until he saw the other ship's lights with his own eyes before changing course on the *Stockholm.*

Underwood questioned him closely on the course of the *Stockholm,* how he had turned his ship from eighty-seven to ninety-one degrees to compensate for the currents. He had the young officer draw his radar plot of the *Doria's* approach. Carstens explained that he first sighted the *Doria* visually when she was 1.8 to 1.9 miles away, about twenty degrees to his port. He then turned his ship some twenty-two degrees to starboard to increase the passing distance and to give the other ship a better chance to see the red light shining on the port, or left, side of the *Stockholm.*

The acrimonious undertone in the courtroom which had been marked by legal objections and bickering on translations, the meaning of words used and demands of "yes or no" answers, came to the fore when Underwood, standing at his table more than twenty feet from the witness box, pointed his index finger at the end of his extended right arm and shouted: "I suggest to you, Mr. Witness, that the reason you

261

found it necessary to show your red light [port side of the ship] more clearly was that the *Doria* was actually dead ahead or a little on your starboard bow! Isn't that a fact?"

Haight, the Swedish Line attorney, jumped to his feet before the question could be translated. "Just a moment," he asserted. "I ask counsel be instructed not to yell at the witness or at the interpreter. There is no reason to raise voices in that manner."

Mark MacLay, the special master presiding, said impartially, "We will let it stand. But Mr. Underwood is cautioned accordingly."

"I will try to curb my enthusiasm," Underwood offered.

Then some of the lawyers waiting impatiently for their turn to question the witness spoke up.

"Under the circumstances," said Leonard T. Matteson, attorney for the shippers suing for lost cargo aboard the *Doria*, "I don't think Mr. Underwood's tone or manner is improper."

Haight, his ire rising, insisted Underwood's shouting at the witness was "not fair or proper," whereupon Raymond T. Greene, representing several passengers, commented acidly, "It seems strange after four days that Mr. Haight always picks an acute time to get up and give his little speeches."

The hearing master rejected the lawyer's suggestion that Haight make his objections *after* the witness answered the question. "The proper procedure," said the hearing master, "is to move to strike it out before the answer is given."

Haight rose to his feet, his eyebrows twitching, but his voice perfectly modulated. "If I may say just one word in answer to Mr. Greene's comment? To the best of my recollection this is the second time Mr. Underwood has raised his voice. The first time occurred the first or second day. I did not object then because it seemed to me proper to let it

262

pass once. But if it happened again, I had in mind to make my comment. This is when it has happened. I am not picking any cute or acute time."

The Italian Line attorney had the last word. "I would like to say in my own behalf, while we are making speeches, in view of the provocation I have had, if I have only raised my voice twice, I think my behavior has been particularly good."

"Let us get on," said the special master from the judge's bench.

"I would like an answer to my question." Underwood said. The court stenographer read back the question: Was it true that the *Doria* had been dead ahead or a little on the starboard side of the *Stockholm* before Carstens made his first turn to starboard?

"No," said Carstens flatly.

Carstens admitted that after his first twenty-odd degree turn to the right he took his eyes off the *Doria* in order to answer the telephone. He did not see the *Doria* turning to the left until it was too late and then he ordered an emergency hard right turn and full astern.

"Have you ever calculated how far you would have passed astern of the *Doria* if you had not changed your rudder at all?" asked Underwood.

"I have not calculated it, but I have thought about it," Carstens answered carefully, "and I should not have passed astern of her; I should have passed right into her."

Underwood, then reviewing Carstens' testimony concerning his three RDF fixes at 10:04, 10:30 and at about 11 P.M., at which time he sighted the *Doria* radar pip for the first time, pointed out the impossibility inherent in the third mate's calculations. It would mean that he sighted the pip only nine

263

minutes before the collision, which he timed at 11:09 that night.

"At your speed of about eighteen knots, how far would the *Stockholm* advance in nine minutes?" the lawyer asked.

"Let me see now—2.7 miles," Carstens computed in his head.

"If the *Doria* were ten miles away, nine minutes before the collision, and if the *Stockholm* advanced 2.7 miles in the same time, then the *Doria* had to cover 7.3 miles, did she not?"

"Yes," said Carstens, "but what I understand from this question, you mean 2300 as a fixed time, but I have said it was about 2300."

Disregarding the answer, Underwood went on to drive his point home. According to the third mate's calculations, it would mean the *Doria* was traveling at a speed of forty-seven knots, an obvious impossibility. Not only was there something wrong with either the distance or the time as set forth by the third mate—they weren't even close if they had the *Doria* traveling at forty-seven knots. Carstens admitted he was not sure of the time and that it probably was before 11 P.M., but he insisted he first plotted the *Doria* when the ship was ten miles away.

If one took the distance of ten miles to be accurate, then Carstens must have seen the *Doria* on radar fifteen minutes before the collision, based upon the approximate speeds of the two ships: the *Stockholm* at eighteen knots and the *Doria* at twenty-two knots. But, as Underwood sought to prove, if one took the times as accurate, then Carstens must have first seen the *Doria* on radar only six miles away.

Carstens' testimony was corroborated by the three seamen on his deck watch. Sten Johansson, the lookout in the crow's-nest, Ingemar Bjorkman, the bridge lookout, and Peder Larsen at the helm, testified they saw no fog, that Carstens plotted the approach of the *Andrea Doria,* and all three said they saw the ship off to the left side of the *Stockholm* before she swung across the *Stockholm* bow just before the collision. Larsen even agreed with Carstens' statement that he allowed his attention to wander away from the compass. He said, in effect, that he was more interested in watching the officer at the radar to his right than keeping his eye on the compass which was to his left.

In the midst of Larsen's testimony, even the subjects of sex and crime entered the admiralty proceeding. Larsen, testifying in Danish which was the bane of three different interpreters, at first flatly refused to say whether he had ever been in jail. Later he admitted he had served time because of "trouble with a girl" in 1955. But further than that he would not say, and Judge Walsh, when the matter was taken before him, ruled that the seaman's sexual indiscretions had no bearing on the cause of the collision.

Carstens' testimony also was corroborated by the *Stockholm's* course recorder, that mechanical device located in the ship's chartroom which inked on graph paper the heading of the ship every minute the vessel was under way. The graph of the course recorder, probably the most important single piece of evidence, showed that Peder Larsen had allowed the ship to yaw some two or three degrees on either side of the course line before the first of the two starboard turns.

It showed that about two and one-half minutes before the collision, Carstens had made his first starboard turn of twenty-four degrees. Two minutes later (time enough to answer the telephone call) he made a hard starboard turn, and about a half-minute later, the collision occurred. The point of collision is indicated on the course recorder graph by a jog or bump in the line where the pen apparently jumped off the paper at the point of impact. Then, presumably when the two ships were jammed together, the *Stockholm* swung to the right another sixty degrees in twenty seconds time. This is a turn so fast that no ship could do it alone under her own power. It could be accomplished only if the *Stockholm* were propelled or pushed by another force (presumably the *Andrea Doria*.)

Carstens-Johannsen remained in the witness box eleven court days stretched over a period of almost three weeks. Eleven different lawyers questioned the young officer on every phase of events leading up to the collision. What one lawyer forgot, the next pressed. It soon became evident that this hearing would not be completed in six weeks, as originally planned, and because of the crowded court calendar, the hearing was moved first to the assembly room of the New York County Lawyers Association Building and later to the museum room of the Seamen's Church Institute in New York.

As the hearing wore on, Carstens, who had been nervous and shy the first few days, seemed to thrive in the limelight of the witness chair. He began to enjoy matching wits with the various attorneys who sought to trap him into some admission damaging to himself or the cause of the *Stockholm* or the Swedish Line. As the hearing progressed with the concomitant publicity, it became evident that more than financial damages were at stake. Witnesses for both ships were testifying in behalf of their own personal reputation and that of their ship and, indeed, the prestige of Sweden and Italy as seafaring nations.

Carstens testified he had no idea the *Andrea Doria* would

be in those waters at the time of the collision. But it made no difference, he insisted. He had standing orders to be careful of all ships, large and small, which were encountered by the *Stockholm*. Neither did he try to communicate by radio with the *Doria* when he spotted the pip of the ship on radar twelve miles away. "There is no one who can know what ship is coming when you see a pip on the radar," he said.

Two important questions—or series of questions—bearing on responsibility for the collision, Carstens said, could better be answered by Captain Nordenson than himself. Why was the *Stockholm* steaming eastward against traffic on the so-called recognized or recommended westbound lane for ships going to New York? Was it or was it not the customary practice for the *Stockholm* to go at full or unreduced speed through fog?

The question of speeding in fog was perhaps the most important and fought-over point of the trial. For if the *Stockholm* could be shown to have been following a practice of speeding in fog and was doing that at the time of the disaster, then she would be as negligent and as guilty as the *Doria*. Early in the case, it became known to all attorneys—although not to the public—that the Italian Line would admit speeding in fog, and *per se*, at least partial blame for the collision.

Carstens displayed Teutonic stubbornness in his denial that the *Stockholm* always continued at full speed in fog. He insisted that on the night of the collision he, first of all, was not in fog, and secondly, even if visibility was only two miles, he was not speeding because the diesel-motor *Stockholm* could be stopped dead in the water in less than one mile, or less than half the distance of visibility as required by law.

267

Leonard Matteson, the shippers' lawyer who became the hearing's expert on speed in fog, pointed out that in the *Stockholm*'s logbook dating back from July 25 to June 6, there were sixty four-hour watches in which fog was noted. Not once in those sixty watches was there a notation that the speed of the *Stockholm* had been reduced, the lawyer said.

But Carstens said he believed the *Stockholm* did reduce speed once in fog somewhere around England on the previous voyage from Sweden to New York. Matteson, with the logbook in his hand, was stymied. He asked Haight if he would concede that the logbook showed the *Stockholm* had not reduced speed in any of those sixty watches. But the Swedish Line lawyer declined politely. "Mr. Matteson, no, I am not going to make any such concession." He would have to prove it by questioning every officer of the *Stockholm* about those entries in the logbook, the *Stockholm* lawyer said.

As for the customary practice of the *Stockholm* when in fog, Carstens pointed out that he had been on the ship only three months and he did not stand watch twenty-four hours a day. "It is the captain who can give answer to that," he said.

Carstens also plotted the course taken by the *Stockholm* on the night of the collision and the so-called recommended or recognized route for eastbound ships. Measuring the distance between the two courses at the point of collision, he testified they were approximately nineteen and one-half miles apart, and the newspapers reported that the *Stockholm* had been nineteen and one-half miles off course at the time of the collision. But Carstens said he was merely following the course ordered by his captain.

268

"I'm Also Wondering About That"

Captain Nordenson, undergoing a fierce barrage of questions on his opinion of Carstens' acts and decisions on the night of the collision, blacked out at the end of his third day on the witness stand. While the lawyers engaged in their usual arguments about the propriety of questions, Captain Nordenson sat drumming a pencil eraser on a pad of yellow paper. With Underwood asking the questions, Matteson held his pocket watch in his hand, announcing the time it took the captain to compute the time involved for the two ships traveling at a combined speed of forty knots to converge from ten miles apart. The captain's mind went blank, as he described it afterwards, and he forgot where he was. The lawyers, so busy arguing, failed to notice the change in the witness' demeanor. When Captain Nordenson said in a slight voice, "I don't feel well," he was hastily excused.

Captain Nordenson spent two weeks in a hospital and four more weeks recuperating from what doctors diagnosed as possibly a slight cerebral thrombosis, a clot in one of the capillaries of the brain. What none of the attorneys realized at the time was the tremendous fatigue of this sixty-three-year-old sea master who had attended the testimony of Carstens and Captain Calamai who preceded him and then spent long night hours aboard the *Stockholm*, which was being repaired in the Bethlehem Steel Shipyard in Brooklyn, studying to prepare himself for his turn on the witness stand.

Captain Nordenson resumed his testimony after his recovery, but testified only briefly each day in order to conserve his strength. He gave the appearance of a tired, old man who appeared more like the grandfather of six children, which he was, than a strict sea captain.

But he was unflinching in his defense of Carstens. He insisted that Carstens had done nothing wrong on the night of

269

the collision. The young officer had every right to wait until he saw with his own eyes the lights of the other ship two miles away before changing course on the *Stockholm*, said the captain. He added the weight of his experience and his own reputation in saying that Carstens should not be expected to suspect fog as the reason for not seeing another ship's mastlights before two miles distance.

As for the route taken by the *Stockholm*, Captain Nordenson said "I have been thirty-six and a half years in the Swedish-American Line and all that time we have followed that route, except during the ice period, springtime." There was no law, no agreement to prevent him from taking the *Stockholm* on that route. The Swedish Line knew of the route. The reason for taking the route, he explained, was that it was the shortest way to get to Nantucket Lightship, from where he always turned the ship northward (on a course of 66°) to head for Sable Island, off Nova Scotia, and then to Cape Race, Newfoundland, and across the Great Circle Track to Scotland and the North Sea to Scandinavia. It was safer, he said, to meet westbound ships head-on than to take the westbound route twenty miles south of Nantucket Lightship and then head north, cutting the westbound traffic of ships at right angles.

Captain Nordenson swore it was the practice on his ship to reduce speed in fog. He was as tenacious on that point as Carstens. This time, however, Underwood questioned the captain on each of the sixty watches in which fog was noted in the ship's log.

Point by point on each watch, Captain Nordenson was forced to admit that the log showed all fog precautions had been taken, such as posting extra lookouts, sounding the fog whistle and maintaining a radar watch, except that the speed of the ship was not slackened. At the end of this line of questions, Underwood asked:

"Now, Captain, we have been through this log and I would like to ask you again: do you admit or deny that it was your practice to continue at substantially full speed in fog at sea?"

"Well, it depended on the density of the fog," answered Captain Nordenson. He insisted through hours of questioning on this point that the *Stockholm* had "tremendous backing power" to allow her to go at eighteen to nineteen knots at times when fog was noted in the logbook.

One officer of the *Stockholm,* however, did admit what was apparent to most observers at the hearing. The *Stockholm's* chief officer, Herbert Kallback, was questioned on each of the same sixty watches between June 6 and July 25 in which fog was noted. In conclusion, he was asked:

"Is it not a fact—I want your testimony—it was not the practice—don't look at Mr. Haight [which the chief officer was doing at the time]—Answer to your own conscience, when you answer my question, is it not a fact that it was not the practice on the *Stockholm* to reduce speed in fog?"

The chief officer, in a soft, resigned voice, answered, "I must say yes."

Captain Nordenson testified there was no particular reason why he could not have been on the bridge at the time of the collision. He was in good health, not overly tired, and he had not been drinking, he said. He went to his room simply to work on some papers and he was there "sitting standby" so that he could be called if needed in a matter of seconds. He had not retired for the night, he said. He intended to return to the bridge for the approach to Nantucket Lightship and the subsequent change of course to Sable Island.

Why did the *Stockholm* only have one officer on watch

when most transatlantic liners used two? the captain was asked. Simply because that was the policy and practice of the Swedish Line. Under questioning, Captain Nordenson admitted that two officers on watch would be better than one, but that one officer could adequately handle a bridge watch by himself.

Because of his illness, the captain was the final as well as the second witness for the Swedish-American Line. During his recuperation, the three seamen on watch, the radio officer, the engineering officer and three motormen on watch testified as well as the ship's chief officer and chief engineer.

Captain Nordenson's testimony, which consisted largely of a defense of the seamanship of Carstens-Johannsen, might be considered to have passed his final judgment on the young officer when he was asked if he would have confidence in an officer who did not even think of fog as one possible reason for not seeing the lights of an oncoming ship five miles or less away.

"I know now that you blame Carstens-Johannsen for being too young, and you also called him inexperienced, because compared with my experience of more than forty-five, soon forty-six years at sea, you can call him inexperienced," declared Captain Nordenson. "But, on the other hand, there is a difference between inexperience and incompetence. And as far as I can see, he has not shown any incompetence in handling the ship."

272

Chapter Fourteen

"DO I HAVE TO ANSWER?"

WHILE THE COMMANDERS of these two ships
which collided were remarkably alike in their introspection
and quiet demeanor, it would be difficult to imagine two men
more dissimilar than Ernst Carstens-Johannsen and Piero
Calamai. One was youthful, energetic, with the look of an
adolescent; the other a man made old by tragedy, whose
sallow complexion and sagging posture gave him the appearance of a sick man who had lost weight too rapidly. He had
in fact spent nine days in a hospital following his return
to New York.

Unlike the twenty-six-year-old Swedish officer, who wore
an immaculate dress blue uniform and starched white shirt

273

in the courtroom, the master of the lost *Andrea Doria* wore mufti. Unlike the voluble answers given by the loquacious Carstens, Captain Calamai testified in low, almost inaudible, monosyllables. His characteristic pose in the witness chair was to support his head by cupping his chin in the crook of his thumb and forefinger, resting his elbow on the arm of the chair. His manner was that of one who had been through so much that nothing more could hurt him.

Yet the captain was every bit as good a witness for the Italian Line as Carstens had been for the Swedish Line. Despite the difference in their demeanors, their backgrounds and their experience, each had been the man solely responsible for the navigation of his ship from the time the other ship had been sighted to the moment of collision and disaster. Each was the star witness for his side.

Swiftly and expertly, Underwood led Captain Calamai in a recitation of the events leading up to the collision: how the *Stockholm* had been sighted on radar seventeen miles away and slightly to the right of the *Doria* and had maintained a course which would have resulted in a safe starboard-to-starboard passing if the *Stockholm*, without sounding any signal, had not turned suddenly to her right and into the hull of the *Doria.*

Haight, after warming up with some preliminary questions, asked the captain about the use of radar on the *Andrea Doria.*

"Captain Calamai, had you yourself had any special training in the use of radar?"

"No," came the immediate answer.

"Had Captain Franchini had any special training in the use of radar?"

"I don't think so."

274

Had any one of the three officers on the bridge plotted the radar observations of the oncoming *Stockholm?* No, was the answer, "it was a parallel course and it was not necessary."

The captain conceded that the only way to accurately determine the course and speed of another ship by radar was to plot two or more successive observations. The book of instructions for the radar set called for plotting, the captain admitted. But the plotting device, a Marconi Locatograph, was not used ordinarily on the *Doria* and had not been used that night because it was not thought to have been necessary.

In cross-examining the master of the *Andrea Doria,* it appeared that Haight had adopted a sympathetic approach toward the man who had lost his ship. Captain Calamai in return seemed to answer forthrightly as if he were too weary to attempt to parry questions.

One of the most controversial aspects of the hearing was what had happened to the logbooks of the *Andrea Doria.* In the exchange of pertinent documents before the hearing, the Italian Line informed the court that all the important logs went down with the ship. The only papers saved were the captain's accounting log, two secret books of the North Atlantic Treaty Organization, the complete file of the crew's sailing papers and a strip of the ship's course recorder graph, the Italian Line reported. But the Italian Line offices in New York and in Genoa had told the newspapers shortly after the collision that all the logbooks had been saved and had been sent in a diplomatic courier's pouch from New York to Genoa.

When asked about this at the hearing, Captain Calamai said, "Reading the newspapers, amongst the many inexact things, I also noticed this. But I made myself the conviction that what the newspapers reported as to the saved logbooks, they intended the seamen's passports."

Navigational logs are of course of primary importance in an attempt to reconstruct a marine disaster, which was the task of this "discovery" proceeding. The important work was the plotting of the courses of the two ships to determine their true position prior to the collision. Thus, one or the other ship could be found primarily at fault for making the disastrous turn.

Questioned at length, Captain Calamai explained how the logbooks came to be left on the sinking ship. At about 2:30 in the morning, he had given the general order, "Save the books." He had said those words, he remembered, but to no one in particular. First Officer Oneto and Third Officer Badano were nearby on the bridge and he had assumed one or the other would see to the books, the captain said.

He himself had gone down to his cabin and had carried the two NATO books and his own logbook up to the bridge where he had given them to Mario Maracci, an officer cadet. Later, there had been a "misunderstanding," the captain said. He told Third Officer Badano to take the course recorder graph. Badano in haste had ripped off the final twelve-hour section of the graph and given it to Maracci. And, as Badano later testified, the officer asked the cadet, "Do you have the books?" meaning the deck logbooks, and the cadet had replied, "Yes, I have them," meaning the NATO books.

The logbooks actually must have fallen to the floor of the chartroom in the midst of a stack of papers at the time of the collision, the captain said. He learned that the logbooks had not been taken off the ship soon after he climbed into lifeboat No. 11, Captain Calamai said. Both Oneto and

Badano were in that lifeboat although he did not remember who told him about the logbooks at the time.

"After you learned that the ship's books had not been taken from the ship," Haight asked, "would it have been possible for a man, an officer or a man, to have gone back aboard the ship to get the ship's books and documents?"

It was one of the few times Captain Calamai leaned forward in his chair. "Today I can say yes, because the ship went down at ten o'clock [four and one-half hours after he had left the ship]," the captain said intensely. "But at that moment I didn't know if the ship would have gone down immediately, contemporaneously." He paused and then softly added, "I was so shocked by the tragedy of which we were an object, that is why I didn't even think."

Did either Badano or Oneto volunteer to go back for the books, or did he order them to? No, said the captain, "I felt badly . . . we didn't discuss it any more."

What happened to the Engine Room logbooks? They had been completely forgotten when the engineers abandoned the Engine Room. The radio logs? "The wireless operator, when he received from me the order to abandon ship, he thought it was an immediate thing," Captain Calamai testified. The radioman had left his logbook and file of messages behind.

The questions went on and on and Captain Calamai conceded that Italian law required the captain of a sinking ship to save all logbooks before abandoning ship. Italian law also required a captain who lost his logs to reconstruct a temporary log for the last watch of his ship, the witness admitted, but that had not been done.

Haight then presented the captain's accounting log to him, in which the only entry for July 25 was the temperatures of the ship's freezers, and asked him whether or not anything else had been noted in that log for that day, such as fog precautions? "I don't remember," said the captain. "There is nothing else written here." The captain explained that he had not finished writing the events of July 25 because of the collision.

"I see. Just one more question about it, Captain," the Swedish Line attorney said casually. "When you wrote the log up in your cabin was it in the same physical condition that you now see it? And I direct your attention to various places in the cover and pages which show that the book, as I see it—if I am wrong, correct me—has been taken apart and restapled together."

"I object to this question," thundered the Italian Line attorney, jumping to his feet, "and if Mr. Haight wishes to take the stand, I would love to cross-examine him on this assertion."

After argument back and forth between the two lawyers, the hearing master ruled that Captain Calamai should answer the question. But Underwood pressed his objection. Striding to the witness stand and taking the logbook from Captain Calamai's hands, Underwood said, "I want a moment to cogitate and see whether I will submit to that." He had the right to press his objection before Judge Walsh. Inspecting the logbook, he walked up and down the front of the room, turning the pages one by one. While the whole courtroom watched, the logbook fell from the lawyer's hands to the floor. Several pages skidded across the floor.

Haight protested vehemently. He wanted an answer to his question. What had just happened, he asserted, made no difference because his office had photographs of the logbook as it had appeared before. Was the book in the same condition it had been on the afternoon before the collision? he demanded.

"No," replied Calamai impassively. "May I explain?"

"Yes, anything you wish," said the lawyer.

"As I said before, I took the book from the floor of my cabin and gave the logbook to the cadet Maracci, who put it under his jacket. And I heard later in New York that the logbook had become wet and that it was not in the condition as before."

"Did you hear how the logbook became wet?" asked Haight.

"Probably while the officer [cadet] was going in the lifeboat there was water," answered the captain.

The question of the logbooks recurred again and again during the cross-examination of Captain Calamai and other officers of the *Andrea Doria*. If the logbooks and navigation charts had been available, they would have gone far in reconstructing the positions and course of the Italian ship prior to the collision, and thereby solving the mystery of the hearing: how could the radar on the *Andrea Doria* show the *Stockholm* to her right and the radar on the *Stockholm* show the *Doria* to be to the left? The answer simply was that either one of the radar sets had been wrong or the men interpreting the radar on one of the ships had been wrong. Such a mistake, whichever navigator made it, must have been an honest error. One must assume that neither Carstens nor Captain Calamai would deliberately steer his ship into the path of another vessel. The problem of the lawyers was to determine which officer, Carstens or Calamai, had been in error.

279

As the hearing progressed, the transcript of the testimony accompanied by the lawyers' briefs was sent to the principal owners of the two ships whose representatives were engaged in secret negotiations in London attempting to settle the countersuits before the case came to actual trial. The *Stockholm* was owned by the Brostrom Concern, a huge private shipping company of which the Swedish-American Line was a subsidiary. The *Doria* was owned by the Italian Line of which the Italian Government was the principal stockholder. The negotiations were complicated beyond the issue of responsibility by the large number of insurance firms who were at cross purposes in the attempts to settle the case out of court. Insurance firms with money invested in both lines sought the speediest settlement possible since they would pay no matter which side won and legal fees were mounting up at approximately $2,000 a day. Those insuring only one ship held out for the best terms possible. The basic question in the settlement negotiations was, in short, how much would the *Stockholm* people pay toward the $30,000,0000 value of the lost *Andrea Doria?* The answer depended on the results of the testimony at the hearing in New York.

In the witness chair, Captain Calamai tacitly admitted at least partial responsibility for the collision when he testified the *Andrea Doria* was proceeding through dense fog which limited visibility to one-half mile at substantially her full speed. The practice aboard the ship as long as he had been master had been to reduce the *Doria*'s usual cruising speed of 23.3 knots to 21.8 knots by cutting the pressure in the boilers. The captain conceded too that reducing boiler pressure saved fuel but also reduced the available emergency backing or stopping power of the ship. It was possible to retain the full backing power by keeping full pressure on the boilers but throttling down the nozzles feeding the steam into the turbines. But this meant more fuel consumption and hence greater operating expenses. The captain surprised the court, however, when he admitted that he did not know the stopping power of his ship. He also said he did not know how much distance the *Andrea Doria* required to make a full ninety-degree turn. That data had not been tested during the trial runs of the ship in 1952 or since. It was like saying he was driving a car without knowing the stopping power of its brakes.

But it was clear nevertheless that steaming at 21.8 knots, the *Andrea Doria* was not complying with the rule of the road which requires a ship to proceed in fog at a "moderate speed" or one in which it can be stopped in half the distance of visibility ahead. It has been estimated that to stop the *Andrea Doria* dead in the water from a speed of 21.8 knots would take about two miles. Half the distance of visibility that night was one-quarter mile.

The Swedish Line attorney devoted almost half of his lengthy cross-examination of the captain to the stability of the *Andrea Doria* and the measures taken to save the ship after the collision. This was in line with his attempt to prove that the *Stockholm* was not responsible for the sinking of the luxury Italian liner. He argued that the *Andrea Doria* should have been able to withstand the damage of the collision.

But on stability matters, Captain Calamai displayed a surprising lack of knowledge, answering question after question with "I don't know" or "I don't remember." The *Andrea Doria,* he said, was a two-compartment ship, built in conformity to international standards. She was supposed to remain afloat with any two of her compartments fully or partially flooded. The latter condition is by far the worse, for water sloshing inside a ship threatens to capsize it as surely as would an equal weight of loose iron cargo rolling from one side of a ship to another.

The captain admitted that at no time after the collision did he give the Engine Room any instructions on measures to be taken to save the ship, although the chief engineer on duty was a replacement for the regular chief engineer, on vacation.

He agreed with Haight that the best way to correct the starboard list of the ship would be to flood the deep-fuel tanks on the port side of the ship. But he said this was impossible for some reason he did not know.

He admitted that he was told the engineers were pumping water out of the flooded double-bottom tanks on the starboard side of the ship and that, in theory at least, this increased the danger of capsizing by further reducing the weight at the bottom of the ship. But he did not order the men to stop that pumping. He left the entire effort of saving the ship to his engineers, Captain Calamai said. Asked if it would have been possible to flood the deep-fuel tanks on the high port side to equalize the weight of the ship by pumping water from the sea into them, Captain Calamai said he did not know but he understood that maneuver also had been made impossible by the severe list to starboard. The indication was that the sea intake valves on the port side of the ship's bilge line had risen out of the water when the ship went over on her right side.

Captain Calamai said that the *Andrea Doria* had on board a certificate of safety, issued by the harbor master of Genoa, but that it too went down with the ship. Asked if the certificate had any conditions attached to it in regard to whether the fuel and water tanks of the ship were required to be ballasted at any time, the captain said, "The safety certificate did not have any elements, any data, to this regard."

Pressing his questions as to why the *Doria* took an immediate list of 18 to 19 degrees, Haight asked if the Italian Line had supplied the captain with information on the stability of the ship under emergency conditions. The captain said he did not remember. Had the Italian Line warned him that excessive heeling might result if the *Doria* should sustain unsymmetrical flooding approaching New York? The captain said he did not remember.

The Swedish Line attorney, after quizzing Captain Calamai about stability of his ship, called upon Underwood and the Italian Line to produce various plans and blueprints of the *Andrea Doria,* as well as all the instructions for operating the ship under various load conditions given to the Italian Line by the Ansaldo Shipyard which built the ship. Underwood said he would comply although it might mean moving the entire home office of the Italian Line in Genoa to New York. He protested though against Haight's request that the chief engineer of the *Andrea Doria* testify at the hearings, arguing that the chief engineer had been asleep in bed at the time of the collision and could contribute nothing to explain the cause of the collision. But he was overruled by Judge Walsh who agreed with the *Stockholm* attorney that the chief engineer should explain what was done to save the *Andrea Doria* after the collision.

Haight questioned Captain Calamai for almost two full days on the stability of the *Andrea Doria,* before he went on to navigational matters. Captain Calamai readily conceded that when he first sighted the *Stockholm* seventeen miles away there had been sufficient time and sufficient deep water around his ship to turn the *Doria* to the right for a standard port-to-port, or left-to-left, passing. "Yes, I could have changed," he said, "but I did not deem it necessary because I considered that the two ships were going green-to-green [starboard to starboard]."

The captain insisted that as the two ships came together from seventeen miles apart, his second officer, Franchini, at the radar repeatedly told him the other ship was on a parallel course and would pass to the starboard. Franchini did not tell him the exact bearings except for the 4° bearing at seventeen miles and 14° bearing at about three and one-half miles when he turned the *Doria* four degrees to port. He saw the "glow" of the other ship's lights when it was about 1.1 miles away and about 20° to 25° to starboard.

Asked if he had expected to see the lights at that angle, the captain replied, "I didn't compute the bearing, but I was so convinced that the ship would pass on our starboard side that it was not followed, it was not checked, when, in fact, we saw the glow."

Haight, then setting out to prove that even by the observations made aboard the *Andrea Doria* the two ships were not on parallel opposite courses to pass starboard-to-starboard, approached the witness chair and handed the captain a pad of plotting paper. He asked the captain to plot the radar observations, as remembered, aboard the *Doria*.

Captain Calamai took the paper, looked at it and said softly, "It is the first time I see."

"Do you know how to use this kind of a plotting sheet?" asked Haight.

"I am not very familiar because this is one work I let the officers do," said Captain Calamai.

Underwood protested that the captain should not be forced to do something which he admitted he was unfamiliar with and left to his officers. Haight insisted, arguing that in order to use radar and check on his officers, the captain of the *Andrea Doria* had to know how to interpret radar. The matter was referred to Judge Walsh, who ruled in favor of the Swedish Line attorney.

After several hours of objections and arguments, Captain Calamai plotted the significant distances and bearings at which the *Stockholm* was observed before the collision: seventeen miles and 4° to starboard, five miles and 15° to starboard and 1.1 miles and 22½° to starboard.

When that had been done, Haight asked: "My question is, is it not correct that the radar observations, distance and bearing, as set forth in your report to the Italian Line, show that in fact the *Stockholm* was not on a course parallel to the course of the *Doria*?"

"I renew my objection unless a time is fixed," said Underwood.

"I think he can answer," said the presiding hearing master. "Go ahead."

There was a silence in the room and then Captain Calamai answered in a soft, pathetic voice. "I can see it now from the maneuvering board."

The plot on the maneuvering indeed did show that the *Stockholm*, according to the radar observations, would barely clear the *Doria*. It showed a collision course.

Haight then set forth another plot based upon the captain's testimony that he made the 4° turn three and one-half miles away from the *Stockholm* instead of five miles. The captain

285

had written in his first report to the Italian Line that the 4°
turn had been made at a distance of five miles from the
Stockholm. But in his court testimony, he said that although
he remembered the distance as five miles both Franchini and
Giannnini, who had been on the bridge with him, said it had
been three and one-half miles. The second plot showed also
that despite the *Doria's* 4° turn, presumably widening the
passing distance, the passing distance shrank noticeably into
a collision course.

"When you saw the glow of the *Stockholm's* lights bearing
about twenty-two and one-half degrees on your starboard
bow at a distance of about 1.1 miles, if Captain Franchini
had reported to you that even though you had altered the
Doria's course four degrees to your left, the passing distance
had closed from .8 mile to .2 miles," Haight asked, "would
you have continued ahead with the *Doria* at 21.8 knots ... ?"

"If I would have had that information," Captain Calamai
replied, "I would have stopped the engines immediately,
giving then full speed astern and coming possibly to the right,
giving the signal of a turn to the right."

The commander of the *Andrea Doria* finally was saying that
if his second officer had plotted the radar observations of the
Stockholm when she was three and one-half or five miles
away or had remained to watch the radar pip when the
Stockholm turned to its right two miles away, Captain Calamai would not have lost his ship.

When Second Officer Franchini took the witness stand, he
testified he did not plot radar observations because it had
never been the practice to do so in open sea under Captain
Calamai's command. Franchini, after working out substantially the same plots on the maneuvering board as had Cap-

tain Calamai, said that if he had plotted that night he would have seen the *Stockholm* turning to starboard.

At no time that night as he watched his radar scope did he suspect that the *Stockholm* was making a turn, he said, admitting that after he had left the radar it must have shown clearly that the *Stockholm* was on a collision course. He left the radar, he explained, when he heard the captain and Giannini discussing sighting lights of the *Stockholm*. It is easier to see how another ship is maneuvering by seeing her lights visually rather than by interpreting radar, Franchini said.

"Before you left the radar, did you at any time realize that the passing distance was closing?" asked Haight.

"No."

"If you had plotted . . . you would have realized that the passing distance was closing, would you not?"

"Yes."

"If you had told the captain that the passing distance was closing, what do you think he would have done?"

"I don't know," said Franchini.

"Have you been told that Captain Calamai had testified that if you had told him that the passing distance was closing that then he would have stopped and reversed and gone right?"

"Yes, sir . . . he told me so," said Franchini.

The Swedish Line attorney walked up to the witness chair and pointed to the radar plot which Franchini had worked out showing the two ships converging. "If the captain had not been on the bridge and you as watch officer at the radar had seen by plotting that the passing distance was closing," asked Haight, "what would you have done?"

Franchini hesitated and tried to duck the question. "It all depends," he said. The Swedish Line attorney pressed this question and Franchini, somewhat abashed, finally asserted, "I would not like to answer because it takes me in a position to criticize eventually the maneuver of the commander. Whatever I would have done, I would not want to answer, because the captain did his maneuver."

There was an electric silence. Underwood, his hands clasped behind his back, paced the floor. Haight, in a compassionate tone of voice, told Franchini who was looking around the room for help, "Mr. Franchini, I respect your not wanting to in any way criticize the captain's maneuver, but each one is in this court to answer questions as best as he can, and I do, please, want an answer to my question."

Franchini looked despairingly at Underwood. "Do I have to answer?" he asked.

The Italian Line lawyer replied bluntly, "Captain Franchini, if you understand the question, you should answer it."

"Academically speaking," said the second officer, pausing for breath, "most probably I would have inverted the motion of the engines and I would have turned to one side."

"To which side would you have turned?" asked Haight.

"Probably to the right," came the reluctant answer.

This left unanswered the basic question of whether the ships actually had been right-to-right or left-to-left before their last-minute desperate turns. It has remained a source of controversy because the question is not susceptible to a direct and absolute proof. Ordinarily in admiralty cases the logbooks, navigational charts and course recorder tapes provide enough information for the lawyers and experts to reconstruct a marine accident by plotting the courses of the ships involved. But in this case, with the logbooks of the

Andrea Doria not available, the information on hand was too meager for such plotting.

If one takes a navigational chart of the Nantucket waters and lays off the course of the *Stockholm* heading for the Nantucket Lightship, as plotted by Carstens, and then lays off the remembered course of the *Andrea Doria* away from the lightship, one finds the ships were approaching one another head-on, or nearly head-on. The lines would show the ships to have been in a slightly crossing situation, with only one or two degrees separating their being head-on to one another. In such a position, it would be possible for the radars to show one ship off to the right and the other one off to the left. This is so because radar beams travel in a straight line and reflect from the highest point of a ship sighted, a mast or a funnel, and do not show an entire ship on the radar screen. However, drawing two straight lines on a navigational map can at best only approximate the position and courses of two ships. Ships do not travel in straight lines. They yaw from side to side and are set off course by currents, tides and winds.

The best source of information in reconstructing the collision, if correlated with the testimony of the officers of both ships, is the course recorder graph of each ship. Even the honest testimony of eyewitnesses on the bridges of the two ships must be viewed critically because people honestly see things differently, particularly those caught up in the frenzy of an accident. But course recorders, which record every single heading and turn of a ship underway, are mechanically objective, subject only to the normal deviations of a mechanical instrument, which can be corrected by the testimony of witnesses.

The graphs of the course recorders of the *Stockholm* and

289

the *Andrea Doria* were interpreted for the hearings by the same man—William R. Griswold, sales manager of the Marine Division of the Sperry Gyroscope Company, manufacturers of the course recorders used on both ships. Mr. Griswold, an impartial expert, put into words the meaning of the graphs, but he carefully refrained from any interpretations, obvious though they might be.

The course recorder graph of the *Stockholm* correlated closely with the testimony of Carstens-Johannsen, allowing for normal deviations on time and bearings with the ship's clock and gyrocompass.

The *Stockholm* course recorder showed that:

Ship's Recorder Time	Recorder Mean Heading	Maximum Yaw	Compass Heading According to Carstens' Testimony	Remarks
8 P.M.	92°	(94-89)	90°	(Course from N.Y.)
9:40 P.M.	90°	(92-88)	87°	(Capt's change of course)
10:10 P.M.	91°	(94-89)	89°	(CJ-first change of 2° to offset drift)
10:40 P.M.	92°	(96½-89)	91°	(CJ-2nd change of 2° which CJ thought was about 11 P.M.)
11:07 P.M.	94½ held for 90 seconds			(CJ insists this was a yaw—not change of course)
11:08½	altered right to 119° for 2 minutes			(A 25° turn to right which Carstens estimated at 22½° upon sighting lights of the *Doria*)

The reading of the course recorder was broken down into fractions of minutes for the time immediately preceding the collision. A sharp jog in the pen motion indicated the impact of collision, recorded at 11:11 p.m. course recorder time. Subtracting the two minutes difference for the 11:09 p.m. time of collision noted by Carstens, the course recorder shows that:

At 11:06½ the *Stockholm* made a 25° turn to the right to 119°, which it held for two minutes (correlated to the 22° turn estimated by Carstens when he first saw the lights of the *Doria*).

At 11:08½ p.m. the *Stockholm* began a hard right turn. At about 11:09 ship had turned 13° to a heading of 132° when the pen was jogged, indicating the point of collision, and then continued right to a heading of 150° at 11:10 p.m.

In the next 20 seconds approximately, the *Stockholm* turned sharply farther right from 150° to 210°—a 60° turn in a third of a minute. This would be an impossible turn for any ship the size of the *Stockholm* without the push of an outside force (presumably the *Doria*).

From 11:10 to 11:11½, the *Stockholm* turned another 18° to the right and then began to swing left, right and left out of control. . . .

The course recorder graph of the *Andrea Doria*, containing the crux of the controversy on the positions of the ships before the collision, was more difficult to interpret. Nowhere on the graph was there a clear and definite jog of the pen to indicate the point of collision, such as there was on the *Stockholm* graph. A final decision on whether the ships were right-to-right or left-to-left before the collision would depend upon the interpretation of the graph of the *Doria's* course recorder.

Only the section for the twelve hours before the collision was saved, and although the Swedish Line attorneys argued that there was no way to prove that the undated graph was that the final voyage of the *Doria,* it contained enough information to reconstruct the important events preceding the collision. The graph did not correspond to the times or heading of the *Doria* as testified to by Captain Calamai and his watch officers. But the differences were explained. Captain Calamai and the others testified that in Naples the recorder pen ran dry and Second Officer Badano reset the pen and graph paper so that it no longer was synchronized with Greenwich Mean Time. The day before the collision, when the ship was heading at 267°, which was near the edge of the paper, First Officer Oneto moved the pen 10° ahead so that it would record away from the edge of the paper.

Even so, the graph can be read according to the correct time and sequence of events by correlating it with the time of 10:20 P.M., when the *Doria* was abeam of the Nantucket Lightship.

The graph shows that at 9 P.M., the *Doria* was on a steady course of 278° (corresponding with the 267° testified by Captain Calamai); at 9:40 P.M., ship turned 6° to the left to 272° (corresponding to the 261° course for the fifteen-mile approach to the Nantucket Lightship); at 10:20 P.M., the ship turned right to 279° (corresponding to 268° upon coming abeam of the lightship).

At 11:05 P.M., the graph clearly shows the 4° turn to the left and the gradual bearing off to the left in response to Captain Calamai's order "Nothing to the right."

Some five minutes later, at 11:10½ P.M., the *Doria* began a hard left turn in which the ship turned 110° in three minutes, going from 275° to 165°. It was a "fairly uniform" rate of turn, according to the Sperry Company analysis, with the *Doria* turning 55° in the first ninety seconds and 55° in the

292

last ninety seconds of the three-minute turn, The left turn ended at 11:13½ P.M., at which time the *Doria* then swung sharply to the right, going 173°, or almost halfway around the compass, in the next thirteen minutes.

In that left turn lies the controversy. The *Doria* officers say their ship was struck by the *Stockholm* at about 11:10 when the *Doria* had swung only ten or fifteen degrees at the beginning of the hard left turn. They dispute the Sperry Company's analysis that the left turn was a uniform rate of turn and shows no indication of collision.

The Swedish Line says the collision occurred at the end of the *Doria*'s three-minute left turn. It was the *Stockholm* plunging into the side of the speeding Italian ship that broke the left turn and pivoted the ship to the right, says the Swedish Line. It would follow necessarily that if the *Doria* turned left for three minutes before the collision, she must have crossed the *Stockholm*'s bow, starting the turn from a port-to-port position. For if the ships had been starboard to starboard and the *Doria* turned to her left at almost twenty-two knots for three minutes, the slower *Stockholm* never would have caught up to her. According to this theory, both ships began their turns three minutes before the collision when they were about two miles apart. Since it takes a turning vessel two, three or more ship lengths for rudder action to take effect, it would explain why Carstens did not see the *Doria* begin her turn before answering the telephone call from his lookout. It would also account for Captain Calamai seeing the *Stockholm* to his right if the *Doria* had been swinging across the *Stockholm* bow.

Charles Haight contended for the Swedish Line at the hearing that the collision must have occurred at the end of the *Doria*'s left turn at 11:13 P.M. (course recorder time) because it would take the *Doria* going at 21.8 knots some 53 minutes to go the 19.5 miles which separated the point of collision from the Nantucket Lightship. The *Doria* was abeam of the lightship at 10:20 P.M., according to Captain Calamai's testimony. Fifty-three minutes sailing time at 21.8 knots would put the *Doria* at the end of the three-minute turn at the time of collision.

Of vital importance in this connection was the point at which Captain Calamai had made his 4° turn prior to the collision. The recorder graph clearly shows the turn was made at 11:05 P.M. but the question was whether the ships were three and one-half or five miles apart at the time. Captain Calamai wrote in his report on the collision, which was prepared on the destroyer escort *Allen* on the way into New York, that the turn was made when the *Stockholm* was five miles away. In his testimony, the captain said that although he remembered the distance as five miles, both Franchini and Giannini remembered it as three and one-half and the captain then thought the two younger officers were correct. The importance of this rests in the arithmetic fact that it would take the *Doria* 5¼ minutes to go three and one-half miles and 7½ minutes to go five miles. In the first instance, 5¼ minutes from the 11:05 P.M. turn would place the collision at about 11:10 P.M. at the start of the hard left turn, as the Italians contend. If the distance had been five miles, 7½ minutes would put the time between 11:12 and 11:13 P.M., at the end of the big left turn, as the *Stockholm* people contend.

With these facts and theories, the layman, the man of the sea, and the maritime expert can reach an informed judgment as to whether the ships were port-to-port or starboard-to-starboard prior to the collision. But it will only be an opinion, for in the final analysis only a court of law can make a conclusive and binding determination on so controversial a matter. And this case, one of the most complex and most expertly handled in admiralty law, never did and never will reach such a final judgment, for in January, 1957, shortly before the engineering officers of the *Andrea Doria* were scheduled to take the witness stand, the case was settled out of court.

Chapter Fifteen

"I LOVED THE SEA—NOW I HATE IT"

REPRESENTATIVES OF THE ITALIAN LINE and the Swedish Line and their insurance underwriters were sitting in London as a jury on the case. Their deliberations had begun soon after the start of the hearings in New York. The negotiators followed the case through the voluminous record of testimony which was sent regularly from New York to London. The hearing transcript also was sent to the Italian Line in Genoa, the Italian Government in Rome and the Swedish Line in Gothenburg. The hearing record thus served as the basis for argument and negotiation in Europe on the primary financial question of how much the Swedish-American Line should pay toward the loss of the *Andrea Doria*.

The deadlock in London in the settlement negotiations was broken when the cause of the *Doria*'s severe list immediately after the collision and hence the primary cause of her sinking came to light.

The break came on January 8, 1957, three and one-half months after the start of the hearings. On that day Underwood, on behalf of the Italian Line, submitted as court exhibits twenty-six different books and charts pertaining to the ballasting, piping, cross-flooding and other stability data on the *Andrea Doria*. The information had been demanded earlier by the Swedish Line as necessary for the cross-examination of the *Andrea Doria*'s engineers, who were scheduled to take the witness stand shortly. The *Doria*'s principal deck officers, who had knowledge of the collision—Captain Calamai, Franchini, Giannini and Badano—had completed their testimony. The helmsman was scheduled as the next witness and the engineers were to follow. But three days after the Swedish Line attorneys gained possession of the stability calculations, the hearings were abruptly ended. It was only a few days before the engineering officers of the *Andrea Doria* would have taken the witness stand to explain how and why the Italian luxury liner sank.

The explanation no doubt was contained in a report on stability instructions for the *Andrea Doria* prepared for the Italian Line by the builders, the Ansaldo Shipyard of Genoa. Whatever the Swedish Line lawyers found in that stability report and sent to the London negotiators, however, never was made public.

But the House of Representatives Committee on Merchant Marine and Fisheries, which had conducted an independent investigation of the collision, made public its report that same month. The committee, whose expert consultants had analyzed the Ansaldo stability report declared:

"Briefly, the analysis shows that the Andrea Doria met the subdivision [compartmentation] requirements of the 1948 Safety of Life at Sea Convention by a very narrow margin. It is stated in the 'stability report' that the ship also could meet the stability requirements of the 1948 convention provided she was kept ballasted with substantial and specified quantities of liquids in her various tanks. It does not appear possible to account for the behavior of the ship immediately following the collision on July 25, 1956, except on the assumption that she was not in fact ballasted in accordance with this information."

In fact, Captain Calamai had testified he knew nothing of any shipyard requirements pertaining to ballasting of tanks. Franchini had testified that while certain fresh-water tanks were ballasted during the voyage from Genoa to New York, no fuel tanks of the *Andrea Doria* ever were refilled with sea water. The deep fuel tanks in the compartment ripped open by the collision, were empty, he had testified.

The reason for not ballasting fuel oil tanks with salt water is fairly obvious. It is a matter of money. Putting salt water into fuel oil tanks pollutes the tanks and requires that they be scrubbed clean at the end of each voyage lest a diet of oil and salt water ruin the ship's engines. Furthermore, if fuel tanks are ballasted with salt water, a ship is prohibited from dumping dirty ballast into harbors such as New York lest the residue oil in the tanks pollute harbor waters. Hence, unwanted ballast must be emptied into a barge and carted away to a safe dumping area, which is a costly and time-consuming operation, avoided whenever possible by all steamship companies.

299

When the *Stockholm* bow struck the particular compartment of the *Andrea Doria* where the deep-fuel tanks were located, the lack of ballasting probably meant the difference between staying afloat and sinking. The congressional committee report estimated that the *Andrea Doria* at the time of the collision had "perhaps only one-third" the stability required by her builders. It concluded "that while the *Andrea Doria* was apparently built within the requirements of the 1948 international convention, there is a clear presumption that her stability at the time of the accident was substantially less than that envisaged by her designers."

If the *Andrea Doria* had been adequately ballasted, she should not have listed more than 7°, or at the very worst 15°, as set forth in the international convention on ship stability. Then, the portside lifeboats could have been launched, although they might not have been needed. The ship's pumps probably would have been able to keep up with the water entering the Generator Room, even with the vital door between the two compartments missing. Flooding could then have been confined to the two compartments—the fuel-tank compartment and the Generator Room. The *Andrea Doria* would then have been able to sail into New York under her own power, or if that were not possible, surely she would have been able to reach shallow water where she could have been repaired without undue cost. In short, it appears that the *Andrea Doria* went to the bottom of the sea, a total loss, not because of the collision alone but because of her instability due to improper ballasting. The lack of a watertight door between the damaged compartment and the Generator Room made a bad situation worse by permitting the rapidly rising water to knock out one generator after another, progressively crippling the pumps. This information must have indicated to the Italian Line interests that if the case continued to the end of a full trial, they might well lose the right to limit their liability as well as incur the bad publicity involved.

With the consent of the Italian government, the principal stockholder, they accepted the basic Swedish Line terms. The Swedish Line would pay nothing toward the loss of the *Andrea Doria*. It was a bitter pill but the Swedish Line was then in the better bargaining position. All the *Stockholm* witnesses had testified publicly in the pre-trial hearings. Thus, the Swedish Line could no longer be hurt by further publicity. But the Italian Line still had the *Andrea Doria* engineers to put on the witness stand in addition to the helmsman and lookouts and hence everything to lose and little if anything to gain by continuing the hearings.

The settlement, as finally worked out, provided for both lines to drop their damage suits, ending all legal action against each other. Thus the Italian Line and its insurers absorbed the loss of the $30,000,000 ship. The Swedish Line interests dropped their countersuit, absorbing the cost of the $1,000,-000 new *Stockholm* bow and the estimated $1,000,000 loss of business during repairs. The personal injury liability funds of both lines were available to cover the cost of all third-party claims, which included damage suits for deaths, personal injuries, baggage, cargo and mail losses. The Swedish Line put up its fund of $4,000,000 representing the value of the *Stockholm* after the collision voyage and the Italian Line put up its fund of $1,800,000, representing $60 per gross ton of the 30,000-ton *Andrea Doria*. The two steamship lines agreed to pool these funds and to co-operate in settling out of court the approximately 1,200 third-party claims. It was believed at the time that all these suits could be settled within the limits of the $5,800,000 combined funds. Any costs beyond the funds would be shared equally. An integral part of the settlement agreement was that its terms were to remain secret and that there would be no assessment of blame upon either the *Stockholm* or *Andrea Doria*.

The secrecy provision of the agreement soon broke down because of the large number of persons necessarily a party to it and the vigilance of the press toward a front-page story. On January 24, the two steamship lines announced in open court before Judge Walsh that a settlement between them had been reached and that they would co-operate in negotiating a settlement of each and every third-party claim.

Judge Walsh congratulated both the Italian and Swedish-American Lines and their counsel for ending the case in less than six months from the date of the collision. They had set a speed record for settlement of a major admiralty case.

Lawyers for both lines worked for another two years in investigating and settling the 1,200 damage claims for deaths, personal injuries, and baggage, property and cargo losses involving both ships. The final total figure for all third-party claims came to a sum approximating the combined liability funds of $5,800,000.

The Swedish Government announced meanwhile that it would hold no inquiry into the sea disaster. It said through its proper authorities that the testimony at the New York hearings had been reviewed in Sweden and no cause had been found warranting criminal prosecution against any of the *Stockholm* crew for negligence in handling the ship.

The Italian Government had appointed a special commission of maritime experts who over the course of a full year interviewed each and every one of the 572-man crew of the *Andrea Doria*. The conclusions of that commission have not yet been made public.

Since the end of the New York hearings the *Stockholm*, outfitted with a new bow in the Bethlehem Steel Shipyard in Brooklyn, is still sailing the same route between Gothenburg, Copenhagen and New York. The *Andrea Doria* lies on her side on the bottom of the North Atlantic some fifty miles south of Nantucket Island, a tempting challenge to men who dream of bringing the luxury liner back to the surface.

The Swedish Line, in a bold demonstration of its confidence in its men, rewarded Captain Nordenson and Third Officer Carstens-Johannsen by immediately assigning them to the new flagship of its White Viking Fleet, the 23,500-ton *Gripsholm*, which had been built in Italy at a cost of $14,000,000.

Captain Nordenson commanded the new *Gripsholm* from her maiden voyage across the North Atlantic in May, 1957, to June, 1958, when he retired upon reaching the mandatory retirement age of sixty-five. Carstens, promoted from junior to senior third mate, continued on the *Gripsholm* until later in 1958, when with the vestiges of the collision stigma apparently still in the air, he left the Swedish-American Line to sail as chief mate on a small freighter of the Brostrom Concern.

While the other officers and men of the *Andrea Doria* were reassigned to other ships, Captain Calamai never sailed again. He was kept on the active rolls of the Italian Line in Genoa until he reached the mandatory retirement age of sixty. Then in December, 1957, without having been given command of another ship, he was quietly retired. It is extremely doubtful whether Captain Calamai, after his tragic experience, would have accepted command of another ship if it had been offered. He had expressed his views on one

303

occasion after the collision when he said, "When I was a boy, and all my life, I loved the sea; now I hate it."

The *Andrea Doria–Stockholm* collision probably will have repercussions for many years. It has already brought about several changes toward the safer operation of ships. The Swedish-American Line not long after the collision assigned two officers instead of one to every bridge watch. Radar manufacturers pushed the development of a new type of radar, one which showed the true motion instead of relative position of other ships. One of the first true-motion radar sets sold, one which gave a real bird's-eye view of all ships and objects around in true perspective, was installed on the Swedish Line's new *Gripsholm*. Virtually all maritime nations have increased the training of maritime officers in the proper use of radar, and Great Britain has taken the lead in making a certificate of proficiency in the use of radar a prerequisite for obtaining an officer's license in the merchant marine.

The *Andrea Doria* disaster, above all, has led to the widespread demand among maritime experts for another convention of the major seafaring nations to modernize the laws of the sea.

Real reform can come only through another International Conference for Safety of Life at Sea at which the maritime nations of the world can hammer out by treaty agreement new laws designed to reduce the chances of another *Andrea Doria–Stockholm* collision. Maritime experts are agreed that the calling of a fourth Conference is overdue. Various agencies of the United States Government, such as the Coast Guard and Navy, are preparing proposals for such a meeting, as are other nations.

While it is easy to recite needed reforms, it is indeed difficult to propose new uniform laws for shipping which would be acceptable to some thirty-odd different and sovereign nations, each of which has the prerogative of signing or not signing treaty agreements. But just as the sinking of the *Titanic* in 1912 led to the first International Conference which set the first standards of stability for ships, required the use of radio and prescribed the number of lifeboats to be carried, so the sinking of the *Andrea Doria* must necessarily lead to new laws governing the use of radar, higher stability standards and some kind of practical enforcement of the laws of the sea.

The next Conference must come to grips with the question of whether radar should or should not relieve the master of a ship from the present requirement of reducing speed in fog so as to be able to stop his ship in half the distance of visibility. The present law certainly is violated with the impunity which characterized Prohibition in the United States, and perhaps the time has come for its repeal. An alternative would be to permit a ship equipped with radar to continue at full speed in fog so long as it maneuvers to keep at least five miles away from any other ship at all times. A five-mile safety margin (or six or seven miles, if need be), rigidly enforced, would do more to prevent collisions in the open sea than the current practice of ships passing one another with only one mile separating them, allowing no room for error.

While changing any of the Rules of the Road is a complex problem involving considerable study, there seems little reason why the next Conference could not require every deck officer to use his ship's radar properly, something radar experts claim is not done by more than 90 per cent of navigators. This would make the plotting of relative-motion radar observations mandatory under law. At present, there is in reality no law governing the use of radar. The 1948 Conference decided that radar then was too recent an innovation to be the subject of binding regulations—but that was eight years before the collision of the *Andrea Doria* and *Stockholm*.

United States authorities no doubt will press at the next Conference, as they did at the last, for higher stability requirements for passenger ships, matching those in this country. While it is physically possible to build an absolutely unsinkable ship by intense compartmentalization, that extreme must be reconciled with the need for passenger comfort and the high cost of building such a ship. Some compromise must be found between the truly unsinkable ship and the feasible, profitable passenger liner which private companies would be willing to build and operate.

Yet whatever success there be in this regard, the next Conference must face the question of how to enforce its stability requirements. Strangely enough, at present each country administers the stability code of the Conference, and in nations such as Italy, where the shipping industry has been nationalized, this means that the government, which is the shipowner, passes upon the standards of construction of each of its own ships.

For the safety of the 50,000 men, women and children who are estimated to be traveling daily on the North Atlantic, an international agency, perhaps under the United Nations, must be empowered to pass upon the design, construction and stability of all passenger liners. Every passenger ship also should be subject to periodic checks as to its construction, ballasting, watertight compartments and doors, its alarm systems, lifeboats and other items bearing upon the safety of its passengers. Whether or not foreign nations and shipowners would submit to such international supervision is another question. But if they refused, it would seem that the United States could then argue for the right to pass upon all construction stability matters which bear upon the safety of American citizens, who constitute the majority of passengers on ships that ply the North Atlantic.

Mandatory sea lanes across the North Atlantic is another problem for the experts to solve, if possible. Any acceptable solution would have to rearrange the present recommended tracks to allow Scandinavian and northern-bound vessels to use the northern-most (and shortest) route across the Atlantic, shifting English Channel and Mediterranean-bound ships to a more southerly and longer route. This is indeed a most difficult problem in logistics, but for any solution to be of any value, the new routes must be binding upon all ocean-going ships, which are not subject now to any track agreement, for cargo ships and oil tankers are as liable to cause collisions as are passenger vessels.

To correct the total lack of enforcement of the rules of safety on the high seas will require the highest statesmanship at the next Conference. While airplanes, railroads, buses and even automobiles are governed by policing agencies, there is no one with the authority to compel sea captains to obey the basic precepts of prudent seamanship. Court action after a collision or shipwreck hardly provides preventive law enforcement. This could be accomplished by an agency established within the United Nations, but only if the thirty-odd maritime nations of the world consented to relinquish that much of their sovereignty. Ships could be required at little expense to carry motion picture cameras which continuously photograph radar observations. The film could be checked periodically by the UN agency as a monitor insuring good seamanship and, in the event of an accident at sea, the film would serve as convincing proof of who is to blame. Yet it must be recognized that captains will not readily agree to carrying aboard their ships such telltale cameras, which have been available and not used for many years.

In the light of the *Andrea Doria–Stockholm* disaster, the next International Conference will no doubt wish to review the efficacy of present-day lifeboat operations, loudspeaker systems, abandon-ship plans and a host of other questions.

There can be no doubt that new laws are needed to make ship construction and operation safer. Lloyd's of London has published statistics showing that an average of nearly three ships a day collide throughout the world—or more than 1,000 ships, each of more than 500 gross tons, a year. In addition, it has been conservatively estimated that there are about three "near misses" a day, in which ships narrowly avoid collision by emergency last-minute action.

Yet there remains a limit to what any law, rule or regulation can do to reduce the risk involved in any means of travel. The primary responsibility for safety of life at sea remains, where it has always been, with the navigator on the bridge of each and every ship.

It would be remiss not to point out the obvious: travel on the modern ocean liner is by far the safest means of mass transportation in the world today. The collision of the *Andrea Doria* and the *Stockholm* was the first such disaster in history involving two passenger liners. It broke a peacetime safety record dating back to the end of the first World War. The Trans-Atlantic Passenger Conference, an association of passenger shipowners, points out that in the peacetime years since 1919, regular passenger ships carried approximately 27,000,000 persons across the North Atlantic without losing or injuring a single passenger because of collision or shipwreck. This adds up statistically to 81,000,000,000 passenger miles without such an injury or fatality.

Thus, with the statistics of Lloyd's of London and those of the Trans-Atlantic Passenger Conference at hand, one can only speculate on the likelihood of another *Andrea Doria–Stockholm* type of disaster. Circumstances and carelessness may combine tomorrow, or not for a generation, or perhaps never again, to bring about another improbable but possible collision in the open waters of the North Atlantic. One cannot foretell.

Chapter Sixteen

SALVAGING THE *DORIA*

Twenty-five years later, the *Andrea Doria* lies quiescent, still settling down in her briny grave upon the sandy bottom of the North Atlantic some fifty-three miles southeast of Nantucket Island. The fatal forty-foot wound in her starboard side is beneath her and out of sight, covered now with three or four feet of sand and silt.

But in all those years, the *Andrea Doria* has not been forgotten. At considerable risk to their own lives, teams of underwater explorers have dived down 200 and 240 feet in search of whatever they could find out about the luxurious Italian liner. Men have planned and plotted and dreamed of bringing the ship back to the surface for all to see again, or, short of that, of salvaging the treasures buried aboard her.

In the busy shipping lane leading to and from New York, ships pass over her grave every day. There is not a navigational officer who does not personally recall or know about the sea disaster of our time, of the *Andrea Doria* and the *Stockholm*. A good many navigational charts are still marked with a tiny red X to note the site where the *Andrea Doria* went down. And yet, with all that open sea around them, with all the lessons that should have been learned, the officers of other ships continue to disregard collision courses—and time after time they pay the consequences.

I sailed aboard the *Stockholm* in the spring of 1957, shortly after the ship had been repaired and returned to service, and once again the *Stockholm* found herself on a collision course. It was the first night out of New York, approaching the Nantucket Lightship once again. Dessert and coffee were being served in the dining room when the *Stockholm* suddenly shuddered and rumbled, like a heavy truck bouncing on wet cobblestones with the brakes applied. None of the other passengers seemed aware of the tell-tale signs. But the waiters knew. One could not resist rushing to a porthole to peer out into the black night.

The following night, taking an after-dinner brandy with the captain and other passengers in the lounge, I leaned over and whispered in his ear: "Did you reverse engines last night?"

"Yes," he replied softly. "I'll tell you about it later."

In his cabin the next morning, Captain Nordenson confided in me: At a distance of about twelve miles, a ship was sighted on radar, its course and speed plotted on the radarscope, traveling at nineteen knots on a reciprocal course, head-on or nearly head-on, to the *Stockholm*. Captain Nord-

enson called for a course change to starboard for a safer
passing. He had one of his officers plot the course of the
other ship again. They were still on a collision course. He
ordered a clearly perceptible twenty-degree change of course
to the right. He plotted again. The two ships were still on a
collision course. He could hardly believe this was happening.
The other ship was turning to its *left*. That was contrary to
all the Rules of the Road, contrary to even the rudiments
of good seamanship, contrary to anything sensible under the
circumstances. Captain Nordenson ordered a third, more
radical change of course to starboard. He plotted the other
ship on radar and had visions of the *Andrea Doria*. It seemed
to him as if the whole disaster was being played out again.
The unknown ship bearing down upon him had changed its
course further to port. They were still on a collision course.
In the dead of night when the lights of the other ship hove
into sight, Captain Nordenson, a calm man under most circumstances, shouted out his order: "Hard starboard rudder!
Full astern!"

The *Stockholm* rumbled and shook with the sudden re-
versing of the engines. Her bow swung sharply to the right.
At the end of her turn, the Swedish liner had come completely around, 180 degrees, and was heading back to New
York. The other ship slipped by within a quarter-mile of the
Stockholm. Then she was gone, gobbled up in the blackness
of the night. Captain Nordenson speculated that the other
ship was a freighter. More than that, he did not know. It
had been a near miss, a near catastrophe. If there had been
a disaster, who would believe Captain Nordenson's tale of
another collision at sea?

On my return from Europe aboard the Italian liner *Conte
Biancamano*, I asked an officer on the bridge how the radar

worked. He replied innocently that you could see the blip of another ship on the radar screen and trace its course in your mind's eye. No, he said, there was no need to plot the positions of the other ship on the graph. That was unnecessary work. On the second day out, I asked my room steward if I absolutely had to go to the lifeboat- and abandon-ship drills. "Oh, no, sir," he replied with a conspiratorial grin, "Just stay out of the way of the officers."

Just ten days after *Collision Course* was published (on March 16, 1959), the newest and most luxurious of the Grace Line's cruise ships, the *Santa Rosa*, smashed into the superstructure of the 10,000-ton oil tanker *Valchem*. It was three o'clock in the morning with variable fog in the North Atlantic, twenty-two miles due east of Atlantic City, New Jersey, and seventy-five miles south of the tip of Manhattan. Another collision on the open sea. Four crewmen aboard the *Valchem* were killed. I was assigned to cover the Coast Guard investigatory hearings as a reporter for The Associated Press. Once again I heard the same tale of woe and human error as I had observed in the *Andrea Doria–Stockholm* pretrial hearings.

The $25 million luxury liner, heading back from a Caribbean cruise to New York City with 247 passengers and a crew of 265 aboard was speeding in fog. At FULL SPEED AHEAD, her two giant steam turbine engines were turning her twin propellers 118 revolutions per minute. The *Santa Rosa* was making 21.5 knots through the water. Captain Frank Siwik, who had twenty-nine years' experience at sea, all with the Grace Line, had been called to the bridge when visibility became low. The radar was turned to the six-mile range as the *Santa Rosa* maneuvered to overtake a slower freighter, also bound for New York. No one bothered to switch the radar back to the customary sixteen-mile range. So, when another ship was spotted on the radar, at a distance of about five miles, the second mate on watch had time to plot only *two* sightings. He could see that the other ship was heading towards the *Santa Rosa*. With their combined speeds, the two ships were closing fast. Thick fog was settling down upon them. Visibility was reduced to about one-half mile. Captain Siwik called for a slight turn to port, to the *left* in anticipation of a starboard-to-starboard passing. Then he called for another turn to port, a slight one. And then another. But all this time no one aboard the *Santa Rosa* knew or could know that the other ship was turning to its starboard for a port-to-port passing. The second mate would have had to take three sightings of the other ship and plot them out on his maneuvering board in order to see that the other ship was turning—and turning toward the *Santa Rosa*. But there was no time for this. When the other ship hove into sight, less than half a mile away, it was too late. Captain Siwik saw the lights of the ship as she was crossing his bow. He cried out, "Hard right!" The second mate rang up FULL SPEED ASTERN on the engine telegraph. But a ship does not have the brakes of a car.

The *Santa Rosa* sliced into the left side of the aft superstructure housing of the *Valchem*, just forty feet ahead of the stern. The liner's bow cut more than halfway through the tanker's boiler room and crew's quarters. Two crewmen, asleep in their bunks, were killed upon impact. Another was swept overboard and lost. A fourth was pulled out of the wreckage and flown by a Coast Guard helicopter to a hospital in Jersey City. He died enroute. Minutes after the collision, the *Santa Rosa* lowered eleven of her lifeboats and picked up seventeen crewmen of the tanker who had fallen or jumped overboard. The *Valchem*, adrift in the water, fortunately was not loaded with oil. Having delivered her cargo in Jersey City, she had been enroute to Texas in ballast. If the *Valchem* had had oil aboard, both ships could have been engulfed in a raging fire that would have taken more lives than had been lost on the *Andrea Doria*.

Human error was also blamed for the collision between the American Export liner *Constitution* and the Norwegian freighter *Jalanta* just outside New York Harbor on March 1, 1959. Once again it was FULL SPEED AHEAD in dense fog. Captain James W. La Belle told the Coast Guard hearing that he was relying upon his radar for safe passage, but he was not plotting the pips of other ships seen on his radar-scope. As the *Constitution*, coming from Newport News, Virginia, headed towards the mouth of New York Harbor, Captain La Belle noted on his radar that he was in a head-to-head situation with a ship leaving the harbor (which was the Norwegian freighter *Kingsville*, bound for Savannah, Georgia). For a safer port-to-port passing, Captain La Belle ordered a 20° turn to starboard.

The *Constitution* ran right into another ship, the *Jalanta*, which Captain La Belle had not seen at all. The *Constitution* hit with such force that it sliced off part of the *Jalanta*'s bow. Captain La Belle was found at fault for his failure to search. Without plotting *all* the pips on his radar scope, there was no way he could tell what other ships were doing in the area. Despite his thirty-two years at sea, the captain had no defense. He was charged by the Coast Guard with negligence, his master's license was suspended for one year.

The *Andrea Doria-Stockholm* disaster, if it did nothing else, convinced just about every shipping company of the need for every one of its watch officers to be trained in the proper use of radar. New radar schools were opened in the United States and in most major seafaring nations of the world. In the United States, a man had to complete a radar course before he could qualify to stand a watch on the bridge. As a result, we now have a whole generation of navigators who have never sailed a major ship without radar. Radar is recognized today as the biggest advance in navigation since the chronometer. At the 1960 International Conference for Safety of Life at Sea, the delegates tried to legislate the proper use of radar in navigation. It was not an easy task. To a limited extent, for the first time, radar was recognized in international law as a valid instrument of navigation, extending the eyesight of seamen on watch. But it was not until the next International Conference, in 1972, that important and major clarifications of the Rules of the Road, as they applied to the use of radar, were actually put into international law.

The new Rule 19 provides that in restricted visibility "a vessel which detects by radar alone the presence of another vessel shall determine if a close-quarters situation is developing and/or risk of collision exists. If so, she shall take avoiding action in ample time. . ." With this new rule, there was now no mistaking that maritime law required ships using radar, which included virtually all major ships at sea, to take early and positive action to avoid collisions or even the risk of collisions. With the use of radar, ships were allowed to proceed at a "safe speed," rather than the previous "moderate speed," so long as navigators obeyed all the other rules of the roads in avoiding collisions. In effect, the new rules were saying to all captains: If you use radar, you can proceed at a "safe speed" in fog, obeying all the other rules. If you did not use radar, a legally defined "moderate speed"

317

in dense fog might well oblige you to stop dead in the water in dense fog.

Despite the new navigational rules, despite the new and more sophisticated technology in radar and other aids to navigation, despite the improved training of ship officers, down through the years, ships of all sizes, shapes and configurations have continued to collide with one another in the open sea and upon inland waters. In 1979, the Norwegian oil tanker *Team Castor* and the Liberian flag tanker *Gino* smashed into one another off the coast of Brittany, France. The *Gino* sank, spilling much of her 40,000 tons of oil into the Atlantic. Another 10,000 tons of oil were lost when the tanker *Fortune,* collided with the U.S. aircraft carrier *Ranger* in the South China Sea. Two Japanese tankers, the *Miya Maru 8* and the *Daikoku Maru 18,* collided in Japan's Inland Sea and fouled the waters with 540 tons of crude oil. With the increased oil transport industry of recent years, tanker collisions, some major and some minor, are an almost common occurrence, numbering more than a thousand in each year of the last decade.

In 1980, the U.S. Coast Guard suffered its own worst sea tragedy. On January 28, at 6 P.M., the 180-foot Coast Guard buoy tender *Blackthorn* set out in Tampa Bay, Florida, for a return voyage to her home port of Galveston, Texas, following a routine month-long overhaul in a Tampa shipyard. The night was clear and moonlit. Traffic in the bay was not particularly heavy. And yet, as the buoy tender passed under the Sunshine Skyway, an extraordinarily long bridge which spanned the bay, no one on the Coast Guard ship's bridge, including her captain, Lieutenant Commander George Sepel, apparently saw the navigational lights of the 605-ton tanker *Capricorn,* steaming down the deep water channel leading into the bay. The *Blackthorn* was attempting to cut across the channel into open water. The tanker, expecting the *Blackthorn* to turn into the channel, maintained the course and speed for which she had the right of way. The *Blackthorn* smashed into the big tanker at an angle, portside to portside, with such force that the 180-foot buoy tender flipped over and sank to the bottom of the bay within a minute or two. Twenty-seven Coast Guardsmen were fished out of the black water; twenty-three men went down with the ship.

In another remarkable first, in heavy seas in the dead of night off the southern tip of Japan, the most technologically advanced and sophisticated of ships, the U.S. nuclear submarine *George Washington,* traveling beneath the surface, rammed into a small Japanese freighter, the *Nissho Maru,* and sent her to the bottom of the Japan Sea. The captain and the first mate were lost at sea. No one aboard the *Nissho Maru* had the slightest warning of the approach of a submarine. The collision became an international incident when it was reported that the *George Washington* "hit and ran." The U. S. Navy did not acknowledge its submarine's involvement in the sinking for a full thirty-six hours after the collision. It also touched off an international politically embarrassing question as to what a nuclear-armed American submarine was doing in Japanese waters.

As for the collision itself, human error was to blame once again. Few details were made public, but as reconstructed by knowledgeable maritime experts, a great many different innocent factors combined to bring about the disaster. Each factor alone was understandable; combined they led to catastrophe. The *George Washington* apparently was traveling beneath the surface at great speed, probably twenty knots or more, because a nuclear submarine is a very uncomfortable, rolling ship when cruising on the surface. At that speed, a sub's periscope vibrates so much that it is useless for sighting other ships. At high speed, the sub's sonar is unreliable because of the noise of the sub's own propellers. So, as a matter of practicality, the usual technique for cruising a nuclear submarine at full speed underwater is to surface every thirty minutes or so, take a quick radar check to determine that the way is clear, and then to dive and cruise on underwater for another half-hour—blindly.

From the extent of the damage reported, it is clear that the *George Washington* was proceeding at considerable speed. When the top of her conning tower hit the Japanese freighter, she probably lost the use of most of her navigational aides: her periscope, radar, loran, upper steering station, searchlights and her radio antenna. Surfacing after the collision, she might well have been a half or a full mile away from the sinking freighter. There would be no way the sub's crew, using only hand flashlights, could see any of the Japanese seamen in the water, or their ship, on a dark, foggy night at sea. Only the following morning could the captain of the *George Washington* have had the sub's radio antenna repaired so that he could report in.

Thus, as reconstructed, there was little under the circumstances that the *George Washington*'s crew could have done that they did not do. They did not purposely leave other seamen to drown after the accident. Nevertheless, it is clear in admiralty law that a submarine, any submarine, is the "burden" vessel in any collision. After all, surface vessels in peace time can hardly be expected to steer clear of submerged submarines they cannot see. The U.S. Navy accepted full responsibility for the collision. The officer of the watch aboard the *George Washington* was given a severe reprimand; the captain was relieved of his command.

There is, in short, no cure for human error at sea. Accidents occur again and again in all modes of transportation and in all walks of life. Almost all of them are the results of human error. It is man who is imperfectible. Ship collisions are seen as particularly extraordinary because they are just that—unexpected and extraordinary. With the thousands of ships at sea every day, it is remarkable that ships at sea are as safe as they are.

There is little likelihood of there ever being another collision at sea like that of the *Andrea Doria* and the *Stockholm*. The day of the transatlantic luxury ocean liner is past. In the years that the *Doria* and the *Stockholm* sailed in and out of New York, there were sixty-one passenger ships plying the North Atlantic, carrying some fifty thousand passengers at any one time. Now, only the *Queen Elizabeth 2* of the Cunard Line makes regular crossings—and then only during the summer months. Once, it had been a way of life to travel to Europe or to New York on a Cunard, French, Scandinavian, Italian, or American liner—a bit of elegance, a special adventure, a voyage to be remembered and cherished. Today's generation knows nothing of that bygone age; few if any have ever seen those behemoth floating palaces, much less travel aboard one of them. They are gone —not because of any collisions at sea or similar disasters. They are gone because they had become too expensive to operate (largely due to the increased cost of fuel), because they were too slow, because people no longer have the leisure time to spend five or six days crossing the Atlantic. Jet engine and supersonic aircraft now cover the distance in a matter of hours rather than days. The luxury ocean liner

321

has been relegated to the role of a floating hotel, with her gourmet dining rooms, fashionable cocktail bars, nightclubs, and dancing salons—going nowhere in particular in what is euphemistically called a cruise. These sailings are strictly designed for rest, relaxation, and romance.

In such an economic climate the transatlantic liners could not survive. They became deficit ridden and soon were sold off, briefly as cruise ships and then for scrap metal. The Italian Line discontinued sending any of its ships to the United States. The *Cristoforo Colombo,* sister ship of the *Andrea Doria,* has been sold for scrap. The *Ile de France* has been junked in Japan. The Brostrom Concern sold the *Stockholm* to East German interests, and they, in turn, after cruising the small liner between Colombia and Venezuela for some years, sold her to a Japanese company, which reduced the ship to scrap iron and steel. In 1975, after a long and bitter dispute with Swedish unions over transferring its passenger ships to the Panamanian flag for economic reasons, the Brostrom Concern simply dissolved the entire Swedish-American Line, sold off the *Kungsholm* and the *Gripsholm,* and went out of the passenger line business.

America's ocean liners fared no better. The *United States,* which had been the pride of this country's transatlantic passenger fleet since 1952, was decommissioned in 1969 and laid in mothballs in Norfolk, Virginia, for twelve years. Then in 1981, she was converted to a cruise ship for service between the West Coast and Hawaii. The *Independence,* of the American Export Line, was bought by C. Y. Tung, the Chinese shipping magnate, and refitted as a cruise ship between San Francisco and Honolulu.

With so many of the other ships of that era gone, it is the *Andrea Doria* that has remained alive in the memory and imagination of those who cherish ships. The *Andrea Doria-Stockholm* collision was such an unexpected and spectacular event that people old enough at the time remember well where they were and what they were doing when they first heard the news. For those whose lives are associated with the sea, especially the men in the diving and salvage business, the *Andrea Doria* remains tantalizingly close—just fifty-odd miles off shore and reachable in thirty-three fathoms of water.

For twenty-five years, deep-sea salvage experts and aficionados have pondered the problem of how to raise the 29,000-ton Italian liner from the depths. A little more than twenty-four hours after the sinking, Peter Gimbel, the twenty-eight-year-old son of the head of the Gimbel Department Store chain, was the first man to dive down to the *Andrea Doria.* An amateur scuba diver at the time, with six years' diving experience behind him, Gimbel swam down to the sunken ship, accompanied by another amateur diver, Joseph Fox, and photographed the ship lying on her starboard side upon the coarse yellow sand of the ocean's bottom.

The *Doria* looked like a carefully embalmed corpse, stretched out upon her right side, her slender bow up off the ocean floor, her forty-foot-wide wound hidden beneath her, as though she were just resting there, unhurt, in pristine condition, her paint and decks still gleaming, her overall appearance still luxurious, still beautiful.

How to raise her? That was the question.

Obviously, she was too big, too heavy, to be hauled up to the surface like some playboy's sunken yacht. What kind of cables or chains could lift a 29,000-ton ocean liner? What kind of winches could handle that weight? What size ship or ships could you have on the surface from which to operate the winches and cables? The standard method for salvaging large ships is to send divers down to her, to seal off her openings, or most of them, and then force the sea water out of her sealed compartments by pumping in compressed air until she floats back to the surface. That is the textbook theory. As a practical matter, no ship of the size and weight of the *Andrea Doria,* or even half her size, has ever been salvaged from that depth.

But that has been the real challenge for salvage experts around the world: Salvage the *Andrea Doria* and you can demonstrate with worldwide publicity your ability to refloat hundreds of valuable ships with all of their sunken treasures from the briny deep. Anyone who could devise a practical method of raising a major vessel from a depth of one hundred feet or more would capture a very lucrative market of deep sea salvage. The *Bon Homme Richard,* a flagship of John Paul Jones, sunk during the Revolutionary War, has been located in 180 feet of water in the North Sea, off the coast of England, waiting to be raised. The Civil War's famous old ironclad, U.S.S. *Monitor,* has been found and filmed on the bottom of the Atlantic off Cape Hatteras, North Carolina, in 220 feet of water, but no one has figured out how to raise her. Then there are the ships sunk during World War II, reputedly carrying vast war treasures to the bottom of the sea. One of them is the Japanese *Awa Maru,* which went down in 185 feet of water in the Formosa Strait with a cargo of diamonds and gold plundered from occupied territories, said to be worth more than $500 million.

The salvage value of the *Andrea Doria* has ranged over a wide spectrum of figures, including such wild schemes as converting the huge steel hull into millions of highly polished steel cuff links to be sold as souvenirs to an eager public. Actually, the Italian government and the insurance underwriters who paid for the insured portion of the ship have looked into every feasible way to recoup their losses. Once the court case was settled, they invited confidential bids for the salvage value of the Italian liner, and they also gathered estimates on the feasibility and the costs of attempting to raise the ship. The results were so disappointing that they were never announced. The Italian government and the insurers abandoned any hope of raising and selling off the one-time flagship of the Italian Line. The cost of attempting to raise the ship was prohibitive. The bids on buying the ship, if she were raised, were too low to warrant even an attempt at salvage.

This did not stop others from making and announcing plans to raise the *Andrea Doria*. They cropped up in the news from all over the world and from all walks of life. Fill the ship with Ping Pong balls and she'll float to the top. That was one of the very first plans. A former navy captain in Detroit announced a scheme to float the *Andrea Doria* by pumping 2,500 tons of liquid plastic into the ship through its portholes. The plastic, lighter than water, would instantly solidify and the *Andrea Doria* would float gently to the top. Then all he would have to do was to close off the hole in the side of the ship, cut away the plastic, and the *Doria* would be as good as new. This method has been used to salvage downed Navy aircraft, but is considered impractical for refloating ships which are so much larger and heavier.

A Canadian salvage group announced that it had a secret chemical that it would add to the oxygen given to divers which would enable them to work under the great depths of water for longer than normal—an hour or more—but no

325

one said what the divers would do underwater to raise the *Doria*. A team of four Italian divers, headed by a television producer, announced plans in 1968 to raise the *Doria* and actually made two dives to the ship before they gave up and were heard from no more. An entrepreneur in Coney Island, New York, built a homemade forty-foot submarine, with which he said he would work on refloating the *Andrea Doria*, but the little submarine itself almost sank upon launching in 1970. Because it is so dangerous and so expensive to have deep-sea divers working at such depths, there have been various schemes to work on the *Andrea Doria* from the confines of a miniature submarine equipped with robot arms or tentacles. But no one, as yet, has been able to devise such a submarine.

The most grandiose scheme for raising the *Doria* was promulgated by a New Jersey salvage company, financed by a wholesale liquor dealer. His idea was to raise the *Doria* by slipping four-inch-thick steel cables beneath her hull and attaching the cables to two giant Great Lakes iron ore ships. The ore ships would be flooded with sea water until they were partially submerged; the cables would be tightened; the sea water pumped out of the ore ships so that they would rise to the surface, pulling up the *Doria* from the bottom. Once free, the *Doria* would be towed beneath the water some eighteen miles to the South Davis shoal, where divers could more easily repair the stricken liner. No one, however, explained how those steel cables would be slipped under the huge ship or the odds against successfully lifting and towing a 29,000-ton ship submerged through the treacherous crosscurrents and rough seas off Nantucket. The attempt was never made.

To raise the *Andrea Doria* is not technically impossible.

It is only that no one as yet has figured out a way to do it that would have a reasonable chance of success and at reasonable expense. Any single one of the problems relating to a salvage operation—the heavy seas, the exasperating currents beneath the water, the heavy fog, the uncertain weather, the pressure at that depth of water, plus the size of the ship, the forty-foot hole in its side, and the many openings in the interior of the ship itself—poses a considerable obstacle, but combined they virtually insure defeat. It would require many divers to seal off the seventeen interior stairways, the open portholes, and finally that forty-foot wound. And there is just not enough room down there for that many men working at one time. They would get in each other's way. These are only the most obvious obstacles facing anyone attempting to salvage the ship. There are, according to the experts, many other technological barriers. And then there is the stumbling block of money. . . .

All of the plans, practical and otherwise, have failed thus far because of the prohibitive cost of even making an *attempt*.

The best estimates from experienced salvage firms for refloating the *Andrea Doria*—with no guarantee of success—range from $3 million to $6 million; to repair and refit her "in class" so that she could sail again would cost another $6 million to $12 million. What would the *Andrea Doria* really be worth if all that were done? No more than $9 million. So, at the very best, one could hope only to break even. That was why the Italian government and the ship's insurance underwriters decided to leave the luxury liner where she lay. More than $11 million was spent to salvage the French liner *Normandie* after she was devastated by fire and sank at her pier in New York in 1942. And the *Normandie* went down in only forty feet of perfectly calm water. A goodly number of people have invested their money over the years in various attempts to salvage the *Doria*, intrigued with the exaggerated stories of treasures, prizes, and fame, and they, in a manner of speaking, have come up with nothing.

The one man who has been consulted on the subject more than anyone else has been Captain Bruno J. Augenti, a salvage expert for more than forty years who was a key technical consultant during the U.S. court hearings on the collision. Augenti has done all he could ever since to dissuade men from undertaking any attempt to salvage the *Andrea Doria*. He has turned away several would-be salvagers with a stern warning: "If you solicit funds to salvage the *Andrea Doria*, I will report you to the District Attorney for attempted fraud." Augenti, a former submarine officer in the Italian Navy insists: "The value of the *Andrea Doria* will not justify the expense of the salvage." Twenty-five years after the sinking, this feisty sea captain, who loved the *Andrea Doria*, has not changed his mind: "As far as I am concerned, I do not know of any new technology to do the task."

Short of bringing the *Andrea Doria* back up, the next best thing was to go down to her and retrieve her treasures. Divers have gone down to the *Doria* alone and in pairs and in groups of four, some with elaborate support systems, others on a strictly adventurous scuba dive to the most glamorous wreck within reach. Over the years, more legends have come up from the depths than riches. There was said to be more than $1 million in cash in the safe and a cache of personal jewelry in safe deposit boxes in the First Class Purser's Office on the Foyer Deck. There was more cash and jewelry in the Cabin Class Purser's Office further aft on that deck. There was a bag of industrial diamonds somewhere on

328

the ship. There were stories of diamonds and gold in various passenger cabins. There was a solid silver plaque, estimated at a quarter of a million dollars, in the First Class Foyer, and other silver plaques still adorning the walls in various other public rooms. There were oil paintings and sculptures still worth a fortune. And souvenirs. A place setting from an *Andrea Doria* dining room was said to be worth at least $5,000 on the collector's market. And the china. And the wine cellar. And . . . Estimates of the potential retrievable treasures ran from $2 million to $4 million. And, it was all down there—for the taking.

But that is the stuff of which legends are made. It is all within the realm of possibility. Personal jewelry and cash and whatever contraband a passenger might have carried aboard would not appear on the ship's manifest. However, according to the *Doria's* pursers and the insurers and the lawyers involved, there is nothing *known* of jewelry, cash or other valuables approaching the million dollar mark. No one has put in an insurance claim for any such remarkable treasure lost aboard the ship. The highest personal property loss claim paid was for $100,000 for unstrung pearls in the First Class Purser's vault. In all there were 3,222 claims filed for losses aboard the *Andrea Doria*. That included claims for the losses of life, personal injury, cargo losses, seamen's claims for their losses and 1,134 passenger claims for the loss of personal effects. While these claims may have added up to $85 million, they were all settled for a total of $5,877,399. Thus, the average single insurance payment came to a mere $1,800. That is hardly a figure in which a treasure can be hidden.

The Italian Line and the Italian government, along with the insurance underwriters, looked very closely into the question of what had been lost aboard the ship. At the Italian hearings, the pursers who had served on that last voyage of the *Doria* testified that, as far as they knew, virtually all the passengers had taken their valuables out of their safe deposit boxes before the collision. The previous night had been the traditional next-to-last night at sea, celebrated with the gala Captain's Night dinners and parties. It was the "dress-up" occasion of the voyage and women had worn their finest jewelry and clothes on that night. The festivities had continued until about 2 A.M., long after the pursers' offices had closed for the night. So, no one could return any jewelry that night and the pursers told the court that they could not recall anyone returning valuables to their vaults the next day. Purser Emilio Bertini said that he remembered that only one safety deposit box in the First Class Purser's Office was still in use at the time of the collision. He had noticed, he said, women having difficulties lowering themselves off the ship by way of the rope ladders because they were still clutching their purses and handbags while climbing down. Most of the passengers were in their cabins at the time of the collision and would have been expected to have taken their valuables with them upon leaving the ship. Most other passengers had had ample time to return to their cabins to retrieve their money or jewels before the general abandoning of the ship.

But legends die hard or not at all. Treasure hunters have tried to find their way to that First Class Purser's Office on the Foyer Deck and get into the safe there. None have succeeded thus far. Peter Gimbel on his first expedition down to the ship in 1956 sought only to photograph the doomed ocean liner. He succeeded so well that *Life* magazine ran his photographs and sponsored a more elaborate venture to photograph the ship in color the following year. By that time, Jacques Cousteau, the most famous underwater explorer in the world, made a dive to inspect the *Doria*. He emerged with the pronouncement that he would have nothing more to do with it. The underwater environs were too deep, too shark-infested and the currents made any future dives too tricky for safety and good health.

Deep-sea diving is a risky business at best. At the depth of the *Andrea Doria*, the water is blue-black and cold, visibility next to nil, and the temperature ranges from a numbing forty to forty-eight degrees. The pressure upon the human body is about six times greater than normal atmospheric pressure. Anyone scuba diving to the *Doria*, carrying his air supply in tanks upon his back, is limited to only about fifteen or twenty minutes underwater. The ship lies in about 240 feet of water and with its ninety-foot beam, the diver is at 150 feet when he reaches the uppermost part of the ship. The farther down he goes, the more dangerous it becomes and the longer he must spend in decompressing. Beyond a depth of one hundred feet, diving becomes dangerous. Only the most experienced and expert divers can venture down to two hundred feet and beyond. Over and beyond these difficulties, the *Doria* happens to lie at the cross section of about six different oceanic currents. The water is never calm there, on the surface or two hundred feet down. There are no regular tides, high, low or slack. The currents constantly swirl around at different speeds at different times of the day. They are never still. A diver must keep moving to stay in one place.

Gimbel had planned five or six dives to the *Doria* in the summer of 1957 to photograph what changes a year under the sea had wrought upon the luxury liner. Coming up from his second dive and decompressing some ten or twenty feet from the surface, he was attacked by a sleek, silver-blue, twelve-foot shark. It came in a straight, slow line for his belly. When the shark was about a foot from his body, Gimbel thrust his knife to the hilt into the shark's head. The shark swung about violently, reversed direction and swam away. Gimbel called off the remainder of his planned dives. The ship, one year after the sinking, still looked in remarkably good condition. Only close up could one see the slime, the barnacles, and the incrustations which had begun to adhere to the hull of the ship. The teakwood decks looked like new. Oil was still leaking somewhere from the innards of the ship's tanks. Tiny air bubbles still were escaping from some unseen closed areas.

Other divers explored the wreck as the years went on, and in 1964 two divers from Norfolk, Virginia—George Merchant and Denny Morse—came up with the first salvage prize from the ship, the four-hundred-pound bronze statue of Admiral Andrea Doria, which they had removed from the First Class Lounge. That feat alone took them fifty-four separate dives.

The most elaborate and serious attempt to get at and into the *Doria* was made in the summer of 1973 by a group of experienced divers from San Diego, California, who incorporated themselves under the name of Saturation Systems, Inc. They spent more than a year and a half and some $350,000 in preparing for their diving expedition. Rather than "bounce dive" to the ship and then decompress after each descent, these men designed and built a twelve-ton steel "habitat" which they took down and attached to the *Doria*. Equipped with food, beds, air, and communication lines to their surface ship, the twelve-by-five-foot chamber enabled two lead divers to remain underwater for as long as two weeks without having to go through the protracted periods of decompression. They called their underwater habitat "Mother." Two navy trained deep-sea divers, Don Rodocker and Chris DeLucci, worked inside the *Doria,* while a third diver, inside "Mother," handled the life and communication lines. Their plan was to reach those safe deposit boxes and the vault in the First Class Purser's Office, roam the ship for other treasures, and come home with $4 million in booty. They had carried the habitat three thousand miles cross-country on a flatbed truck, and then another eighty miles on a fishing trawler from Fairhaven, Massachusetts, to the site of the *Andrea Doria.* They spent twenty-three days at sea, an expedition of twenty-six people, and the principal divers spent five of those days cutting a four-foot-square hole through the hull so that they could directly reach the safe in the Purser's Office.

But seventeen years under water had taken its toll. The *Andrea Doria* was draped with huge nets ripped off fishing boats that were bottom fishing (most of them believed to be illegal Russian ships), and those tangled nets were still catching fish aboard the *Andrea Doria.* Moreover, it soon became obvious to the divers that once fish were caught in the nets, sharks were coming there almost regularly at night to feed off them. The outer hull of the *Doria,* swept by the currents, still was in good shape; the teak decks still showed no damage. But when the divers reached their goal and entered the Grand Foyer of the *Doria* they were appalled. The place was in shambles. The interior walls of the foyers and lounges, built of thin wood, were hanging askew from electrical wires; the plywood ceiling was drooping low, the floor was covered with rubble. There was no access to the

333

Purser's Office. It did not seem there was any Purser's Office left intact. Tons of debris covered the entire area of the safe and deposit boxes.

They roamed the ship and finally, in utter disappointment, they called it quits. Chris DeLucci's and Don Rodocker's accomplishment, however, was proving that with an underwater habitat like "Mother," they could spend 191.07 hours underwater and be brought back to the surface safely. It would point the way for future efforts. The only treasures they retrieved, however, for all their efforts, were a few badly worn silver-plate platters and one bottle of (very expensive) French perfume in good condition.

Two years later, Peter Gimbel returned to the *Andrea Doria,* backed up this time with the latest sophisticated diving equipment, and diving experts from International Underwater Contractors, one of the largest and most successful salvage companies in the world. It was to be an "in-depth" exploration of the *Doria,* an attempt to discover-on-the-spot evidence of why the presumably unsinkable ship had sunk. Underwritten and sponsored by the Xerox Corporation, the exploration was filmed and presented in color in a one-hour CBS television special in March, 1976.

On this exploration, Gimbel found the *Doria* to be no longer the gleaming, clean ship he had seen before. Now she presented what he called a "hostile environment," highly dangerous to anyone delving into her innards. The ship, still structurally in good condition, was swarming with fish of all kinds. Fishing nets torn from other ships were still strewn all over the ship's superstructure, trapping fish for marauding sharks; the steel hull was encrusted with barnacles and rust; the interior walls of the ship had collapsed, sea dust had settled upon everything inside the ship.

Gimbel tried to make his way down to the Engine Room to find "the missing door," but there were so many turns, so many stairways, and the way so dark and so deep, that he never got to the location he sought. He did, however, descend to the floor of the ocean in order to inspect the point of impact of the collision. He found there that the *Stockholm* had indeed, as suspected, ripped open the double bottom tanks as well as the deep fuel tanks at the point of impact. It helped explain why the *Doria* had taken that sudden and drastic list immediately after the collision.

Gimbel was not treasure hunting. He was exploring and filming his exploration as he moved through the ship. As such, his expedition was eminently successful because his television program, "The Mystery of the *Andrea Doria*," was unique: Never before had the public ever seen an ocean liner upon the floor of the Atlantic twenty years after a sea disaster that had shaken and intrigued the world.

As if to remind the world of the quarter century gone by, in July, 1981, one of the *Doria*'s portside lifeboats broke free of the mother ship, floated to the surface and made her way alone to New York. The forty-two-foot empty lifeboat drifted some two hundred miles to reach Staten Island, where she washed ashore at Consolidated Edison's generating plant in New York harbor. "It's a strange piece of sea history," commented Con Ed spokesman Larry Kleinman. "It got here by a happenstance of the tides, and it's weird."

On the date of the twenty-fifth anniversary of the sinking, July 26, 1981, Peter Gimbel set out once again to explore and film the wreck of the *Andrea Doria*. It had become an obsession with him. Swimming out of a diving bell anchored fifteen feet above the *Doria* and living in a pressurized habitat aboard a salvage ship, the *Sea Level 11*, Gimbel and his diving colleagues will spend a full month in a pressurized environment, as if they were 140 feet underwater at all times.

Working with the most modern and sophisticated deep-sea diving equipment, five commercial divers and four diver-cameramen, Gimbel hopes to film for an updated television special the deep interior of the *Andrea Doria* and, in particular, the site of the watertight door between the deep-tank compartment and the generator compartment. Was the door there or was it missing? Was it closed tight or was it bolted open? The department store heir has elaborate plans to hoist the two safes from the First Class Foyer Deck and settle the question once and for all: Is there really a treasure of $1 million-plus in those safes or nothing at all? "It's a once-in-a-lifetime opportunity," said seaman Tim Gerard, one of the forty people in the Gimbel expedition.

Like the *Mona Lisa* with her inscrutable smile, the *Andrea Doria* continues to intrigue the world and to beckon adventurous explorers underwater. Peter Gimbel was not alone in his quest to fathom the sinking of the *Andrea Doria*. A group of New Jersey divers also announced plans to explore the Italian liner sometime in 1981. A forty-year-old amateur diver, John Barnett, of Pound Ridge, New York, lost his life in the summer of 1981 diving to the *Doria*. His body was found on the bridge of the ship some two hundred feet beneath the surface of the Atlantic.

It is ironic that while the *Stockholm*, the *Ile de France*, and all the other ships involved in the disaster have gone to the scrapheap, the *Andrea Doria* lives on beneath the sea. In her prime, she had been one of the most beautiful ships conceived by man. Now she remains the most glamorous, intriguing, accessible, and divable wreck available to man. She seems to be just lying there on the ocean's bottom, within man's reach but beyond his grasp.

Chapter Seventeen
REVISITING THE *DORIA*

ON A BEAUTIFUL, CLEAR AND SUNNY MORNING in July 2002, the captain of the dive boat *Seeker*, Dan Crowell, cast a large floral wreath into the calm ocean above the sunken wreck of the *Andrea Doria*, commemorating the forty-sixth anniversary of the sea disaster of that generation. A crew member read aloud the names of the fifty-one passengers killed aboard the *Doria* and the five seamen who perished aboard the *Stockholm*, and in memoriam recalled:

> Forty-six years ago this month two ocean liners met at the same
> point in space and time and changed the lives of many. The collision

of the *Andrea Doria* and the *Stockholm* was hailed as a great sea rescue and indeed it was; however, we are here on behalf of the survivors and friends to remember the passengers and crew who lost their lives.

July 26, 2006, will mark a half-century that the Italian flagship went down to her watery grave some fifty-three miles southeast of Nantucket. The years have certainly taken their toll upon the once-proud luxury liner. Ironically, though, while the other trans-Atlantic liners that plied the Atlantic Ocean in that era have been sold or scrapped into oblivion, the *Andrea Doria* lives on— deep beneath the waves—in the hearts and minds of those men and women who love the sea. Survivors of the *Doria* and children and grandchildren of those survivors keep in touch through Friends of the *Andrea Doria*, which arranges reunions and publishes a newsletter in order to remember and memorialize the tragedy that shaped their lives. The organization was headed by Anthony Grillo of Monroe, New York, who was three years old when he survived the collision on the Italian liner. The U. S. Merchant Marine Academy at Kings Point, New York, a maritime college for training merchant marine officers, has built an elaborate simulator of the bridge of the *Andrea Doria* where professors and students can re-enact the possibilities of what went wrong on those fateful and controversial days of July 25 and 26, 1956, and learn from that experience. Books and magazine articles have been written over the years delving into the smallest details of the event, and the Internet contains well over a hundred thousand references to the *Andrea Doria*.

The ship grew to be revered like a martyred head of state assassinated before her time. She became the "Grand Dame of the Atlantic," and the "Mount Everest" challenge for scuba divers throughout the world. Lying on her starboard side upon a soft seabed of sand 240 feet beneath the surface of the ocean waves, she was by far the largest, deepest shipwreck accessible to any amateur scuba diver brave and skilled enough to venture to that depth. Swimming down to the *Doria* with about two hundred pounds of air tanks and equipment strapped to your back, breathing compressed air, was like climbing Mount Everest, the highest peak in the world, difficult, arduous, dangerous, even life threatening, but something that could be done.

Blobs of her thick fuel oil still manage to float up occasionally to the surface of the ocean, giving divers the eerie feeling that the *Andrea Doria* indeed is still alive. Inside, the supply of souvenir dishes, cups, saucers, lamps, ashtrays, and artifacts seem to be inexhaustible. Swirling underwater currents, especially every winter, continue to give the wreck a good shaking, which turns up more collectibles. Forty-seven years after that fateful collision and the sinking of the *Andrea Doria*, scuba divers can still find a cup, a dinner plate, or an artifact to take home as a collectible and treasured evidence that they dove to the *Doria*.

The man who showed the way was Peter Gimbel, the department store heir, who became obsessed with underwater exploration. He was the first explorer of the *Andrea Doria*, diving down to her the day after she sank, then returning several weeks later with underwater photographers for a spectacular magazine display of the sunken ship in *Life* magazine. He demonstrated that it could be done. Then Gimbel worked years to organize a major venture, hiring some of the nation's best divers and salvage experts to bring back to the surface the ship's first class safe in 1981. Gimbel arranged to televise his bold attempt to swim through the ship and to find and retrieve the safe, reputedly containing many millions of dollars in cash, jewelry, and other valuables. He brought up the Bank of Rome safe from the First Class Purser's office, but the paper money turned out to be mush and no valuables were found.

But the dive was not a complete failure. Peter Gimbel's lasting legacy to the *Andrea Doria* was the dive itself and the hole his crew had burned through the port side of the ship's hull, the size of a double garage door, through which they had lifted the safe. It became known as "Gimbel's Hole" and served for some twenty years as the favored entryway into the wreck for the hundreds of divers who came after him. The man-made hole gave easy access into the First Class foyer in the middle of the ship, from which one could swim to the nearby gift shop, dining room, or farther forward to the bow or back to the stern of the ship.

There is a world of difference, of course, between casual scuba diving in the clear blue waters of the Caribbean, and the skill and expertise required to descend beyond the dark depths of 100 or 130 feet. Beginners swim not far below the surface but deep enough to get the feeling of weightlessness and the pleasure of gliding along with a variety of harmless fish, taking in the wonders of underwater life, coral, reefs, brilliant colors, knowing that if anything goes wrong they are within an easy swim to the water's surface and precious fresh air. That's pure recreational diving. But to dive deeper than 130 feet, particularly for the pleasure of exploring sunken ships, a diver risks serious injury from oxygen toxicity, nitrogen narcosis, the bends, and even death. Gimbel's exploits, however, made deep scuba diving more and more popular.

The 1980s also happened to mark a whole new world of so-called "extreme sports," which afforded amateurs the added lure of extreme physical danger. One could try mountain climbing, rock climbing, auto racing, parachute jumping, or deep-sea scuba diving. Any one of these sports would test the extreme limit of one's skill, physical strength and mental discipline— and at the risk of death. Of course, the further you ventured, the greater the gratification of knowing that you were going where very few, or perhaps no one, had gone before. Sir Edmund Hillary was the first to climb Mount Everest in 1953 "because it was there." (He stayed there for only fifteen minutes.) For the same reason, scuba divers from many parts of the world have practiced, prepared, and equipped themselves at considerable expense and effort for the personal challenge of exploring the most intriguing of all accessible shipwrecks.

In the 1980s, after Gimbel, only professional or serious sports divers who had close to ten years of experience ventured down to the *Doria*. They wore small tanks of compressed air, giving them no more than fifteen to thirty minutes total bottom time under deep water to find their way in and, more importantly, out of the *Doria*. They were pioneers, learning a new skill. But those early divers were treated to a rare view of a marvelous ocean liner, which appeared immense and awesome, longer than two football fields, a sunken city, her name still visible on the bow and on the stern, her brass fixtures still gleaming, her portholes still intact, her teak decks almost like new. The ship, however, was covered with sea growth and bright anemones that made it look like a floral garden. Lost trawler fishing nets blanketed parts of the ship with steel cables or hemp fishing lines.

Inside the ship the large public rooms were in violent disarray. With the ship lying on her side, the floor and ceiling became her walls; everything was at an angle. Swimming inside the ship was difficult and dangerous. Lighter pieces of furniture had floated to the ceiling; curtains floated sideways in the seawater. The walls and ceilings in many areas had collapsed, exposing and loosening tangles of electrical cables. There was a surreal, spooky feeling in the water-filled interior of the ship, especially as fish and debris drifted casually by and dangling wires and exposed electric cables threatened to snag divers. But

341

there were souvenirs all around, there for the taking. All about was dead silence, except for the hiss of air and bubbles being expelled by the diver himself. Some divers described it as the closest thing to a haunted house where real people once had lived and died. Others thought of it as a time capsule of a bygone age of trans-Atlantic luxury liners.

In those early days of deep wreck diving there were few minor mishaps, like cases of the bends, but no deaths. Those pioneer divers were experienced and knew full well not to exceed their time limits, or their own physical limits. They knew that deep underwater pressure increased the amount of nitrogen absorbed in the blood, and that made one euphoric, like being a little drunk and carefree. It affected one's judgment. Some compared the effect to the taking of so-called laughing gas at the dentist. The divers knew not to do anything at all foolhardy when swimming down to the *Doria*, its upper hull some 190 feet below the surface of the sea. It took these divers years to learn how to function rationally at such deep depths, taking into consideration that the deeper and longer one swam underwater, the greater the build-up of nitrogen in the blood stream.

From about 150 feet down, the diver starts getting more and more reaction from the nitrogen. The pressure is six to eight times the normal air pressure at the surface of the ocean, and that pressure forces nitrogen to dissolve in the blood and tissues. When you come up, the gas in your body can form little bubbles that can settle in your joints, your spine or your blood, and this can cripple or kill you. Prevention is fairly simple. You come up slowly, stopping a minute or two at various depths, and then complete the compression at 20 feet and then at 10 feet below the surface. For a fifteen to thirty minutes bottom time, a diver would have to spend sixty to ninety minutes coming back to the surface, decompressing. That would allow the body to flush out the excess nitrogen and bring the pressure in the body back to normal. The length of time you decompress and the depths at which you do it depend upon how deep you've dove and for how long. It is, in short, an exacting sport.

For those who practiced or indulged themselves in deep sea wreck diving, there was a special feeling of awe, of being alive and aware in a strange element, of living the moment to its fullest, of being akin to all the great explorers of the past. The early divers of the 1980s became a small, close society of men who knew and dove with one another, and they played a significant role in the early days of deep-water explorations. There was Gary Gentile, who put together a team with Bill Nagle aboard the *Seeker* that recovered the auxiliary bell of the *Doria* in 1985—a remarkable achievement at the time. He called the ship's bell "the ultimate artifact from the ultimate wreck." John Moyer, who crewed with Gentile on that venture, capped ten years of diving in 1993 by retrieving three Guido Garbano art frescos, weighing seven hundred pounds, from the wall of the ship's Winter Garden Room. Others in this group of "old-timers" exploring the *Doria* included Bart Malone, Steve Gatto, Mike Boring, John Chatteron, Jon Hulbert, and David Bright, who is reputed to have the largest collection of artifacts of them all from the *Doria*, including two lifeboats, one surviving deck chair, *Doria*-inscribed life rings and life preservers, and thousands of china dinnerware, lamps, jewelry, portholes, glass windows, and just about one of each of everything brought back to the surface from the *Doria*. Knowledgeable and with degrees in physiology, biology, and German, Bright worked full time for Pfizer, Inc., and spent his spare time diving, exploring, and studying sunken wrecks, including the Civil War's *Monitor* off the coast of North Carolina, the *Titanic*, and some 113 dives to the *Doria*, and lecturing on what he had learned.

343

COLLISION COURSE

In 1988, when he was thirty-one, Bright decided to try exploring the Tourist Section of the *Doria* simply because a survivor, Liliana Donner Hughes, had asked him to bring her something to remember from that section, if possible. It occurred to him that the Tourist Class dining room had been unexplored; almost all divers entered the ship through Gimbel's Hole and concentrated on the First Class forward section of the ship. With about thirty previous dives to the *Doria* under his belt, Bright teamed up with Ed Suarez, thirty-six, who worked for the IRS in Washington but loved to dive anywhere there was water. Ed was a jovial, swashbuckling character who told great diving stories, and an expert diver and instructor whose eccentricity was to "bring the store" down with him to any shipwreck. He would bring down so much redundant equipment for safety's sake it would seem like he had a whole dive store with him.

Here is David Bright's account of their dive:

> Log: July 5, 1988
> Dive Boat: *Seeker* ; Captain Bill Nagle
> Weather: Sunny, warm, 85 degrees
> Hook: Promenade, slightly distal to Gimbel's Hole.
> Dive Partner: Ed Suarez
> Bottom time: 23 minutes; Total Dive time: 99 minutes
> Temp on bottom: 45 degrees
> Visibility: 20 feet (dark); Max Depth: 217 ft.

We decided to try to find the Tourist Class dining room on this dive. We had to swim from Gimbel's Hole to the stern of the ship. There was a slight current, so we decided to swim through the Promenade to the end, come out of the Promenade and follow a ship railing to the stern bridge wing. The wing has a huge trawler

344

net attached to it, so we decided to avoid that area and dropped down into the stern area. . . . We came across a room that we felt was the dining room but could not access it. We looked through the windows and saw what we felt were dining room tables of many different shapes. . . . We tried to find a way into this room, but there was a solid metal bar that prevented us from getting in. We saw a Tourist Class saucer through one of the windows that was taunting us to find a way in, but we couldn't. Since we still had a long swim ahead of us (with the current), we decided to end our dive.

David and Ed, feeling very pleased to be the first ones to locate the Tourist Class dining room, decided not to share their find with anyone else. They agreed to meet and to carefully plan their next dive to the *Doria*. When they boarded the *Seeker* at Montauk two weeks later, they learned that a diver, Joe Drozd, had died the previous week diving to the *Doria*. Perturbed by the death and disturbed that five inexperienced deep divers were aboard for the trip, David joined with the mates of the *Seeker* in determining the lack of diving experience of these five men and then managed to scare them so much that three of the newcomers loaded their gear back into their cars and drove home. The other two dove just once to touch the hull of the *Doria* and they decided they had had enough. David and Ed persuaded Bill Nagle and his crew to tie up to the stern section of the *Doria* rather than at Gimbel's Hole, and they went down the line with a concealed hacksaw.

Log: July 17, 1988
Dive Boat: *Seeker* ; Captain: Bill Nagle
Weather: Sunny, warm 85 degrees
Hook: Stern area near Bridge wing
Dive Partner: Ed Suarez
Bottom time: 25 minutes; Total Dive time: 115 minutes

Temp on bottom: 45 degrees

Visibility: 15 feet (dark); Max Depth: 205 feet

> We found the dining room site very easily. . . . We proceeded to pull
> out the hacksaw and started cutting through the far right side of
> the bar. We took turns doing the cutting as we didn't want to get
> too narc-ed (nitrogen narcosis). We made a slight dent into the
> steel and realized that it was going to take us a bit of time to do the
> cutting. Ended the dive and decided that we needed a better plan.

Their better plan was to split up so that each one would spend
the entire time sawing through the steel bar. They each made
three dives and by the end of the trip they had cut only an inch
and half into the steel bar.

Their despair and the fact that they did not come up with the
usual artifacts did not go unnoticed.   David's friend, John
Chatterton, who was serving as the secondary captain and dive
mate on the *Seeker*, asked why he was so quiet. David told him he
and Ed were working on a project and did not want to talk about
it to anyone. Chatterton inquired no further, as per diving eti-
quette. But when he returned from his final dive of the trip, he
approached David. "Now I know what you guys are doing!" He
said he had come across the nicked bar and offered to help cut
through the bar with a cutting torch he used as a commercial
diver. David welcomed him to the project. They planned to get
into the dining room at the start of the diving season next year.
But a few weeks later, Chatterton telephoned him, "David are you
ready to go now?" Without hesitation, David agreed and the two
divers planned a full excursion down to the *Doria* with eight sea-
soned *Doria* divers in mid-August, rather than wait a year. That
was taking a great risk on the chancy weather beyond the usual
diving season.

A tremendous amount of preparation went into that late season dive. The operations portion of this expedition was lead by John Chatterton because of his experience as a commercial diver. They planned to cut through the bar using an underwater blow torch and magnesium rods; for working underwater they needed to bring with them huge cylinders of oxygen, many electrical batteries, hundreds of feet of hoses, electrical cable, and duct tape. The eight-man team worked through the night preparing everything on the night trip out to the *Doria*. They were lucky. The morning dawned in pure summer splendor, cloudless and calm. They split the work as planned in three teams of two divers each, taking turns going down and working to cut their way into the Tourist Class dining room. Below, conditions were unusually perfect; visibility was sixty-five feet, the current was nil and amber rays of sunlight actually reached the wreck. "It was the best visibility that I have ever seen on the *Doria*," David recalled. "It was like diving the deeper waters of Florida, and I will always remember that day because everything had to be perfect, and it was." As was appropriate, David and Ed were the first team to enter the Tourist Class dining room.

Log: August 17, 1988
Dive Boat: *Seeker*; Captain Bill Nagle
Weather: Sunny, warm, 80 degrees
Hook: Stern area under Bridge wing
Dive Partner: Ed Suarez
Bottom time: 25 minutes; Total dive time: 135 minutes
Temp on bottom: 47 degrees
Visibility: 65+ feet (light); Max Depth: 220 ft.

We came down the anchor line and I entered the dining room first, followed by Ed. All the tables were sticking out of the left side of the

347

ship and were of various sizes and shapes. We decided to go forward through the dining room staying at the mid-ship level. As I came across the bulkhead at the end of the forward portion of the dining room, I observed a corridor that led to the pantry, but there were fallen cables blocking the entrance to the pantry. As we tried to explore the corridor, Ed's regulator got caught in the cables and I had to come in and clear his regulator of the cables. Going slowly through the corridor, we saw several pieces of porcelain china, silverware and silver service trays. At the end of the corridor were many cables that looked very spooky, so we decided to turn around and go out of the corridor and back into the dining room. Just before the end of the corridor, I decided to lift up and went into the pantry.

As I looked around, there was nothing but wall-to-wall porcelain china.   I shrieked with joy. I reached down and grabbed Ed to come up and see where I was. I could see his eyes getting bigger and bigger as we started to dig into our "prize." We were so excited that we stirred up the silt and we had limited visibility. We continued to bag our porcelain dishes without vision but by feel. At the zenith of our euphoria, I realized that it was time to go . . . . Because of our earlier dives and extended current dive, we had a long decompression.

At the end of the first day, the team had recovered forty-eight pieces of fine porcelain china. They were all extremely tired but excited to dive the whole next day retrieving china. But it was not to be. The next morning the weather changed dramati-cally. The sea was rough with high waves and a wicked wind. The men decided wisely to pull the hook, unshackle the *Seeker* from the *Doria* and to leave the area as quickly as possible. Going back to Montauk, the *Seeker* took a good beating from the weather. The stern of the dive boat took on a heavy amount of water, and a few men were dumped out of their bunks when waves hit the sixty-five-foot boat broadside. The running joke that night was that other divers would be diving the sunken *Seeker* just to get their hands on the porcelain they had taken from the *Doria*. The men agreed to divide "the loot" evenly among themselves, and they vowed not to say anything to anyone about the project so that they could complete the excavation of the china early in the next diving season in 1989.

But, of course, the secret did not last long. The men heard rumors that the *Wahoo*, a rival dive boat, was planning to go out to the *Doria* earlier in 1989 than it had ever done before. The assumption was that the *Wahoo* divers were going to jump the claim to all that china. So the original dive team and other invited experienced divers sailed early on the *Seeker*, mid-June, and they reaped the spoils. David and Ed retrieved more than seventy-five pieces of choice china, and before they left, to protect their find, John Chatterton bolted a grate over their access hole leading into the dining room and attached a slate which said: "Closed for Inventory." When the divers from the *Wahoo* got to the site a week later they were extremely angry. But the *Seeker* men felt they were entitled to first dibs. Later that summer, they unbolted the grate and allowed free access to the area. But that act started a rivalry that went on for years between the *Wahoo* and *Seeker*, the two principal dive boats for the *Doria*. David Bright collected so much china from the Tourist Class dining room that he found it easy to give one or two souvenirs to each of the many *Doria* survivors he had met over the years. He also began exhibiting notable *Doria* artifacts to various maritime museums, principally the one on Nantucket Island.[1]

What really opened deep sea diving to the amateur scuba diver was the introduction in the late 1980s of a new mixture of compressed gas developed by the U. S. Navy to be used

[1] Ed Suarez died in a cave-diving accident in West Virginia in July 1994. He was 43.

underwater called Tri-Mix, which added helium to the mixture of oxygen and nitrogen. Tri-Mix made deeper diving more safe and accessible. It largely did away with the dangerous euphoria of nitrogen narcosis; it doubled the "bottom" time a diver could spend on a wreck to thirty or forty minutes; it thereby increased the margin of time to get out of dangerous situations. At the same time, there were vast improvements in all diving equipment, and more and more recreational divers across the country, and, in fact, around the world, took up deep scuba diving. A wide variety of diving clubs sprang up in almost every state, catering to all kinds of divers, including shore, boat, kayak, wreck, and cave divers as well as photographers and videographers. The National Association of Underwater Instructors (NAUI), organized in 1953, with headquarters in Tampa, Florida, now trains and certifies diving instructors in more than five thousand diving clubs, who in turn train and certify sports divers at different levels of competence. On a worldwide basis, the Professional Association of Diving Instructors (PADI) also trains and certifies diving instructors through its 106,000 professional members, who issue more than 500,000 certifications each year signifying the standards for training, experience, and equipment for each danger level of scuba diving.

Tri-Mix brought about a transformation in deep diving similar to the evolution of flying a plane by the seat of one's pants to flying with instruments. Deep scuba diving became known as "technical diving." One could study mathematical tables for the proper proportions of breathing gases (oxygen, nitrogen, helium) at different levels of dives, and then one could dive deeper and deeper until qualified to reach down to the *Andrea Doria*. It leveled the playing field to some extent, requiring less actual experience to dive the *Doria* than the old timers had. Because diving certification took less time, it opened the way for many more men, and some women, who wanted to make that ultimate dive. Anyone who could pay the fare and had open-water certification could go. Boat charters became readily available. As a consequence, because so many of them lacked real cold water, deep and wreck diving experience, it increased the likelihood of serious injury and death.

Through the 1980s, there were perhaps twenty or thirty serious divers who made it down to the *Doria*. With Tri-Mix available in the late 1980s, the number of individual divers increased significantly, most probably to more than two hundred, though no one really kept a reliable count. Of course, most of these divers made many more than one or two dive trips each season and from one to four, five, or even six dives per trip. Whatever the number, a lucrative cottage industry developed on the north shore of Long Island, in which professional divers ran competing dive boats to take the recreational divers out to the *Doria's* grave. Dive boat captains could make their whole year's profit just by sailing to the *Doria* every week from late June to early August. The two leading "research" vessels were the *Wahoo*, captained by Steve Bielenda, a native of Brooklyn in his sixties, who had himself made more than one hundred dives into the *Doria*, and its arch rival, *Seeker*, captained by Dan Crowell, a salty sea dog in his forties, who took over from Bill Nagle and ran the most popular dive boat in the area. The *Seeker* was the more comfortable boat with air conditioning, television, videos, and an atmosphere of joie de vivre. It became the favorite of diving clubs that would charter the whole boat for its own members a year or more in advance. The *Seeker* carried a captain and a crew of two or three and usually from seven to ten paying divers per trip.

Extreme sports are almost always inconvenient and expensive, unlike tennis, golf, or bowling. To qualify as a "certified technical diver" someone would need to pass diving tests and written examinations with about one hundred dives observed and certified by a certified instructor. The three to five compressed gas tanks, plus the breathing regulators, the dry suits, the ropes, the knife, the dive computers, the depth and tank pressure gauges, the buoyancy compensator, the underwater lights, perhaps a camera or video camcorder—all this could easily run $10,000 or more for the best and latest equipment. Then there's the cost of the trip to New York for an out-of-towner or a two- to four-hour drive to Montauk at the northern tip of Long Island. The 107-mile boat ride to the site of the wreck takes ten to twelve hours, depending on the weather, usually leaving late Friday night, returning late Sunday night or early Monday morning. Trip cost? About $1,000.

The sense of adventure began after leaving shore, bouncing on the open sea with fellow divers, sharing stories, advice, and a feeling of something new and exciting to come. Captain Crowell on the *Seeker* and Captain Beleinda on the *Wahoo* might try to check each diver's credentials, experience and know-how, but in practical terms that was nearly impossible. They would say frankly, "Just because you're certified does not mean you're qualified." Divers signed waivers that they were diving at their own personal risk, absolving the dive boat, its crew, and their own instructors from liability. Divers were taught they had to depend upon themselves in diving; they could not expect another diver, even a diving partner, to risk his or her life to save their own. But despite efforts, there has been no way to guarantee safety.

For most divers, to touch the hull of the mammoth ship at a depth of 190 feet or perhaps to venture to the opening of Gimbel's Hole and look inside is a notable dive in itself. To swim into the ship and to explore its decks, its large public rooms and return perhaps with a memento of the dive—a cup, a saucer, a lamp—that raises your dive to a whole new level of pride and bragging rights. There is never enough advice and knowledge you can absorb to achieve complete safety. The number one rule is that the most important thing you can bring back from the *Doria* is yourself. To do that you must train yourself to never, never panic. You have to plan your dive and dive your plan. Know your limits. Only after you have studied the ship's deck plans can you venture farther and farther into the wreck on each successful dive. You have to know where you are, where you are going, and how you are going to swim out— all within the limits of how much compressed gas you are carrying with you. If you get lost, you can run out of gas. If you get tangled in some loose cable or trapped underneath falling debris, you can run out of gas. If the silt on the bottom of the floor of a particular room is stirred up, visibility can be cut to zero. If you cannot see where you are, do not panic; just stay still until the current clears the water around you. If one regulator does not work . . . If you are suddenly low on gas supply . . . If . . . . There are so many ifs and buts and so many scenarios of dangerous situations and how to escape from them that each dive to the *Doria* becomes a new and extreme adventure.

Divers all know that the underwater conditions at the site far from shore are just as dangerous as the snow and thin air up on Mount Everest. Strong, bone-chilling currents can carry divers out to sea; water temperatures at 190 feet and below hover around 40 to 45 degrees. The ship itself is cluttered with old, snagged fishing nets that can easily trap a diver. Inside, a maze of corridors, twisted electrical cables, sharp bits of jagged steel, floating objects, and years of accumulated silt on the floor below you, limited cloudy visibility—all combine to tax the skills and threaten the life of a swimmer far beneath the surface of the Atlantic Ocean. Adventurers going out to the *Doria* know that divers before them, some of them more experienced than they, have lost their lives exploring this ultimate shipwreck. The reasons are varied: One diver can not extricate himself from wires wrapped around his ankle; another is trapped beneath a table; another succumbs to a heart attack; another seems to fall asleep or slip into a coma; several somehow miscalculate the time, or become lost and run out of air, or have a piece of equipment fail; others panic for some reason and fail to decompress while swimming to the surface. The latest count is thirteen deaths. Experienced wreck divers insist that almost all these deaths could have been prevented and are due at least in part to human error and inexperience.

The most recent tragedy was that of Bill Schmoldt, fifty-four years of age, a man in perfect health who ran marathons, an avid and experienced diver, a college professor of computer sciences, and a licensed sea captain, who lectured widely on wreck explorations and marine archaeology. In August 2002, while serving as a crew member of the *John Jack*, a very new and advanced dive boat, Schmoldt suffered some mishap underwater and shot up to the surface without decompressing. He suffered an apparent embolism. In excruciating pain, he was airlifted by helicopter within an hour to a hospital decompression facility on land, where doctors tried but failed to revive him. Of the thirteen[2] confirmed deaths, five of them occurred within a thirteen-month period in 1998 and 1999, all divers from the *Seeker*, all of different causes. Word spread

---

[2]John Barnett, July 1, 1981; Frank Kennedy, July 15, 1984; John Omsby, July 31, 1985; Joe Drozd, July 13, 1988; Matthew Lawrence, July 1, 1992; Mike Scofield, July 15, 1992; Robert Santuli, July 12, 1993; Craig Sicola, June 24, 1998; Richard Roost, July 8, 1998; Vince Napoliello, August 4, 1998; Christopher Murley, July 21, 1999; Charlie McGurr, July 28, 1999; Bill Schmoldt, August 4, 2002.

fast and that put a dent in the number of sports divers attempting that ultimate dive to the *Doria*.

By the end of the 1990s, something brand-new and much better in essential equipment became available to deep wreck divers, which promised to open up whole new vistas of opportunities. That was the Closed Circuit Rebreather. It was a complicated, expensive piece of dive equipment, but once a diver learned how to use it, he or she loved it. CCR tanks acted like an extra pair of lungs, taking the exhalation of the diver, scrubbing it clean of carbon dioxide and expelling it, and then allowing the diver to rebreathe a clean mixture of compressed oxygen, nitrogen, and helium. It was a breathing machine, less cumbersome, lighter, and safer. It weighed less than half of the scuba tanks used before; it allowed the diver to stay underwater much longer than before, even up to three hours, if the diver could stand the bone-chilling cold. With CRR tanks, divers had a greater sense of safety and far less danger of running out of air. If one got tangled, or caught, or lost his or her way, there was now more time to be rescued. Within the first few years, CCR equipment became more and more prevalent. Most of the divers venturing into the *Doria* had switched to CCR tanks by the end of 2003.

By that time, with almost fifty years on the ocean floor, the *Doria* had deterio-rated seriously. The entire superstructure down to the Promenade Deck had broken off the ship and lay in a heap of wreckage alongside it on the ocean floor. The pressure of the depth had gradually compressed the entire hull. Gimbel's Hole, once the size of a garage door, had been reduced to a slit no more than a foot wide. Most door openings had become impenetrable. The teak Promenade Deck had buckled and folded in upon itself. A huge crack in the steel hull threatened to break the bow off and another deep crack along the stern appeared equally ominous. With its structural integrity gone, only the corpse of the luxury liner was left, a seven-hundred-foot hull that looked like a sliced half of a mammoth watermelon.

The wreck now offered a different experience to divers. With its upper decks gone, the rest of the ship was wide open along its entire length. Divers could enter anywhere and venture deep within the ship and exit at will. The continuing search for artifacts changed from a search-and-find to a "digging wreck." Divers now went down with sawed-off rakes and gingerly dug in deep silt for small treasures. The days of coming up with a bag full of goodies were long gone. However, divers still believed that the *Doria*, whipped by strong currents, will continue to give up thousands of artifacts over the next fifty years.

On the *Seeker*'s voyage to the *Doria* in July 2002, when the forty-sixth-anniversary wreath was cast upon the ocean, Christina Young, one of the very best of the very few female deep scuba divers to reach the *Doria*, dove from the *Seeker*, wearing a Rebreather, and swam far into the interior of the ship. Christina, a regular among the serious *Doria* divers, earned her living as a manager in a high-tech industry, played at downhill ski racing, horseback riding, flying, and stuck to her first love: wreck diving. With more than ten years' experience, a thousand dives along the East Coast in the past twelve years and sixty-plus dives to the *Doria*, she had become an expert deep-sea photographer.

Here is her account of that dive:

We were tied into a piece on top of the wreck near the second set of lifeboat davits. The area is just aft of the Winter Garden and forward of Gimbel's Hole. We lost the first day of our three-day trip due to bad weather. Left Montauk around midnight, Monday morning. Not very many people got much sleep due to the strain of trying to stay in their bunks in heavy seas, but the forecast was that the weather would lay down. It did lay down, but most people were too exhausted to go diving the next morning.

On Monday afternoon, I did a dive. Reports back from the couple of people who dived in the morning was that the visibility was just between five and ten feet. So I decided not to take the camera. I dropped down to find a big shell of a wreck with different levels of debris fields where the various decks once were. The Promenade Deck was completely missing, just exposed teak planking was all that was left. I dropped down a level to a debris field that was once the Boat Deck superstructure. Nothing was recognizable here as a "ship." I dropped down another level to what was once the Lido Deck superstructure. I saw an intact sink lying on its side amid the mazes of hull plates and beams. I continued dropping down until I was in another debris field around the 235-foot level when something caught my eye. It turned out to be a nice silver bowl lying amongst the conglomeration of rusted steel. After retrieving it, I continued to search around the area and into little cubbyholes that no longer resembled the doorways they once were. The hallways and rooms they once opened up to were crushed, no longer penetrable.

On the way back up, once I got to the Boat Deck level, I saw a hole that was big enough to enter, almost underneath the overhanging hull. I went inside a few feet and saw something remarkable. There was an old boat anchor (fluted) about four feet long. How did it get in here? The only thing I could imagine was that this must have been an anchor for one of the lifeboats.

My bottom time was just about spent. I swam up to the top of the hull and back to the tie-in point. I'm glad that I didn't bring my camera. The previous divers were correct: the visibility on top of the wreck was only about ten feet, and down in the lower debris fields about five.

On the decompression hang, at one point I felt like I was inside a lava lamp. Brownish-black blobs started slowly coming up and around a couple other divers and myself. At first I didn't recognize what they were, but then after touching one (mistake!) I realized that these where blobs of bunker oil from the *Doria*'s fuel tanks. Later, back on the boat, I had to go and wash off with some dish soap.

I had hoped that the next morning would bring better visibility and I would shoot some video then. However, it was not to be. Petey Wohlieben came back from his traditional 6:30 AM dive and had his ass kicked by the unrelenting current that went all the way from the surface down to the wreck. There is no Promenade Deck (or really any other deck) to hide inside any more, and when the current rips, divers are completely exposed in most directions. . . . We waited until almost 10 AM to see if the current would die, but when it didn't a vote was taken to leave the wreck and head back to Montauk.

The silver bowl I found has the classic crown and "Italia" engraved in it, and appears to be a very nice sugar bowl. It will shine up beautifully. I do think that although the wreck no longer looks very much like a grand ship it once was, new places for exploration are being opened up.

And, so the SS *Andrea Doria* lives on.

Index

***Andrea Doria* Officers:**

Calamai, Captain Piero, 13–17,
    23–54, 62, 79, 96–7, 103–6,
    134, 163–5, 177, 209,
    213–4, 220–4, 228, 243,
    248–9, 273–86, 303
Magagnini, Staff Captain Osvaldo,
    65–70, 103–5, 158–60, 220–4,
    228
Oneto, First Officer Luigi, 62, 103,
    221
Kirn, First Officer Carlo, 103, 221
Franchini, Secondo Officer Curzio,
    61–9, 74–9, 96, 106–7, 134,
    160, 284, 286–8
Badano, Second Officer Guido, 62,
    103–7, 186–7, 213–4, 229,
    276, 292
Giannini, Third Officer Eugenio,
    61–79, 96, 106–7, 134, 165,
    208–10, 221
Donato, Third Officer Antonio,
    107, 221
Tortori Donati, Dr. Bruno, 117–20,
    162, 166–9, 206–8, 220, 229

Chiappori, Chief Engineer Alcisio,
    99, 101–2, 164–5, 213
Mondini, First Engineer Giuseppe,
    98
Giannini, Dr. Lorenzo, 117,
    168–9, 206–8, 220
Natta, Monsignor Sebastian, 121,
    197, 223

***Andrea Doria* Crew:**

Balzano, Cabin Boy Gaetano, 118
Bertini, Purser Emilio, 116, 160,
    330
Bonivento, Purser Adolfo, 116
Bussi, Radioman Carlo, 107
Conte, Cadet John, 221
Coretti, Chief Nurse Antonia,
    118–9, 166–8
Domenchini, Helmsman Carlo, 66
Guidi, Chief Radioman Francesco,
    107
Ingianni, Chief Purser Franchesco,
    116
Marraci, Cadet Mario, 221, 276
Pirelli, Cadet Giuliano, 203

359

INDEX

Rovelli, Steward Giovanni, 161, 166–9, 207, 219–20
Spina, Fireman Fortunato, 203
Visciano, Helmsman Giulio, 74, 77

Andrea Doria Passengers:

Ansuini, Melanie, 195
Barton, Gay, 204
Boyer, Mr. and Mrs. Marion, 109–10
Carlin, Mr. and Mrs. Walter G., 110, 151–3
Carola, Margaret, 120, 166
Carola, Rosa, 117–20, 162, 207
Cianfarra, Mr. and Mrs. Camille, 112–5, 161, 166–9, 207
  Joan, 113, 150
  Linda (see Morgan)
Clergy, 161, 197, 220
Covina, Christina, 120, 166
D'Elia, Mr. and Mrs. Giovanni, 196
Dilworth, Mayor and Mrs., 111
Di Sandro, Norma, 190, 245
  Mr. and Mrs. Tulio, 190
Dooner, Mrs. Liliana, 130, 195
Dorneich, Klaus, 195
Fornaro, Mrs. Josephine, 128
Fusco, Franco, 124
Grassier, Christine, 171–181
Grubenman, Jack, 125–6
Grubenman, Mr. and Mrs. Don, 126
Hall, Richard (Roman), 123, 203–4
Hendler, Sylvan, 171–181
Hill, Ellis and family, 128

Hudson, Robert, 118, 166, 222–3
Iazzetta, Mr. and Mrs. Benvenuto, 120, 166
Keil, Morris and family, 204
Krendell, George, 171–181
La Flamme, Theresa, 125
Lilley, Marguerite, 171–181
Lombardi, Antonio, 122
Maggio, Joseph, 195
Merlin, Mr. and Mrs. Kenneth, 111
Morgan, Linda, 113, 149–52, 233
Morgan, Edward P., 113
Novik, Morris, 123
Onder, Mr. and Mrs. Joseph, 117, 119–20, 208
Parker, Edward, 121
Passante, Mr. and Mrs. Max, 115, 218
Peterson, Mr. and Mrs. Thure, 111–5, 161–2, 166–69, 213, 219–20
Pomilio, Giuseppe, 196
Ponzi, Antonio, 122
Rabovsky, Mr. and Mrs. Istvan, 112
Reinert, Jerome, 206
Roman, Ruth, 123, 203–4
Sedja, Mratin Jr., 81
Sergio, Mr. and Mrs. Paul, 130–1
Sergio, Mrs. Ross and family, 131
Theriot, Mr. and Mrs. Ferdinand, 115
  Peter, 115, 162–3, 204, 218–9
Vali, John, 195
Waite, Raymond, 161
Watres, Carl, 245
Wells, Mrs. Fanny, 127, 166

360

INDEX

Stockholm **Officers:**

Nordenson, Captain H. Gunnar,
33–4, 38, 41, 44, 51, 58,
83–92, 145–6, 153, 185,
215–7, 230, 232, 249, 269–72,
303

Kallback, Chief Officer Herbert, 44,
86–7, 90–2, 146, 233, 241,
271

Enestrom, Second Officer Lars,
32–3, 86, 91, 153, 185, 188–9,
232

Abenius, Second Officer Sven, 86,
153, 185, 190

Carstens-Johannsen, Third Officer
Ernst, 31–33, 37–60, 82–84,
86, 153, 185–6, 193–4,
254–268, 303

Assagren, Chief Engineer Gustav,
58, 85, 91

Bjorkegran, Third Engineer Edwin,
85

Svensson, Second Engineer Justra,
58, 85

Dawe, Chief Purser Curt, 88–9,
146–7, 151, 233

Nessling, Dr. Ake, 147–9, 217, 231

Stockholm **Crew:**

Ahlm, Sven, 148

Bjorkman, Ingemar G., 37, 41, 48,
50–2, 57, 258, 265

Claesson, Nurse Karin, 147–9

Eliasson, Chief Bosun Ivar, 233, 241

Falk, Lars, 148, 232

Garcia, Bernabe Polanco, 149–50

Gustavsson, Wilhelm, 148, 232

Hagstrom, John, 146

Hallik, Alexander, 58

Johansson, Alf, 149, 231

Johansson, Sten, 41, 46, 56, 264

Johansson, Radio Operator Sven
Erik, 92

Jonasson, Kennth, 146

Larson, Helmsman Peter, 40–41,
45–60, 145, 258–9, 265

Mellgren, Chief Radio Operator
Bengt, 92

Osterberg, Karl Elis, 148

Reinholdson, Radio Operator Ake,
93

Smedberg, Arne, 232

Steen, Sunne, 146

Trasbo, Valdemar, 152, 191

Stockholm **Passengers:**

Bruner, Miss Colleen, 43

Pettit, Dr. Horace, 59, 81–2

General:

Adams, Frank, 114

Aircraft, 137, 230–2

Ali, Giuseppe, 249

Allanet, Pierre, 141

Allen, destroyer escort, 237, 240,
242–3

Ambrose Lightship, 32, 36

American Export Line, 322

Andrea Doria
condition, underwater of, 323,
328–36
exploration, underwater of,
328–36
plans for raising, 323–8

361

pursers', offices of, 328–30, 333

salvaging, 323–8

estimated cost of, 327

treasure, rumors of, 328–30, 336

value, estimated, 327

Art, 19–21

Augenti, Captain Bruno, 328

Awa Maru, 324

Azore Islands, 66

Barnett, John, 336

Beaudéan, Captain Raoul de, 139–48, 199–202, 216, 228

Blackthorn, 324–5

Blanc, Captain Réné, 139

Block Island, 32–33, 48

Bon Homme Richard, 324

Boyd, Captain Joseph A., 138, 187, 192

Brittany, France, 318

Brostrom Concern, 39, 280, 322

CBS, 334

Cannes, 24

Calamai, Mrs. Pierro, 235–6

Cape Ann, 137–8, 140–5, 165, 186–7, 192, 233, 243

Chinigo, Michael, 236

Claims, court, 329–30

Coast Guard, 134–6, 210, 217, 230, 316, 318

Campbell, 136, 245

Evergreen, 136, 211, 234, 238, 240, 242

hearings, 316

Hornbeam, 136, 237–8, 240–2, 245

Humboldt, 234

Legare, 136, 240–1

Owasco, 136, 240–1

Tamaroa, 136, 240–1

Yakutat, 136, 245

Yeaton, 245

Consolidated Edison (ConEd), 335

Constitution, 316

Conte Biancamano, 313

Course Recorder

Andrea Doria, 291–4

Stockholm, 265–6, 290–1

Cousteau, Jacques, 331

Cristiforo Colombo, 24, 322

Cunard Line, 321

Daikoku Maru, 318

Deep sea diving, 331

DeLucci, Chris, 333–4

Doria, Admiral Andrea, 22

Davis Shoal, 106

Duilio, 105

Erdman, Roger, 237

Failla, S. Charles, 137–8, 143, 186

Fog, 13, 14, 25–6, 28, 32, 61, 67, 133, 141, 154, 187, 200, 259–61

Fox, Joseph, 323

Fortune, 318

Gallo, Armando, 203

Galveston, Texas, 318

Genoa, 23, 24, 235

George Washington, 319–20

Gerard, Tim, 336

Gibraltar, 24

Gimbel, Peter, 323, 330–2, 334–6

Gino, 318

Grace Line, 314

Great Circle Route, 17

Greene, Raymond T., 262

Gripsholm, 303–4, 322

Guillou, Jean Pierre, 203

Haight, Charles S., 254–6, 262, 274–288

Hinrichs, Hans, 218, 227

Hopkins, Robert E., 139, 223, 233

Ile de France, 139–44, 198–202, 217, 220, 227–8, 233, 322, 336

Independence, 322

International Conference for Safety of Life at Sea, 97, 142, 304–8, 317

Italian Line, 242, 244, 247, 249–50, 275, 280, 297, 325, 329

Jalanta, 316

Kelley, Sgt. Jonah E., 134, 234

Kingsville, 316

Kleinman, Larry, 335

Kungsholm, 322

La Belle, Captain James W., 316

Life magazine, 330-1

Lifeboats, 206–10, 222

    Andrea Doria, 103–4, 155, 157–60, 175–181, 183–4, 203–4, 207, 215, 224, 239, 242, 245

    Cape Ann, 187

    Ile de France, 201–2, 217, 227

    Stockholm, 154–5, 185–6, 188–94, 202, 232

    Thomas, 188

Lionne, Norwegian freighter, 138

Lloyd's of London, 247, 308–9

Log Books, 275–9

Loudspeakers

    Andrea Doria, 103–5, 124, 170, 192

    Stockholm, 154–6

Maersk, Laura, Danish freighter, 234

Matteson, Leonard T., 262, 268

Merchant, George, 332

Miya Maru, 318

Mona Lisa, 318

Monitor, 326

Morse, Denny, 332

"Mother," 333-9

"The Mystery of the *Andrea Doria*," 335

Nantucket Lightship, 16–7, 25, 32, 36, 42, 44–5, 48, 51, 66–8, 141, 312

Naples, 24

Nissho Maru, 319–20

Nordenson, Captain H. Gunnar, 312–18

Normandie, 327

Ocean Victory, 118

Parker, Lt. Harold W., 135–6

Pollack Rip Lightship, 46, 48

Preston, Third Officer Robert, 138

Pulitzer Prize, 247

Queen Elizabeth2, 321

Radar, 304–6, 312–18

    Andrea Doria, 62–73, 133, 186, 274–5, 284–7

    schools, 316–7

    Stockholm, 48–54, 255, 263–4

Ranger, 318

Rodocker, Don, 333–4

Rule, 317

Rules of the Road, 52–3, 66, 72, 257, 267, 305, 313, 317

Russian fishing ships, illegal, 333

Salvage, 323–8

Santa Rosa, 314–5

Saturation System, 332

Sepel, Lieutenant Commander George, 318

INDEX

Settlement, 297, 301–2

Sharks, 332–4

Siwik, Captain Frank, 314–5

Special Masters in Court, 253

Speed in fog, 15–6, 25–29, 267, 270–1, 280

Stability

 Andrea Doria, 97–103, 129, 164–5, 211–3, 238–42, 281–3, 298–300

 Stockholm, 87, 90–92, 155

Suits, court, 250–2

Survivors, number of, 244–5

Swedish American Line, 35–6, 242, 247, 249–50, 297, 322

Tampa Bay, Florida, 318

Tarantia, British freighter, 234

Team Castor, 318

Todd, Radioman Robroy A., 135

Thomas, Pvt. William H., 139, 142, 165, 192, 221, 230, 233–4

Tracks, 18–9, 141

Trans-Atlantic Passenger Conference, 308–9

Tung, C. Y., 322

Underwood, Eugene, 254, 256–272, 274

United States, 322

U. S. District Court, 251, 328

U. S. Navy, 319–20

Valchem, 314–6

Walsh, Judge Lawrence E., 253–4, 265, 283, 285, 302

Xerox Corporation, 336

364